FIREBRANDS

Also by Joanna Scutts

*The Extra Woman: How Marjorie Hillis Led a
Generation of Women to Live Alone and Like It*

*Hotbed: Bohemian New York and the
Secret Club that Sparked Modern Feminism*

FIREBRANDS

25 Pioneering Women Writers
to Ignite Your Reading Life

JOANNA SCUTTS

DUCKWORTH

To the seekers in archives

First published in the United Kingdom by Duckworth in 2024

Duckworth, an imprint of Duckworth Books Ltd
1 Golden Court, Richmond, TW9 1EU, United Kingdom
www.duckworthbooks.co.uk

For bulk and special sales please contact
info@duckworthbooks.com

© Joanna Scutts, 2024

All rights reserved. No part of this publication may be reproduced, stored in a retrieval system, or transmitted, in any form or by any means electronic, mechanical, photocopying, recording or otherwise, without the prior permission of the publisher.

The right of Joanna Scutts to be identified as the Author of this Work has been asserted by her in accordance with the Copyright, Designs and Patents Act 1988.

A catalogue record for this book is available from the British Library

Book design by Danny Lyle
Printed and bound in Great Britain by Clays Ltd, Elcograf S.p.A.

Hardback ISBN: 9780715655269
eISBN: 9780715655276

CONTENTS

Introduction   vii

1. Enheduanna   1
2. Murasaki Shikibu   9
3. Christine de Pizan   19
4. Aphra Behn   29
5. Charlotte Lennox   39
6. Olympe de Gouges   49
7. Fanny Fern   59
8. Harriet Jacobs   69
9. George Sand   79
10. Juana Manuela Gorriti   89
11. Sui Sin Far/Edith Maude Eaton   99
12. Alice Dunbar-Nelson   109
13. Renée Vivien   119
14. Mary Heaton Vorse   129
15. Mary Borden   139
16. Jessie Redmon Fauset   149
17. Mina Loy   159
18. Kay Boyle   171
19. Pauli Murray   181
20. Eileen Chang   191
21. Forough Farrokhzad   201
22. Flora Nwapa   211
23. Assia Djebar   221
24. Inès Cagnati   231
25. Lucille Clifton   241

Credits and Further Reading   250
Acknowledgements   272

INTRODUCTION

How many women are on your bookshelves?

Readers rarely set out to exclude whole groups from their reading life, but it's not rare to count up and realise that our personal libraries don't reflect the diversity of the world around us. Especially when we look back a generation or two, the imbalances can be glaring. Even a keen and curious reader might be forgiven for assuming that literature never had a place for women, and that the small handful of familiar names – Jane Austen, the Brontës, Virginia Woolf, Toni Morrison – are exceptions proving the rule. It's certainly true that in patriarchal cultures, keeping girls out of libraries and schools, denying them the ability to read and write, to learn and question, has long been (and continues to be) a powerful tool of oppression. Yet women have always been storytellers, singers, poets and playwrights – the guardians of history and myth, family lore and social ritual. Where they have been excluded, most often, is from the business, judgement and preservation of literature, rather than from its creation.

The careers of the writers in this book were launched by talent, but they were sustained by situation, luck and nerve.

Without positions of power at publishing houses, in journalism, in lecture halls and libraries, women have historically lacked the authority to declare books important, to bring them to readers and keep them in circulation. And without champions, a woman writer's reputation and legacy has always been a vulnerable thing, no matter how widely she was once read – and all the more so when her readers were mostly women, and her subject was the daily texture and intimate struggles of their lives. Scores of once-famous writers have been lost – which is to say they have been overlooked, underestimated, dismissed, neglected and forgotten – in this way. Even Virginia Woolf was shrugged off for years as a minor domestic novelist, until feminist critics reclaimed her works and restored her to her rightful position in the literary pantheon. All too often, though, the passionate advocacy of scholars does not find a broader audience, and too many brilliant, funny, weird and incendiary writers remain obscure. This book sets out to change that, with a diverse array of daring women whose work still has the capacity to shake up our expectations and spark new conversations.

Fittingly, it is Woolf who gives this book its title: it is the term she used in *A Room of One's Own* for women of the past who dared to be writers. Speaking specifically about female novelists of the nineteenth century, and their resistance to the capitalist forces that shaped publishing, she observed, 'One must have been something of a firebrand to say to oneself, Oh, but they can't buy literature too. Literature is open to everybody.' A *firebrand*: literally a burning piece of wood, used to light the way or spark a blaze – the origin of this meaning being roughly contemporary with the fourteenth-century life of poet and political theorist Christine de Pizan. Later, it would also come to describe, figuratively, a person who lit a trail – straight to hell in Christine's case, some of her contemporaries said. A fearsome agitator, both divisive and inspiring. To Woolf, a firebrand was, simply, one lit from within by the conviction that literature should not be hoarded and hidden away, but that it could and should be opened up by her flame.

The twenty-five writers in this selection produced everything from temple hymns to muckraking journalism, via poetry, memoir, drama, fiction, film and innumerable hybrid literary forms. In terms of class and occupation, they include aristocrats and bohemians, workers and warriors, immigrants and servants, farmers' daughters and heiresses. They were married and widowed, mothers and spinsters, straight and queer. Those who were mothers faced the challenge of balancing a creative life with the demands of caregiving and providing for a family, in some cases sacrificing access to their children. Looking at their lives shows how limited our ideas of a literary career often are – founded on fantasies of early success followed by sustained achievement and a retirement of resting on well-earned laurels. Yes, there are early hotshots, but also many instances of fading and resurgence, of fallow years followed by an astonishing late blossoming. Some of these women were in their twenties when they did their best work, but just as many were in their forties or seventies. When our female literary canon contains just a handful of names, it's easy to think that only a certain kinds of women can write. Money makes it possible and children, surely, make it impossible. But here we have Kay Boyle and Lucille Clifton, both mothers of six, and both prolific, prize-winning, politically active writers: perennially short of cash, yet humane and courageous in their art throughout their lives.

The huge variety in the circumstances of these women's lives – stability or constant motion; raising many children or none; having the support of a partner, or being that support; inheriting wealth or losing a home for lack of money – reminds us there is no single way to be a woman writer. And even that label should give us pause. I use it because, for the most part, these writers lived and worked in times and places where sex was destiny, and the gender binary was rigidly enforced and violently policed. Still, several fought its constraints. For the nonbinary Pauli Murray and the gender-rebellious George Sand, in particular, the label 'woman writer' feels neither accurate nor sufficient and says more about the reception of their work than the way they lived in the world.

Several figures in this book also challenge conventional assumptions about the content of women's writing, tackling topics, such as war and politics, traditionally deemed to be masculine arenas. Mary Borden's chilling, laconic war stories, written during her time as a hospital nurse during the First World War, are said to have inspired Ernest Hemingway, while journalist Mary Heaton Vorse was a vital frontline witness to the often violent strikes and labour activism that roiled early twentieth-century America. Others, like the elegant Japanese court writer Murasaki Shikibu and the bawdy Restoration playwright Aphra Behn, put themselves in the shoes of male seducers and rakes, skewering the bombast of individual men and slyly undermining patriarchy's pretensions of superiority. History acts on them all, but for some more dramatically than others. The biographical details of Olympe de Gouges, caught up in the throes of the French Revolution, or of Juana Manuela Gorriti, fleeing across borders amid the turbulence of nineteenth-century Latin American politics, themselves read like stories.

No matter what their subject, women writers across the historical spectrum have found it hard to avoid the question of what it means to be a woman, especially a public woman, in a society organised to silence and exclude them. Many of them used their prominence to push for women's education, and others joined the fight for the vote. Those who lived long before such rights could

INTRODUCTION

be suggested without a roar of laughter, nevertheless imagined alternatives, like Christine de Pizan's jubilant, all-female 'city of ladies' or the flipping of a famous story's hero into a heroine, as in Charlotte Lennox's *The Female Quixote*. The nineteenth-century novelist and journalist Fanny Fern showed there was money to be made as a woman speaking frankly to women – among other things, she was famed for coining the phrase 'the way to a man's heart is through his stomach'. Her sympathetic eye on her readers' everyday lives made her, for many years, the highest paid newspaper columnist in America.

For Harriet Jacobs, Fanny Fern's near-contemporary in pre-Civil War America, the disadvantages of sex were brutally compounded by the horrors of slavery, which robbed women of all bodily autonomy – as Jacobs would boldly testify in her autobiography. Long after emancipation, racism persisted as a burden bound up with gender in multiple, unpredictable ways, as writers as different as Jessie Redmon Fauset and Lucille Clifton make clear in their work. Elsewhere, the work of the Chinese-British novelist Edith Maude Eaton, who adopted the pen name Sui Sin Far, demonstrates how an identity can be both inherited and invented.

Some of these firebrands may be familiar: Christine de Pizan and Aphra Behn have been widely hailed as feminist foremothers, the latter by Virginia Woolf in *A Room of One's Own*, but their work is not always as well known as their names. Others, like the ancient Mesopotamian priestess Enheduanna, who has a strong claim to be the world's earliest identified author of either sex, will likely be new to even the best-read feminist book lovers. Whatever the case, I hope that readers will be inspired to seek out new writing or to crack the spines of books that have languished on their shelves for too long, and that this selection can make a good starting point for discussion, debate and further reading.

The selection here is necessarily idiosyncratic. I began with my particular area of interest and expertise, the literature of early twentieth-century Europe and America, especially New York, Paris and London. Seeking a greater range of voices, I looked first for writers whose works resonated in a female line of succession (as Aphra Behn did for Woolf), and consulted friends and colleagues for their own recommendations. Without seeking to impose narrow standards of feminism on writers from vastly different times and places, I found myself especially drawn to writers who protested women's subordination under patriarchy, as well as those who worked to publish and promote other writers, like the Nigerian novelist Flora Nwapa or literary editor Jessie Redmon Fauset. Since becoming a mother four years ago I am keenly interested in how writing and family life coexist, and in how writers find meaning in the daily minutiae of their lives, as well as in the grand vistas of history. And while I'm always eager for literary gossip, I have tried to downplay the role of more-famous men in these women's lives. Above all, I have tried to showcase writers who are not only worth reading, but well worth reading about.

I am indebted and deeply grateful to the scholars and readers on whose labour a collection like this depends. The biographies and critical sources I used, as well as suggestions for further reading, are included at the end of the book. However, in the profiles themselves, I have prioritised the voices of the writers themselves, rather than the judgements of critics or contemporaries, in the hope that this allows readers to form their own opinions and respond more directly to work that speaks to them.

This book began as an effort to 'feminise' the still overwhelmingly male literary canon, and taken together, these twenty-five firebrands can constitute a new, global, female canon – or at least, the foundation of one. But they do something more

INTRODUCTION

important than that: their stories help us to confront what a canon is, and how it is formed. So many of these writers, from Murasaki Shikibu in the eleventh century to Kay Boyle in the twentieth, were successes by any measure in their day: published, paid and highly praised, their work taught and discussed. Yet over and over again, these figures fade from the record, from literary history, university syllabi and common knowledge. Even the prize-winners. Even the bestsellers. Canons are supposed to reassure us that the cream of the crop will rise to the top by some impersonal movement against gravity. But what if there is no gravity, just human decisions, made over and over – and for most of literary history, made by men? If there's no objective standard of greatness, no agreement about whom we should read – what then?

Such a destabilising possibility, I believe, can be exciting. Nobody here is a writer you *should* know, but individually and collectively they serve as a reminder that the names with which we are familiar since our earliest forays into reading represent only a morsel – a crumb from the banquet. Taken together, these profiles demonstrate the breadth and scope of women's writing and of women's identities throughout literary history. Opening us up to new subjects, experiences and voices, they help us look at the past in new ways, putting paid to our assumptions about silent, cloistered women. In that spirit, this book is an invitation to the pleasure of discovery, to a richer and endlessly rewarding literary feast.

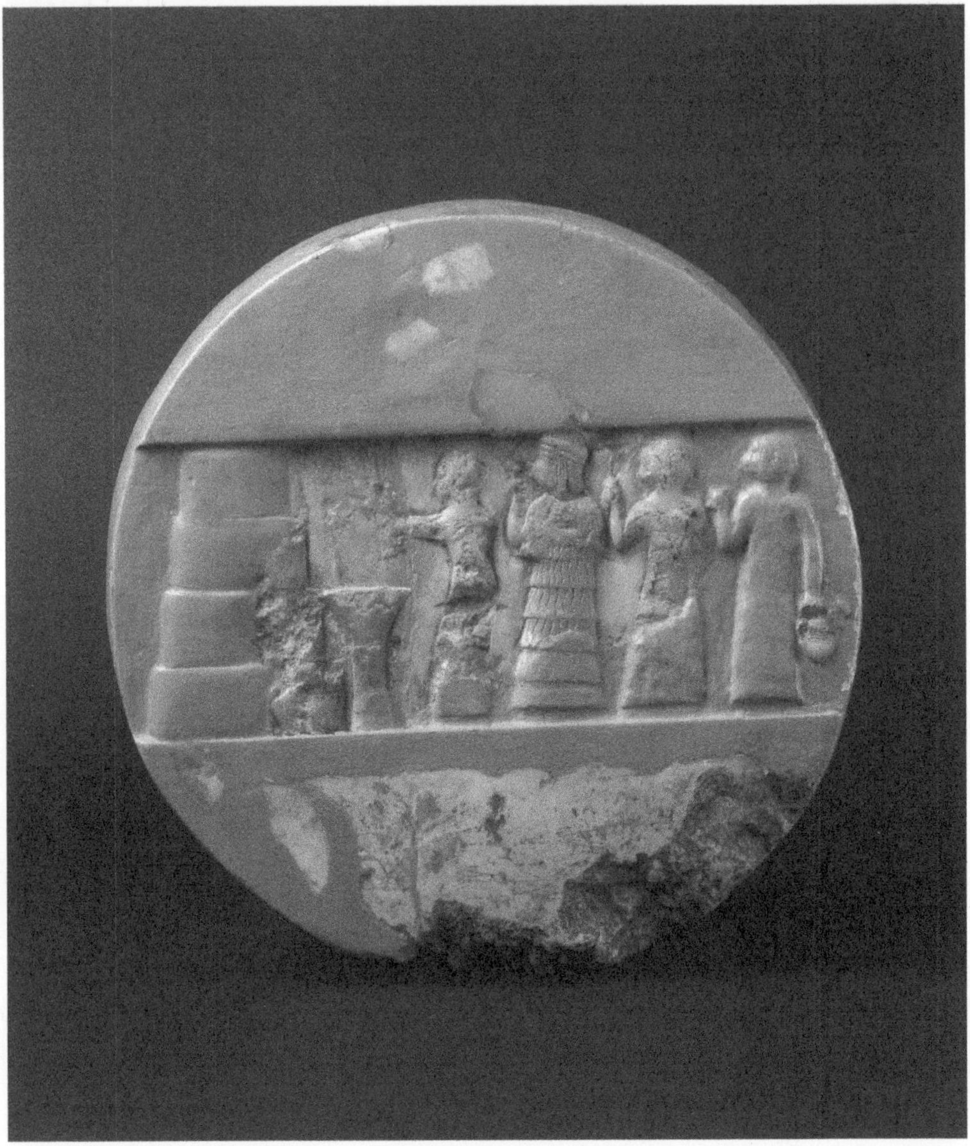

'I, Enheduanna...'

ENHEDUANNA
(*c.* 2286–*c.* 2251 BCE)

What would it mean for literary history if the world's first identified author were a woman? One who, right from the start, was laying claim to her poetic voice, comparing art to childbirth, and crying out in protest against the violence of men? More than four thousand years ago, a solid millennium and a half before the compositions of Homer, a priestess and princess called her own name into history, as the author of a poem, a hymn to her chosen goddess: *I, Enheduanna*. Her exact dates of birth and death are a mystery, as is her mother's identity, and the details of her daily life. And yet, carved and repeated and passed down over centuries, we can still read her words.

Enheduanna lived around 2300 BCE, and the little information we have about her life outside her writing has been gleaned primarily from a small, shattered alabaster disk, unearthed in the ruins of a temple at Ur when it was excavated in the 1920s. There is a picture of her on one side, and the writing on the other identifies her as the daughter of the Emperor Sargon, and a high priestess of the moon god Nanna. A high priestess was a figure who straddled the realms of the human and the divine, with a status akin to royalty. In Nanna's temple, Enheduanna was considered the human embodiment of the god's wife, Ningal, and she addressed most of her powerful poetry to their daughter, the destructive goddess known as Inanna or Ishtar. She was not the temple's first high priestess, but her image on the disk established the iconography of the role: she is depicted as physically taller than her human attendants, and is crowned with an elaborate headdress.

Enheduanna lived at a time of cultural and political turbulence. New languages and writing systems were transforming knowledge and communication, while voyages of discovery and conquest were expanding the parameters of her people's world. Her father, Sargon of Akkad, was the world's first emperor. Beginning in 2334 BCE, his forces swept from the Mediterranean Sea to the Persian Gulf, conquering more than thirty independent city-states across ancient Mesopotamia to forge the Akkadian Empire. Needing help to administer his now extensive lands, he sent his daughter to serve as high priestess in the Sumerian city of Ur, in the southeast of modern-day Iraq – a role that was political as much as religious. There, she was tasked with strengthening ties between the Akkadians and the local Sumerians, who had their own distinct customs, language and deities.

Although other writings that are contemporary with Enheduanna's life survive, the earliest versions of her poems that we have date from some five hundred years after her death. In the Old Babylonian period, around 1894 to 1595 BCE, her poems were taught in schools for scribes and priests, and sufficiently famous and well-regarded that they were being copied by students across Mesopotamia. In dense, tiny, intricate markings, her words were stabbed into wet clay tablets with the kind of back-breaking, eye-straining diligence that is testament to their importance. In contrast to other ancient texts – like the Mesopotamian *Epic of Gilgamesh*, which originated about one hundred years after Enheduanna's time, or the poetry of Sappho, written nearly two thousand years later – there are no lacunae in Enheduanna's poems. The challenge for translators lies not in their fragmentary state, but in the compact density of the language. Indeed, there are more than a hundred extant copies of her poem 'The Exultation of Inanna', which is evidence for its enormous popularity and cultural impact – although, to some scholars, this is proof that the scribes themselves wrote the poems, reaching back into the past to borrow the voice and identity of a high priestess, for reasons that we can't discern but that somehow seem more plausible than the existence of a woman author.

After the end of the First Babylonian Empire, around 1595 BCE, the chain of cultural inheritance snapped, and Enheduanna slipped out of sight, until modern European archaeologists began to dig in the remains of Sargon's empire. In cities dating from the fourth millennium BCE, they found a wealth of tantalising information which gave a picture of a complex, literate, highly interconnected world. In 1922 Sir Leonard Woolley led an expedition on behalf of the British Museum and University of Pennsylvania to excavate Enheduanna's city of Ur. With a team that included his future wife Katharine, he uncovered an extraordinary cache of untouched treasures, including royal tombs, weapons, jewellery and a number of cylinder seals – small, inscribed gemstones that were used to create an impression in clay. These were valued in themselves as works of art, but often served to indicate the identity of individuals and guarantee agreements, much like a modern signature or brand. One such seal gives us the name of the man who worked as Enheduanna's hairdresser. However, in his book about the excavation, despite the fact that it appears on the alabaster disk bearing her image, as well as on tablets found in neighbouring cities, Woolley does not mention Enheduanna's name.

On the site of the moon god's temple in Ur, Woolley's team found tablets engraved with cuneiform script, which could have presented evidence of a school, but images of women led their conjectures in another direction – a cloister, perhaps, or a harem. Other objects also provided clear evidence of women's participation in public life: sculptures and engravings depicting women at work in both urban and agricultural settings, producing textiles and pottery, taking part in religious rituals, and reading. Yet the men directing the excavation of these objects, steeped in their own prejudices about women's social roles, were baffled by these. A small, intricately carved sculpture found in Ur depicts a straight-backed, seated woman with a headdress similar to Enheduanna's and a cuneiform tablet resting on her lap. 'Our specimen carries a tablet on her knees,' the German scholar who unearthed the object dutifully recorded. 'Its meaning is not clear to me.' The tiny, beautiful thing was brushed aside as easily as the idea that there were women readers in this ancient world.

Enheduanna has since been identified as the author of three long poems and a number of shorter hymns in praise of different religious temples. Her poetry cannot be separated from her role as a priestess, and reflects the range and complexity of the Akkadian and Sumerian theological universe. There were several hundred gods, interrelated and vying for power, and they were celebrated as the patron deities of specific cities, communities and households. Worshippers created sculptures representing themselves – some of the earliest known self-portraits – and left them in sanctuaries to hold their place when they could not be there in person. Enheduanna's temple hymns reflect this diversity and form an important piece of the theological puzzle of her time and place. They help illuminate the duties of a priestess in her shrine, which included tracking the lunar cycle and marking the calendar accordingly (a duty that, we might conjecture, held particular importance for women).

Her longer poems address the goddess the Sumerians called Inanna – known as Ishtar to the Akkadians. In two of the long poems, *The Exultation of Inanna* and *A Hymn to Inanna*, Enheduanna calls out her own name in the process of praising the goddess. She describes herself as having given birth to her poem, using a word that can also be translated as releasing, creating, or speaking the poem into existence. Priestesses like Enheduanna were not supposed to bear children, but instead belonged to their own religious lineage, inheriting and transmitting power through their role as temple guardians. So it is striking to see, in one of the earliest literary creations we have, the yoking of bodily and imaginative reproduction and women as the bearers of words and life together.

The Exultation of Inanna addresses the deity as 'Queen of all cosmic powers', using a short word, *me*, that is dense with meaning, signifying both the realm of a god's power and the various objects that are encompassed within it. Although Inanna is nominally the daughter of the moon god Nanna, Enheduanna venerates her as a disrupter of order and hierarchy, a force of chaos, unstable:

'You spew venom on a country, like a dragon.
Wherever you raise your voice, like a tempest, no crop is left standing.
You are a deluge, bearing that country away.
You are the sovereign of heaven and earth, you are their warrior goddess!'

The poet goes on to describe an attack by a rival ruler, Lugal-Ane, who threatens Enheduanna with sexual assault and the desecration of her temple: 'A slobbered hand was laid across my honeyed mouth,/ What was fairest in my nature was turned to dirt.' She rages against the audacity of this invader, who has torn off her sacred headdress and handed her a dagger, saying 'This is just right for you.' She calls upon the goddess for vengeance, a terrifying prospect after the vision she has prepared of Inanna's apocalyptic force: 'Destroyer of mountains, you give force to the storm.'

It wasn't until 1968 that Enheduanna's poems were collected and translated into English, just in time for a burgeoning feminist movement to seize on the idea of an undiscovered female literary progenitor. It's dispiriting, if unsurprising, that feminist enthusiasm for the discovery of Enheduanna was met with even stronger determination to discredit her claim to be, not only the first female author, but simply 'the first known author in world literature' (as she was called in 1978 by an American anthropologist, Marta Weigle). In contrast to the still-murky idea of Homer, who has never been firmly identified as a single, real person, Enheduanna was named and depicted in her own time as an author. Nevertheless, other scholars responded by labelling her a 'wish-fulfilment figure' and cautioning against an 'emotional response' to ancient texts: as though feminists were seizing on her existence in order to rebalance the history of the world and give women equal credit as artists and creators. The focus of the debate quickly shifted away from who Enheduanna was and what she wrote, and towards a critique of what her modern audience was trying to make of her. But to return Enheduanna to literary history does far more than indulge a wish for a new feminist heroine. It allows us to consider the multitude of ways in which literary creation happens, and to question the values that we attach to the idea of an author.

Enheduanna's most recent translator, the Danish scholar Sophus Helle, reminds us that our modern attachment to the author as an individual creator whose work originates in the private recesses of their imagination, is a recent idea – laughably recent, given the scale of history we're talking about here. At some point in seventeenth-century Europe, critics decided that inspiration, skill and genius were the ineffable qualities of a literary artist, who necessarily worked alone. This vision relegated the multitude of intermediaries who are involved in literary creation – scribes, compilers, transcribers, translators, performers, and on and on – to the obscure corners that they occupy today as collaborators, ghostwriters or plagiarists. It's a vision that would have made little sense to the ancient authors whom those Europeans venerated. To Sappho or Plato, as well as to Enheduanna, literary 'inspiration' was a gift from the gods, the spiritual 'authors' who worked with, and through, a human vessel. The 'solitary genius' model turns its back on a wealth of evidence, across divergent cultures and histories, for literature being a collective endeavour, a creative assemblage of other voices, and the threads of the past. Our English words 'text' and 'textile' have the same root, and 'weaving' is among the most potent and ancient metaphors we have for literary creativity. A human weaving cloth is not producing threads like a spider, but gathering and binding them. And, of course, that work has historically been done, most often and most consistently, by women – like Odysseus's wife Penelope, who spent her days at the loom and her nights unpicking her woven cloth in order to keep the story, in which her husband is alive and will return to her, going indefinitely.

Ironically, all this wrangling through the 1970s and 1980s about the authorial status of Enheduanna played out against a backdrop of theories arguing that the 'author' was either dead or non-existent – at best, the arranger of ideas rather than their originator. But still it seemed to be a given that the author (who did not exist) could not be a woman. Why not? A woman of Enheduanna's elite birth had the leisure and space to write, the ancient equivalent of Woolf's room of her own and five hundred pounds a year. Unlike men of her rank, she didn't have to engage in politics, conquer cities or risk her life in war, nor did she have to scratch out a living through manual labour. She belonged to a culture that devoted enormous effort to making art to honour the gods. Why shouldn't her poetry belong to that tradition? 'The compiler of the tablet is Enheduanna,' the poet proclaims in her collection of temple hymns. 'My King, something has been created that no one had ever created before!' The author compiles and creates; the scribes record and revise; the goddess sings. There is not a single way to be an author.

源氏三佳人むらさきの

蹄亭筆

青戦園
笠砂子

さゝ波の
花の山邊も
ゆかしとて
ふみまどひぬる
かきのと
けき

'Among her assemblage of tales she found accounts, whether fact or fiction, of many extraordinary fates, but none, alas, of any like her own.'

MURASAKI SHIKIBU
(*c.* 973–*c.* 1014)

Half the globe and a few millennia away from Enheduanna's temple, we once again find a female author present at the dawn of something: here she is, the author of (arguably) the world's first novel. *The Tale of Genji* is the work of a writer born in Japan, in the city now known as Kyoto, around 973. We have come to know her as Murasaki Shikibu – a pseudonym assembled from the name of her book's central female character and the government ministry where her father worked. She grew up during the Heian period, which spanned the ninth to the twelfth centuries, during which a tiny, internecine group of aristocrats ruled a population of some five million. Hierarchy was everything and gender roles were firmly fixed.

Her mother, it seems, died very young, and Murasaki grew up with her brother in their father's house in Kyoto. As a child she would eavesdrop on her brother's Chinese lessons, and quickly grasp the passages he struggled with, which prompted her father to exclaim, 'What a pity she was not born a man!' Chinese was the language of politics, an arena barred to women, so her intelligence had no practical value. However, her father was a scholar of classical

Chinese literature as well as a civil servant, and took the unusual step of educating his daughter in the language claimed by men.

In imperial Japan, family origins, as well as sex, dictated the course of a person's life. Murasaki was born into the extended Fujiwara clan, who dominated the political scene throughout the tenth and eleventh centuries. Rather than attempting to rule as emperors themselves, the Fujiwara operated as the power behind the throne of various child-rulers, establishing regencies and marrying their young daughters into positions of influence at court. Murasaki's branch of the family was not sufficiently elite for her to make a dynastic marriage, so she married rather late by the standards of her time, in her mid-twenties. Her husband was her second cousin and a friend of her father's who worked in the same government ministry. He was considerably older, and she was widowed not long after the birth of their child, a daughter, Kataiko, in 999. Although she was married for only three years and was not her husband's only or most favoured wife, Murasaki still felt depressed and lonely after his death. As she described later, she found herself moving through life 'from day to day in listless fashion [...] doing little more than registering the passage of time'. But out of grief came a glimmer of liberation. Her late husband had been wealthy, and Murasaki would have had help running her household and caring for her daughter. In a pattern that will repeat for many writers in this book, early widowhood brought with it a measure of privacy and freedom which allowed her to devote time to writing.

We do not know exactly when or why Murasaki began writing the stories that together became *The Tale of Genji*, although the legend that she retreated to a lakeside temple and was inspired by gazing at the moon on a late summer night is almost certainly a poetic fiction. The first instalments, written on paper folded in neat concertina shapes, circulated among the author's friends, and soon found their way to the women of the imperial court. At the time, men composed poetry in Japanese and conducted business and affairs of state in Chinese, but only women openly read fiction in the vernacular. These *monogatari*, or tales, of which *The Tale of Genji* is the most enduring example, were a female domain, designed for entertainment and social instruction. The novel, however, also included almost 800 short poems embedded in the text, a demonstration of their importance in the veiled and coded world of the imperial Japanese court.

By the time she was in her early thirties, at the start of the eleventh century, Murasaki's literary reputation was brilliant enough that she was plucked to be a jewel for the court of the sixteen-year-old Empress Shōshi, to serve as her lady in waiting and tutor. Shōshi had been a consort of the Emperor Ichijō since the age of twelve, a match brokered by her father, a Fujiwara heavyweight named Michinaga who brought Murasaki to his daughter's court. He may have had seduction in mind, but it was primarily an effort to boost Shōshi's status against the Empress Teishi, Ichijō's first wife, whose court boasted the presence of Sei Shōnagon, the author of the wildly popular miscellany *The Pillow Book*. Murasaki judged her chief literary rival to be 'dreadfully conceited', writing in her diary that Shōnagon 'thought herself so clever and littered her writing with Chinese characters' in an effort to impress readers, but that on closer examination these 'left a great deal to be desired'. The sharpness of that judgement suggests self-confidence, but Murasaki also often felt lonely and out of place at court. Although she lived as one of around twenty ladies in waiting, she had trouble making friends, and worried over how she was seen and judged, describing herself as 'perversely stand-offish' and hard to approach. 'Do they really look on me as such a dull thing, I wonder?' she wrote, with a mixture of self-recrimination and defiance. 'But I am what I am.'

The world of the eleventh-century Heian court was deemed 'above the clouds', far above earthly concerns, by those fortunate enough to float in its heights. Daily life was an aerial ballet of signs and gestures, an elaborate performance between men and women who could not look at each other directly, and who fell in love instead with glimpses, with scents, with handwriting, with poetry. As it often is in elite societies, beauty was currency, but here it was also ephemeral, the flare before the fade. It whispered in the sweep of a line of calligraphy, the balance of syllables in a poem, the layering of a perfume and the gradations of colour in a folded sleeve. Although men's and women's social roles were sharply distinguished, their beauty standards overlapped. Pale faces, smooth skin, elegance and physical grace were desirable in both sexes, and men's sleeves, just like women's, were often damp with their tears. The culture was a *mood*, in which the thrill of aesthetic pleasure was always wrapped up in the ache of its vanishing. Or at least, such was the moonlight-dappled fantasy.

Murasaki's diary, however, shows the distance between the ideals of courtly life and its grubbier human reality. Written in vernacular Japanese and focusing on the years between 1008 and 1010, the diary offers rare and detailed glimpses of court life, including the rituals to celebrate the arrival of Shōshi's two sons, and the power struggles between the empress's father and her more reticent husband and between the rival empresses. It also detailed the court's unstable balance of pleasure and propriety: Shōshi warned her ladies in waiting against excessive flirtation, yet 'also begs us not to reject advances in such a way as to hurt people's feelings,' reported Murasaki, who was about twice the empress's age. Convention kept women wrapped in shadow and shielded behind screens and curtains, but there was no real protection from men. Shortly before Murasaki entered Shōshi's court, the Imperial Palace had burned down, so the empress and her entourage moved between various mansions owned by her relatives. In these houses, the women slept on thin futons on the floor of shared quarters, open to the gardens. Murasaki describes waking up one morning to find the empress's father, Michinaga, lurking outside: 'Dew is still on the ground but His Excellency is already out in the garden ... he peers in over the top of the curtain frame.' Self-conscious, she uses the excuse of composing a poem for him – an integral part of courtship – in order to escape his attentions.

Lacking walls to keep suitors at bay, Japanese court women armoured themselves in elaborate formal costumes called *jūnihitoe*, meaning 'twelve layers', although the exact number varied. The robes' multiple layers provided much-needed warmth in winter and also provided an opportunity for fashionable display, as the linings were arranged to peep out in multicoloured arrays, signalling the wearer's taste. Murasaki describes approvingly the get-up of one lady at court who wore 'a plain yellow-green jacket, a train shading at the hem, and a sash and waistbands with raised embroidery in orange and white checked silk. Her mantle had five cuffs of white lined with dark red, and her crimson gown was of beaten silk.' By contrast, a pair of women whose cuff-layering techniques are deemed subpar are ridiculed in her diary for daring to appear in front of other courtiers in such unfortunate colour combinations.

If the ability to compose one's layers was important at court, a flair for composing lines of poetry was indispensable. Those who lacked skill and style in poetry were fatally hindered in the competitive arena of courtship, and copying and memorising poetry was central to any elite person's education, man or woman. And courtship, writ large, is the driving force of the *Tale*, which follows the hero, Genji – nicknamed the 'Shining Prince' – through a dizzying array of infatuations, flirtations, romantic conquests and love affairs, which continues even after his death, with the more sombrely drawn exploits of his descendants. He is the son of an emperor by his most beloved consort, who dies when Genji is a toddler. The grieving emperor wishes to appoint the boy his official heir but, because of his mother's low social status and the opposition of the Fujiwara, cannot do so without enraging the court, endangering Genji and possibly causing wider unrest.

The gradations of privilege accorded to women in the polygamous imperial court were as subtly layered as their colourful sleeves. At the top, there was a single empress, then several wives classed as consorts, and further down the ladder, a group known as intimates. To keep such a delicate system in harmonious balance took a great deal of effort, and an emperor's fairness and equal treatment of his wives, despite personal preferences, was highly valued. When his affection for one woman became too obvious, as it had with Genji's father's for his mother, it aroused dangerous resentment and jealousy. To protect Genji, his father takes the unusual – and narratively useful – step of giving Genji a surname, which designates him as a 'commoner.' He's still one of the elite, but no longer part of the imperial lineage and therefore not tied to the court. This gives the character freedom to roam – and seduce – more widely.

From his childhood, Genji is marked out by his extraordinary beauty, talent and charm. His appeal even troubles the gender binary as 'the other men felt a desire to see him as a woman'. Although his romantic entanglements drive the story, it inverts the traditional Western marriage plot: Genji is married right at the beginning of the story. The wedding is held just after his coming-of-age ceremony when he is around twelve years old. His bride is the daughter of an important courtier, who is a few years older than him and ashamed by her husband's immaturity and low status. The marriage is largely a formality, and the pair do not live together, although the union later produces a son. In the meantime, Genji's other romantic entanglements offer endless opportunities for comedy, tragedy and everything in between, showcasing his skills in the art of seduction and, somewhat less overtly, his moral education. Monogamy may have no place in Genji's world, but his creator praises his loyalty and honesty. Although later, more abstemious generations of readers saw him as a playboy, there is no doubt that Murasaki worked hard to make Genji an ideal of his time – but also to expose the decadence at the heart of imperial Japanese culture that was in danger of refining itself into obsolescence.

At the time of his marriage, Genji's adolescent heart lies with a different woman, Lady Fujitsubo, his father's new wife. The rumour at court is that this young woman bears an uncanny likeness to Genji's late mother. Genji goes on to have a secret relationship with the new consort, and together they have a son, but they can never openly be lovers. Their illegitimate son, however, is recognised as Crown Prince and eventually ascends the throne, a shocking rupture to the fantasy of an unbroken imperial lineage. After a series of unfulfilling romantic encounters and misadventures, Genji retreats from court to the countryside, where he glimpses a child of ten through a fence and falls in love. This girl is Murasaki, the author's namesake, and Fujitsubo's niece – who therefore also, in the chain of resemblance, looks like Genji's own lost mother. Love, in this story, is always a matter of recurrence and echo.

Genji steals the girl away to his own palace and educates her to emulate Fujitsubo. Meanwhile, his wife dies soon after she bears him their son, freeing him to marry Murasaki when she comes of age. His father the emperor dies and is succeeded by his half-brother – and when Genji is found in bed with one of the new emperor's consorts, he is banished from court to the countryside. There, he has another affair that results in the birth of his only daughter. He is pardoned and returns to court, where he sees his secret son assume the throne, a crowning achievement for a man of his rank. Then things start a downward slide: our hero turns forty, and takes another wife, which upsets Murakami. Her death, not long afterwards, breaks his heart, and inspires him to reflect on the brevity of existence. The next chapter has the title *'Kumogakure'* or 'Vanished into the clouds', but is deliberately left blank. When the story resumes, Genji has disappeared from the narrative.

The loss of Genji and Murasaki long before the end of the book can take modern readers by surprise. Although the story continues, following two of Genji's descendants, the disappearance of the 'Shining Prince' from the stage robs the last chapters of the tale of some of its energy. Without our hero's grounding presence, the court seems all the stranger, as coolly remote in its beauty as the moon. Less than two centuries later, that serene realm would be overrun by the march of provincial armies, especially the samurai, who stormed the palace gates of the emperors and smashed their paper-thin ideals. But Genji survived, neither paragon nor pariah, but something else: a labour of love, a window into a vanished world, and a beacon of the possibilities of fiction to entertain, instruct and enchant.

In 1021, just a few years after Murasaki's death, another Heian court diary records the thrilled reaction of a young reader to receiving the full novel in a set of fifty boxed volumes – *The Tale of Genji* is roughly twice the length of *War and Peace*. It would be more than nine hundred years before the delight of the girl unboxing her stories would be shared by readers around the world. As no complete manuscript survives, the text we have today is based on a thirteenth-century compilation of different, fragmentary versions. By that time, Murasaki's formal, poetic language had become hard for ordinary readers to grasp, so annotated and illustrated versions, modern adaptations and interpretations proliferated, infusing the book deeply into Japanese culture even as the decadent Heian period faded into history.

In the late nineteenth century, Europeans fell into infatuation with all things Japanese, as that long-closed society suddenly pulled back its shutters. But Murasaki's particular world remained elusive – an elegant mystery of 'cranes and chrysanthemums', as Virginia Woolf put it – until 1920, when her diary was translated by the American Annie Shepley Omori and her Japanese collaborator Kōchi Doi. Five years later, English scholar Arthur Waley published the first instalment in his landmark six-volume translation of *The Tale of Genji*.

Reviewing the book for *Vogue* in 1925, Woolf marvelled at the historical coincidence that 'while the Aelfrics and Aelfreds croaked and coughed in England', the Lady Murasaki was composing verse for an audience of well-nigh pathological refinement. The Heian court audience, Woolf believed, was comprised of 'Grown-up people, who needed no feats of strength to rivet their attention'. To Woolf, an era when the childish, masculine business of war and politics did not dominate was a mature one, and would be especially nurturing to women. Although the handsome Genji is at the centre of her story, Woolf argued that Murasaki's interest really lay with the women he loves: 'To light up the many facets of [Genji's] mind, Lady Murasaki, being herself a woman, naturally chose the medium of other women's minds.' Genji's pursuit of women may be sexual, but it is also, and more importantly, psychological. His encounters with women are not side plots in the story of Genji's life but the heart of it, and they are narrated not just by him, but through a point of view that slips freely between characters, pursuing the truth about who people are. In a world of veils and illusion, what Murasaki really watched, 'sitting down in her silk dress and trousers with pictures before her and the sound of poetry in her ears, with flowers in her garden and nightingales in the trees', was the life that beat on underneath.

Ci commencent Cent Balades.

'There is not the slightest doubt that women belong to the people of God and the human race as much as men.'

CHRISTINE DE PIZAN
(1364–c. 1430)

In fifteenth-century France as in many other places and eras, from Victorian England to Iran in the 1950s, it was scandalous for a woman to publish love poetry under her own name. But Christine de Pizan, the first professional woman writer in Europe, found that scandal plus skill can be a lucrative formula. Far from concealing her gender, Christine made a feature of it, diving into the debates raging around her (mostly between men) about the intellectual and moral capabilities of women. She called out the injustices of patriarchy and, through her writing and her own fame, showed what a woman could do. According to Simone de Beauvoir, Christine was 'the first time we see a woman take up her pen in defence of her sex'. But she also tackled traditionally masculine subjects, becoming a respected writer on politics, war and military strategy. She wrote a biography of King Charles V of France and conduct manuals for queens, but she also championed the moral virtue of ordinary women, as neither sluts nor saints.

Although she spent most of her life in France, primarily at the royal court, Christine was born in the Republic of Venice in 1364. Europe was still reeling from the devastation of the Black Death, which had ended a little more than a decade earlier and wiped out roughly a third of the population. Charles V ascended the throne of France in the same year, in the lull of peace between the first two phases of the Hundred Years' War. The new king was ambitious and intellectual, earning the epithet Charles the Wise. He vastly expanded his library to contain well over a thousand volumes, and commissioned new translations into French of an array of classical works, especially those on the subject of good government. When Christine was five, her father, a respected physician and scholar, was appointed as Charles's court astrologer and moved his family to Paris. She grew up in a world where knowledge was power, and her father, as unconventional as Murasaki Shikibu's in Kyoto almost four centuries earlier, gave her a boy's education which included Latin and the sciences, and encouraged her to read and study widely. Women's education would become a passionate cause for Christine over the course of her literary career. She would argue that women had 'freer and sharper' minds than men, and that the root of their misery lay in their lack of access to learning.

Despite this unconventional upbringing, Christine was married at the age of fifteen to another courtier ten years her senior, the king's secretary Étienne du Castel. The couple had three children and, judging by Christine's later, heartfelt writings in praise of marriage, it seems to have been a happy union. But less than a decade into her marriage, Christine's father died, then a resurgence of the plague claimed her husband, too. Suddenly, she was solely responsible for supporting her family, which included her mother and niece in addition to her own young children. If a widow didn't choose to remarry, she had few other options, but writing – if one were savvy about it – could be both respectable and profitable. A writer at that time relied on patronage, trading flattering portrayals and fulsome dedications for financial support. As a woman raised in the court, Christine knew her wealthy audience intimately and brought that knowledge to bear as she navigated the balance of teasing and praise, substance and sycophancy, that kept their purses open. Patronage was not simply a quid pro quo of praise for coin, however. A brilliant writer reflected her lustre back onto her patrons, making them appear cultured and discerning, and the financial exchange was backed by the growing recognition that writers had the power to shape a reputation and define a legacy.

Christine's early love ballads were powerfully direct, abjuring the games and guile expected of women being wooed. She praised her late husband for his care of her on their wedding night, when 'A hundred kisses I recall he gave/But took no liberties', and grieved him after his death, with the refrain, 'I am alone, a widow, garbed in black.' She dedicated poems to her royal supporters, in particular the 'High, excellent crowned Queen of France', whom she honoured as 'very redoubtable princess, powerful lady, born at a lucky hour'. This queen, Isabeau of Bavaria, was the consort of Charles VI, who had inherited the crown at the age of eleven after the death of his father in 1380, not long after Christine's marriage. As a teenager, married to his equally young bride, the king had begun to exhibit the first signs of the mental illness that would cause long absences from court and overshadow his reign, setting off bloody power struggles among rival noble houses. Christine carefully navigated between these warring aristocrats as her reputation rose. But she also kept her eye on the horizon, where a new audience was gathering.

Over the course of Christine de Pizan's lifetime, the status, availability and physical form of written texts changed dramatically. The manuscript scroll gave way to the bound codex, the precursor to the modern paper book, and materials for bookmaking became far cheaper. This meant that lower levels of nobility could commission writers directly and build their own libraries. Rising literacy rates also vastly expanded the audience for literature and Christine wrote in vernacular French, rather than Latin, ensuring that her work could reach and delight these new readers. Yet books were still lavishly decorated, as much art objects as they were transmitters of knowledge, and Christine made a point of choosing the illustrators for her books and supervising their copying and illumination. She especially championed women, including one illustrator known only as 'Anastasia', who painted ornamental borders, flower details and background illustrations with remarkable delicacy and skill. The author claimed that 'one cannot find an artisan in all the city of Paris – where the best in the world are found – who can surpass her.'

In 1405, as a demonstration of her own unsurpassed brilliance, Christine completed her monumental *Book of the City of Ladies*. The book began as an intervention in the cultural battle then raging over *The Romance of the Rose*, an enormous poem written in two parts over the course of the thirteenth century, and probably the most widely read literary work in Europe at the time. The poem established the conventions of courtly love, which portrayed men as hopelessly in thrall to fickle and unattainable women. Its misogyny of devotion – 'I hate women because my beloved won't love me back' – coloured medieval thought as richly as gold leaf on the pages of an illuminated manuscript. *The Romance of the Rose* inspired endless debate, mostly between men, about the nature of love (cruel) and women (crueller). When Christine de Pizan jumped into this fight, she charged that the poem was immoral and anti-woman, and began a spirited correspondence with its male defenders. *The Book of the City of Ladies* was her final sally in this quarrel and a work that in its sheer scope eclipsed the argument.

The book takes the form of a conventional, popular medieval genre known as the 'biographical catalogue', celebrating famous figures of history and myth. It is modelled on two female-centred collections, Boccaccio's *On Famous Women* and Chaucer's *The Legend of Good Women*, but it subverts those works and the tradition by insisting that 'good women' are not exceptions but the rule. Rewriting history, myth and religion to reclaim women maligned by male authors, Christine de Pizan describes a society enriched by women's virtues. She imagines those virtues, and the women who embody them, as the building blocks of a city rising on solid foundations to an apex of honour and glory. Deliberately named for ladies (*dames*), not women (*femmes*), the 'city' welcomed even its low-born characters into a nobility derived from morality, not birth. The book is the city, and the city is the book.

Like *The Romance of the Rose*, *The Book of the City of Ladies* opens with a dream. The female narrator is reading a learned treatise about women and marriage that is full of examples of female depravity, leading her to 'despise myself and the whole of my sex as an aberration in nature'. But soon a rebellious thought pushes in. If the author of this treatise, and so many virtuous men before and after him, believe that God is perfect, and also that He created nature and everything in it, then 'why would God make such a degenerate creature?' Who is at fault – women, or the God who made them? In her confusion and dismay at the blasphemous possibility that it is God in the wrong, the narrator falls into a trance. Three female figures arrive, the embodiments of abstract virtues. Two are traditional – Lady Reason and Lady Justice – and one is of Christine's invention, Lady Rectitude (*droiture*, meaning right-thinking or right-doing). They task her with nothing less than building the symbolic city in which women's reputations will be transformed.

Lady Reason instructs the narrator to 'take the spade of [her] intelligence and dig deep to make a trench all around' to mark out the city, then offers to help carry away the mounds of dug earth, which represent all the myths about women that the author has wrongly absorbed. Lady Rectitude insists that there is nothing in women's nature that makes them inherently disloyal or unchaste – indeed, those who deceive their husbands 'go totally against nature'. To encourage the narrator, the virtues hold up diverse examples of great female power and skill. Lady Reason celebrates the poet Sappho, the mythic Amazons, the goddess Circe, Mary Magdalene, the Queen of Sheba and various contemporary French noblewomen. Under the eye of Lady Rectitude, Christine goes on to 'construct the houses and buildings inside the walls of the city of Ladies', in which her heroines – 'pagan, Hebrew, and Christian ladies' – will live, and be celebrated for their gifts, which range from chastity and familial devotion to the prophetic visions of Cassandra and the sibyls. The book's purpose occasionally forces Christine into, let us say, generous interpretations of women like Jezebel and Medea, who was renowned in Greek mythology for killing her own children to exact revenge on her faithless husband. But this is a women-only gathering. Implicitly, and knowingly, the author is asking how different these stories might sound if the people telling them were women.

Finally, the narrator and Lady Justice put the finishing touches to the city with stories of female saints, and install the Virgin Mary as the city's queen. The narrator then makes a speech addressed to all women, in which she urges them to defend their city by living up to its ideals, resisting the 'tricks and honeyed words' of those who try to tempt them into sin. Women need to be vigilant against the devil's tricks, as all humans must be in their fallen world, but she insists that women are no more susceptible to the temptations of evil than men. Equally, both sexes have souls capable of grasping the glory of God. Despite this explicitly Christian conclusion, the book demonstrates how highly Christine and her readers prized the modern space of the city and its root virtue of *civilisation*. This is not a cathedral or a cloister of virtuous women, separated from ordinary life, but a place in which art and ideas may be shared and flourish. It's highly fortified and well defended, but within its walls there is energy and freedom.

Exhausted 'by the long and continued exertion' of finishing her monumental book, Christine 'wanted only to rest and be idle for a while'. But the Three Virtues had other ideas. An illustration in her next book shows Ladies Reason, Rectitude and Justice tugging the author out of bed by the arm and prodding her to start work on *Le trésor de la cité des dames* (The Treasure of the City of Ladies), which advises young female readers on how to achieve the kind of moral success and renown for virtue that characterised the inhabitants of the City of Ladies. Dedicated to Margaret of Burgundy, the daughter of one of her patrons, the book circulated widely among European royal and noble families. Its most confrontational idea was that the new civilisation could only come to life if women were given the chance to learn – like the book's multilingual, accomplished author who was an emblem of what women could become with the benefit of an education and access to a world-class library.

In 1405, the year that Christine published these two major works, France's long-brewing political tensions broke into civil war. In 1410, her *Le Livre des fais d'armes et de chevalerie* (The Book of Feats of Arms and of Chivalry) debated military strategy and the laws of war, including details such as how much troops should be paid, how they should be punished for transgressions and how prisoners of war should be treated. Christine shared the widespread belief of the age that war was a divinely sanctioned means of settling disputes, which ought only to be embarked on by kings, as the representatives of God on earth – the following year, the French court barred lesser nobility from raising an army. Nevertheless, she recognised that it was not all glory, but that war gave rise to many 'great wrongs', including 'raping, killings, forced executions, and arsons'.

A few years later, Henry V of England defeated the French at Agincourt on St Crispin's Day, October 25, 1415. According to the peace treaty, he would become King of France after the death of Charles VI, who had become known as 'The Mad'. Christine's 1418 *Epistre de la Prison de Vie Humaine* ('Epistle on the Prison of Human Life') was a bleak letter of consolation to women mourning their dead, in which she argued that life on earth was a kind of hell, from which the soul would be liberated only in death. It was almost, but not quite, her last word.

With the English occupying Paris, it is assumed that Christine spent the next decade, her last, in the convent where her daughter lived at Poissy, a few miles west of the city. Despite Christine's championing of women's education and decrying the practice of sending noblewomen to convents as young girls, her own daughter had joined the Dominican order in 1397, as a companion to the then four-year-old Princess Marie, the fourth daughter and sixth child of Charles and Isabeau. Christine's decision to let her daughter go may reflect her loyalty to the royal family, but convents could also be places of refuge and offer a kind of freedom in violent times. Marie lived out her life at the convent, eventually becoming prioress. While at Poissy, Christine wrote nothing, for reasons we can only guess at, but perhaps her isolation from the drama of court life silenced her.

At the end of the 1420s, however, inspiration roared back, in the belligerent form of Joan of Arc. In 1428 the devout teenager approached the Dauphin, Charles VI's son, with her vision of leading the French to victory. In desperation, the besieged regent allowed her to try, and thanks to her legendary charisma she broke the siege of Orléans, setting up an English defeat and the crowning of the Dauphin as Charles VII in 1429. Christine's poem *Le Ditié de Jehanne d'Arc*, written at the high point of Joan's influence and France's renewed national optimism, was published just a few days after the coronation, and proclaimed that 'in 1429 the sun began to shine again.' The poem, the first written about the future saint, celebrated Joan at her moment of triumph as the fulfilment of both pagan and church prophecies, and the embodiment of Christine de Pizan's own positive view of women and their potential.

> 'I begin to laugh heartily for joy at the departure of the wintry season,
> during which I was wont to live confined to a dreary cage.
> But now I shall change my language from one of tears to one of song,
> because I have found the good season once again.'

Christine de Pizan died around 1430, before the betrayal of Joan led to her capture and execution, and two decades before the French finally drove the English out of France. Christine's books long outlived her, continuing to be read widely through the Renaissance and beyond; *The Book of the City of Ladies* was published in English in 1521, and Elizabeth I was known to have a copy in her library. Christine's work was timely, taking the reins of history and guiding them to her advantage; and it was timeless, capturing the frustrations of women living under patriarchal systems that could be punctured and pummelled but never quite put down.

Riley Pinx. F.W.f.

Mrs Behn.

'A Female Sweetness and a Manly Grace'

APHRA BEHN
(1640 –1689)

A prolific and popular author of plays, poetry and fiction, Aphra Behn lived and worked at society's extremes and, at times, in its shadows. Her biography is full of gaps and feints, facts obscured and veils drawn, often by the writer herself, who was also an actress and a spy. In Harbledown, Kent, in December 1640, a girl named Eaffrey Johnson was born, the likeliest candidate for the future Aphra Behn. She was probably illegitimate, explaining some of the obscurity around her birth, but whether she was raised in comfort or poverty, in the city or the country, it was decidedly during one of the most explosive eras of British history. The Civil War began when she was barely out of babyhood and King Charles I was executed when she was nine. After witnessing her country come the closest it ever would to a revolution that could sweep away the established order of centuries, she reached maturity at Cromwell's death and the restoration of the monarchy. Having grown up under the sway of Puritan zealots who shut down the theatres and cancelled Christmas, she saw the culture lurch back toward decadence and liberty, art and aristocracy in her early adulthood. But, although her work was often political and she championed the royal order, the impact of these formative upheavals is not easy to detect in her writing.

The event that did form her, and on which much of her modern reputation rests, was a close encounter with English colonialism in her early twenties. In 1663, Aphra is believed to have sailed with her father, his wife and a boy who may have been her younger brother, to the South American colony of Surinam (now the country Suriname). Her father may have been a relative of Lord Willoughby, the English nobleman in charge of the colony, a spy for the king, or simply a chancer setting out with his family on Willoughby's promise of land for settlers. At the time of Aphra's stay, which lasted around two years, the English were wrangling with the Dutch for dominance over the sugar plantations they had established on the backs of enslaved Africans. Aphra keenly observed the colony and its inhabitants, and would later draw on her experiences there for her novel *Oroonoko*, published at the end of her life in 1688. By that time, she had spent more than two decades in the hurly-burly of the London literary world, grabbing fame and money at the theatre, and courting praise and prestige with her poetry.

When she arrived back in England around 1664, Aphra met and married a man named Behn. It is plausible that he was a Dutch or German merchant, whose name might equally have been Ben, Bene or Beane. He apparently died within the year – the plague was ravaging London at the time – and left no money. Whoever he was, or indeed whether he existed at all, he bestowed on his widow the name under which she would launch her writing career: Mrs Behn. And, without funds to count on, she needed money. At that time, the newly restored king was at war with the Dutch over access to trade routes and colonies in the Americas, and Aphra landed herself a mission to spy for the English Crown in Holland. Code-named 'Astraea', Aphra arrived on the continent in the summer of 1666 with a fourteen-point lists of tasks, including bringing back to the English fold one 'Celadon', otherwise known as William Scot, the son of Oliver Cromwell's late spymaster. It is possible that Scot had known Aphra in Surinam, and there are hints that the two were, or had been, lovers. Either way, she was to offer him a pardon and a reward from the king, while gathering what information she could on the other English exiles residing in Holland.

The Dutch connections that Behn had made, via Surinam or her husband or both, gave her the language skills and insight that should have made her valuable in such a mission, but she was not valued. She was betrayed by her handlers, who refused to give Scot his promised pardon, and possibly by Scot himself, who seems to have been a triple agent. The cost of living in Antwerp shocked her, and by December she was desperate to come home. After petitioning the king's ministers repeatedly for funds, she was forced to borrow money to return to England, and continued to beg for redress, claiming at one point that she was about to be thrown in debtors' prison. The war with Holland dragged on, before a peace treaty was struck in 1667. The Dutch took control of Surinam in exchange for the North American colony of New Netherland, which sprawled inland from the port that the English had captured and rechristened New York.

The London to which Behn returned was in turmoil. Just over a month after she had arrived in Holland, the Great Fire had ripped through the city, destroying more than 13,000 homes in the dense, wooden-structured medieval core. Even the king was said to have pitched in to extinguish the flames, but the loss of life from the fire, on top of the still-rampaging plague, was devastating. In the wake of the disaster the theatre, which had been virtually banned under Cromwell, surged back to offer Londoners a desperately needed diversion. The Puritans' worst nightmare was realised, as new rules allowed women to appear on stage for the first time, and (sigh) it wasn't long before competitions were being held to judge the prettiest actress. Aphra Behn – young, talented and hungry – fell in with the theatrical crowd. Acting companies were struggling to keep up with the huge demand for entertainment, so she pitched in, transcribing and adapting older scripts, taking roles on stage and, before long, writing her own plays.

The Forc'd Marriage, her debut, appeared in 1670, quickly followed by *The Amorous Prince* and *The Dutch Lover* – titles that reflect the appetite of both writer and audience for romance with a frisson of scandal. A few years later, her play *The Rover* was a smash hit, enough to draw accusations of plagiarism for its resemblance to an unstaged script by Thomas Killigrew, the courtier, wit and playwright described by Samuel Pepys as Charles II's 'court jester'. Killigrew was head of the King's Company, the Drury Lane theatrical troupe that staged Behn's plays, and thus effectively her boss. She rejected the claim that his was the mind guiding her pen. Increasingly, Aphra Behn the playwright stepped out from behind the curtain to give voice, in the prefaces and postscripts that accompanied her printed plays, to Aphra Behn the working writer and self-sufficient woman, who was 'forced to write for Bread', yet 'not ashamed to owne it'.

The 'Bread' was undoubtedly to be found in the theatre, but it wasn't where one looked for lasting fame. Even Shakespeare, whose plays the King's Company held the exclusive right to stage, had his works freely hacked apart to cater to modern tastes. Under her code name turned pen name, 'The Incomparable Astrea' published poetry that earned her wide praise and comparisons, like many women in this book, to Sappho. Yet her writing wasn't timeless – it was always firmly rooted in her own here and now. She draped the thinnest of allegorical disguises over her friends and famous figures of the moment, and aimed her poems directly at an in-the-know reader. Behn wrote with particular frankness about sex, tackling male impotence and women's sexual pleasure in her poetry. To ease these daring subjects into acceptability, she deployed traditional classical and lyrical poetic modes, with lashings of the in-vogue pastoralism that peopled the poetic landscape with shepherdesses and their humble swains.

Androgyny fascinated Behn, and she blurred gender boundaries in her writing. Her own persona was praised in one of the poetic dedications that introduced her 1684 collection *Poems upon Several Occasions*, for combining 'A Female Sweetness and a Manly Grace'. In 'Our Cabal', which offers a parade of poetic portraits of her friends, she described the intimacy between two men as 'Too Amorous for a Swain to a Swain', observing that one 'nere paid/A Sigh or Tear to any Maid', instead bestowing 'all the Love he ever knew' on his male companion. Behn's one-time lover, John Hoyle, also shows up in 'Our Cabal' as a figure who blends feminine and masculine traits: 'His Beauty Maid; but Man, his Mien.' A lawyer who favoured democracy, Hoyle was openly bisexual and a model for the promiscuous hero of Aphra's play *The Rover*. He had a past that itself belonged on the stage, including one criminal charge (dismissed for lack of evidence) for stabbing and killing an unarmed man, and a second in 1687 for the crime of 'sodomy with a poulterer'. It was to Hoyle that Aphra sent her best known poem, 'The Disappointment', accompanied by a letter (often published alongside the poem) which asked him to refute the scandalous accusations she was hearing about him. The poem is explicit, describing an attempted tryst between a man and his beloved, who is tempted but unwilling to surrender her virtue. She falls into a trance, and he throws himself on her body, 'mad to possess', only to find that the gods have conspired to 'snatch his Pow'r, yet leave him the Desire!' The push and pull of power and desire preoccupied Behn, as shown in this poem and others. The amorous grappling of pursuer and pursued was inescapably tangled up in the larger power struggle between men and women in society. Androgyny, or 'hermaphroditism' as she sometimes called it, seemed to offer a chance to escape those constraints and held out the hope of a lover who is stronger than a woman but less dangerous than a man. In her lesbian love poem 'To the Fair Clorinda', the duality of 'fair lovely Maid' and 'Lovely Charming [male] Youth' combined in one body are what makes Clorinda desirable, not least because sex with her can be indulged without the fear of pregnancy. There is no snake in the grass: the lovers may 'Love, and yet be Innocent/ For sure no Crime with thee we can commit.'

In her poetry, Aphra Behn wove fantasies in which love, in all its forms, could offer a refuge from politics, public life and all the pressures that made it so difficult to rest in a beloved's arms. And with the monarchy's hold on power increasingly shaky and London roiling with tension over religion and royal inheritance, those romantic rural idylls seemed all the more fantastical. When the Catholic queen Mary of Modena, second wife of the unpopular James II, fell pregnant in 1687, thus potentially shunting the Protestant daughters of the king's previous marriage out of the line of succession, anti-Catholic and anti-Royalist fever threatened to break out in violence and even a revolution. Instead, just months after the birth of their son, the royal family were deposed and sent into exile. The king's Dutch nephew, William of Orange, who was married to his elder daughter Mary, took power in the glorious – that is, bloodless – revolution of 1688. Fears for the fate of James and his pregnant queen are woven into the fabric of the staunchly royalist Aphra Behn's late, great novel *Oroonoko*. Revisiting her years in Surinam, it explores the complicated morality of colonialism and royal power against a backdrop that struck English readers as enthrallingly exotic. Although presented as a 'true history,' and containing observations plausibly derived from Aphra's time in South America, the novel is thickly layered with Orientalist fantasy, political propaganda, and sensational fiction.

The titular hero is the epitome of the 'noble savage', his handsome appearance blending classical European beauty – straight hair and a Roman nose – with the marked difference of skin admired as 'perfect Ebony, or polished Jet'. His early life, as he relates it through the narrator, takes place in his native 'Coromantee', a region in Ghana. There, he falls in love with Imoinda, a beautiful young woman who is a concubine of his grandfather, the king. After the young couple spend the night together, they are discovered and Imoinda is banished by the furious monarch to Surinam. Our hero is then kidnapped by English slave-traders and taken to the same colony, where he is given the name Caesar, and reunited by chance with Imoinda. This story-within-a-story is the first attempt by an English writer to describe a society in sub-Saharan Africa, but lacking the first-hand knowledge that she brings to the descriptions of Surinam, it relies heavily on stereotypes.

In the colony, Oroonoko's status and appearance mark him out – his beauty, the narrator notes, 'transcending all those of his gloomy race'. His enslavement is also marked by unusual privilege. Rather than manual labour, he leads hunting expeditions and mingles in white society. He is shown participating himself in the slave trade, attempting to barter his fellow Africans, who regard him as royal, for his own freedom. When Imoinda becomes pregnant, Oroonoko presses for their freedom, not wanting the child to be enslaved too. He is told he must wait for the arrival of the white governor, so he tries instead to whip up a rebellion among his fellow slaves, who soon surrender in what

Oroonoko sees as a sign of their natural servility. He is punished with whipping and vows to take murderous revenge on the governor, before things speed to a bloody climax. Oroonoko and Imoinda decide he should kill her in order to protect her from further violence. Weakened by grief, Oroonoko is captured after defiantly cutting out a piece of his own throat, and the 'royal slave' is bound and hacked to death while stoically smoking a pipe. It is an extraordinarily gruesome ending that shocked Behn's early audiences.

Despite the violence, the book is not a treatise against slavery or colonisation as systems, but it does express horror at the mistreatment of a figure as unique as Oroonoko/Caesar. Consistent with other European writings of the time, Behn depicts the natives of Surinam, whom she calls 'Indians', as either exotic, innocent children of nature who might be taught, or savages who need to be suppressed. The white colonists, who include many characters based on real historical figures, are inept and corrupt, able to abuse their positions at a safe distance from the oversight of London. Although the narrator frankly admires Oroonoko and wishes she could save his life, she is limited by her status as a woman and a mere bystander to the events she relates. More profoundly, despite her misgivings, she is still firmly a member of the English colonial class, and she knows where her loyalties lie.

Aphra Behn's final years were spent in a storm of prolific writing, even as she battled illness and poverty. And while she exhibited increased confidence during this time, she was more viciously attacked. Late seventeenth-century literary culture could be savage across the board, but misogyny sharpened some hacks' pens into knives. Rivals and wannabes, all men, mocked her for daring to write about sex and its pleasures at an age when men no longer found her attractive. One turned her earlier praise against her, deriding her now as 'Sappho, famous for her Gout and Guilt', and memorably yoked together qualities that now sound rather different: 'punk and poesie'. 'Punk' then meant something like 'slut', so the pairing implied that her art was tainted by her sexual frankness. After her death, these attacks congealed into a reputation as a bawdy, ribald cautionary figure who could be invoked as a warning to any virtuous woman who wanted to write. As a result, through the eighteenth and nineteenth centuries, English women poets denied any creative kinship with this fallen Sappho.

Aphra Behn's trailblazing life and work were later reclaimed by feminists, particularly Vita Sackville-West, who wrote a biography of her in 1927, in the midst of her passionate affair with Virginia Woolf. Woolf, in her turn, celebrated Behn in *A Room of One's Own* as the first woman writer who was not an aristocrat but 'a middle-class woman with all the plebeian virtues of humour, vitality and courage'. It's qualified praise, perhaps, but it mattered to Woolf, who saw in Behn a bold woman whose freedom of expression was directly connected to her ability to earn her living by writing. 'All women together, ought to let flowers fall upon the grave of Aphra Behn,' she wrote, 'for it was she who earned them the right to speak their minds.'

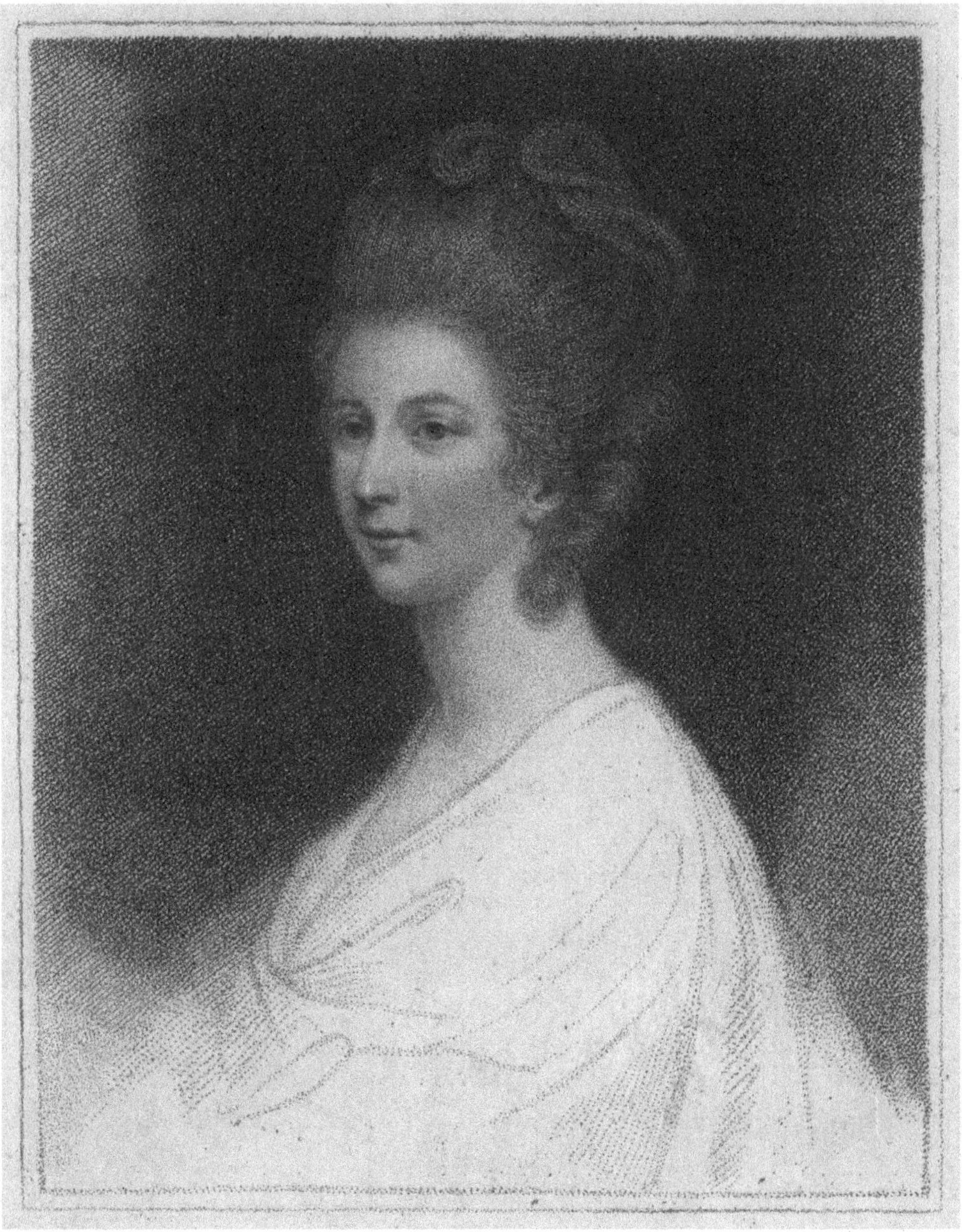

'The ladies must allow me once more to repeat to them that the only means of charming, and of charming long, is to improve their minds; good sense gives beauties which are not subject to fade like the lillies and roses of their cheeks, but will prolong the power of an agreeable woman to the autumn of her life.'

CHARLOTTE LENNOX
(*c.* 1729–1804)

On the surface, the joke was obvious. Any reader in 1752 who picked up a copy of Charlotte Lennox's sprightly bestseller *The Female Quixote* knew what to expect: a gender-twisted take on Cervantes' classic and the multitude of imitators who had, for 150 years, poked fun at romances and their gullible readers. Lennox's heroine, Arabella, was indeed a figure of ridicule, embarking on a series of implausible and amusing adventures to avoid the marriage arranged by her father, and driving everyone around her to the brink of madness before coming to her senses and swearing off the romance books that had skewed her reality. But her story was not quite that simple. There are some powerful cross-currents in the rush of the novel's comedy. After all, weren't women readers supposed to be especially susceptible to the lure of romance – and didn't that mean that any of them might become Arabella? And was her refusal to accept the world as it was and quietly agree to the conventional marriage plot really so ridiculous? Or was there, perhaps, something inspirational in her irrepressible imagination and insistence on bending the world to her will? Was the joke on Arabella – or on those who wanted to tame her?

The answers, perhaps, lay with the woman who created her. For Charlotte Lennox, reading and writing offered an escape from tough circumstances, first through her own imagination and then as a way to make money. Born Charlotte Ramsay, into a military family on the rough outpost of Gibraltar around 1729, she was descended from fairly well-connected Scottish and Irish families. But her parents were without rank or property, so their fortunes lay in the hands of the English aristocrats who directed that nation's actions and ambitions overseas. When Charlotte was around ten years old, her father shipped the family to colonial America, where he took up a senior post in Albany, New York – a formerly Dutch settlement that had been in English hands since the treaty, in Aphra Behn's time, that exchanged New Netherland for Surinam. After arriving in New York City, the Ramsay family travelled 150 miles north by boat up the Hudson river to a town of a few thousand settlers, where there was nothing much available in the way of formal education and certainly not for a girl. If Charlotte had been sent to school, it would have been back downriver in the distant city where – at least going by the scathing descriptions in her novels – the focus would have been on manners and marriageability rather than knowledge.

The barriers to Charlotte's schooling were practical, personal, and ideological. She grew up at a time when girls' education was fiercely debated by men (and women) who questioned how much algebra, Greek and Latin the feminine mind and body could absorb before collapse. At what point did learning render a woman insufferable, infertile or simply unfuckable? For Charlotte, it was her mother, Catherine Ramsay, who stood in the way of her intellectual development. She later wrote that Catherine had 'a high contempt for reading' and would label any keen woman 'with the opprobrious term of being *book-learned*'. Her abandoned Charlotte's education to her father and much older brother, with only the instruction that the girl read nothing that might teach her 'to be undutiful'. It was a rule obviously flouted, back then and throughout her life.

Though it was relatively short, Charlotte's stint abroad came at an impressionable age, and she drew on her observations of the Albany colony for her first and last published novels, *The Life of Harriot Stuart* and *Euphemia*. Those stories give a glimpse of what would most forcefully have struck the notice of a young English girl in America: the vast wildness of the landscape and the unfamiliar diversity of a population in which the English were a minority among Dutch settlers, Africans and Native Americans. Her heroine in the early novel, Harriot, records terror at the sight of these latter 'savages' before her fear gives way to an ethnographic curiosity. She describes the 'ingenious … trinkets of their own making' that they give her as gifts, as well as the way they lived, built their homes, and conducted their political relations with the British. The Dutch, a majority in the Albany of Charlotte's childhood, were frequently stereotyped by the British as poorly educated and ill-mannered. In her mature novel, *Euphemia*, self-consciously refined English women are 'disgusted' by the rudeness of the Dutch, although the heroine herself is more open-minded and does not share their views.

Around the age of thirteen, Charlotte's life was thrown into chaos when her parents sent her back to England to live with an aunt, with the idea of grooming her for a good marriage. She arrived to find the aunt incapacitated by grief over the accidental death of her son, and not far from death herself. Then, back in Albany, her father also passed away. Her mother elected to stay in the colony with her other, more favoured children. 'I have been a wretch since I was thirteen years old when I lost my father,' Charlotte recalled later, adding that, 'adversity is habitual to me.'

Yet if adversity was to remain an all too familiar part of Charlotte's story, so too was luck. The historical record doesn't clearly explain how it was that the young, friendless 'wretch' fell in with the inner circle of aristocratic women at the royal court. Possibly through the support of the Duchess of Newcastle, whose husband oversaw colonial affairs and had appointed her father to his post in Albany, Charlotte came under the protection of Lady Isabella Finch who, uniquely for a woman at the time, owned her own library. Isabella, Lady of the Bedchamber to Princess Amelia, offered Charlotte a place to stay, with a view to training her up as a companion to Amelia and her sister Caroline, the unmarried daughters of King George II. But despite the glamorous trappings, being a lady in waiting was still a job in service: working long hours, exhibiting impeccable conduct and lacking freedom. It was not the future Charlotte wanted. Now that she was in London, she had her eye on a literary career.

In need of money most of all, she turned to the stage. Women had been performing since Aphra Behn's era, but actors and actresses were still characterised by society as 'rogues and vagabonds', and new plays were subject to approval by government censors. Yet, the lingering whiff of scandal only made the theatre more alluring to audiences across the social spectrum. Over the course of Charlotte's career, theatre expanded and democratised, while developments in stage technology and architecture drove the construction of palatial venues in London's West End and elsewhere around the country. Previously a debased and disrespected form, the theatre now laid claim to the heart of British literary culture, and elevated Shakespeare to a national icon. Charlotte not only acted in plays and wrote three of her own, she published works of criticism that challenged Shakespeare's attitude to women and attacked the elitism that placed his works, and those of the ancient Greeks, beyond the reach of the common man (or woman).

For Charlotte, as for Aphra Behn, the theatre kept you alive while poetry polished your reputation, and any successful writer needed both. In 1747, still in her teens, Charlotte Ramsay published a collection of poetry that showcased her versatility as a writer. Her *Poems on Several Occasions* ran the gamut from songs to satire, and was hailed as a triumph. One leading periodical called her, like Behn before her, 'the English Sappho', an epithet that extolled literary brilliance and welcomed her into the female poetic canon. Dedicating the book to her former patron Lady Isabella Finch, Charlotte the poet voices both gratitude and a firm rejection of the offered life of aristocratic servitude. After the dedication, she then turns to her fellow women readers. Instead of treating them, as many contemporary writers did, as weak and in need of moral guidance, Charlotte addressed them as independent thinkers capable of choosing their own path in life – one that, her poems frequently suggest, might be happier travelled solo.

The same year, despite her poetic praise of the single life, Charlotte threw in her lot with a young man named Alexander Lennox. A Scot like her father, he was an apprentice in the publishing trade and claimed to have noble connections. They married in October 1747, and for a time, he may have been a support in her career, using his connections and knowledge of the book business to help her negotiate its shark-filled waters. With a husband on her arm, 'Mrs Lennox' was no longer an unprotected girl from the colonies, and could gain entry into London's literary salons to befriend influential, older male literary figures – like the writers Samuel Richardson and Samuel Johnson – without incurring gossip. It's possible that Alexander was charming, intelligent, and ambitious for both of them. It's certain, however, that he was terrible with money, unreliable, unable to keep a job and yet, under the law, the financial beneficiary of his wife's success for the rest of her life.

Charlotte launched her career at a time when literary culture was shifting from private patronage to the public market, and writers needed to be prolific, adaptable, well connected and visible. A literary reputation was indivisible from a personal one. Many women published anonymously, to avoid the pitfalls of celebrity, but Charlotte Lennox never did. She would even refer to a previous success – 'By the Author of *The Female Quixote*', for example – so there was never any mystery over her identity. She was a working writer, always chasing deadlines and hustling for money. Her correspondence shows her negotiating with the bookseller-publishers who controlled the industry, and trying to raise money to buy back the copyrights of her earlier works so she could reprint them.

Her friendships with men, especially Samuel Johnson, were staunch and vital. When Charlotte's first novel was published, he threw her an all-night party at the Devil Tavern on Fleet Street, with the centrepiece a 'magnificent hot apple-pye' decorated with bay leaves. He placed a crown of laurels on her head, too, 'because, forsooth, Mrs Lennox was an authoress'.

It would be her second novel, however, that truly earned her those laurels. *The Female Quixote, or The Adventures of Arabella* appeared when Charlotte was still barely in her twenties, and at a time when the realistic, moralising, plot-driven novel was in the ascendant. Authors strove to put as much distance as possible between their weighty work and its flighty foreign forebear, the romance – a genre derided for its excesses of emotion and always associated with women. Arabella, the motherless daughter of a rich marquis and 'the Perfection of Beauty, Wit, and Virtue' is a romantic heroine desperately holding back the tide of realism. At the beginning of the novel a suitor appears, her cousin Mr Glanville, who is attractive, kind and approved of by her father. But she refuses to be hustled out of her story, and into matrimony, quite so fast: 'What Lady in Romance ever married the Man that was chose for her?' The down-to-earth Glanville, at first, tries to understand Arabella's love of romance by reading her favourite books, which are a legacy from her dead mother, but 'counting the Pages, he was quite terrified at the Number, and could not prevail upon himself to read them'. In the real world, unlike in her romantic fantasies, Arabella complains, she is 'not allowed any Will of my own'. By the end of *The Female Quixote*, Glanville is on his knees declaring his love, having instigated more than one duel to defend Arabella's honour, and proven himself worthy of her hand. The novel's humour comes from the absurd situations that Arabella sets in motion and by her insistence on seeing all men as dastardly rakes and all women as damsels in distress, but its power lies in her refusal to submit before she has had her 'Adventures'. Although at the very close of the novel, she swears off romance and agrees to marry, the abrupt ending proves that she was right to resist the narrow sphere allotted to women: 'What room, I pray you, does a Lady give for high and noble Adventures, who consumes her Days in Dressing, Dancing, listening to Songs, and ranging the Walks with People as thoughtless as herself? How mean and contemptible a Figure must a Life spent in such idle Amusements make in History?'

Jane Austen admired the book, and its influence is detectible in *Emma*, with its bored and beautiful heroine who tries to enliven her life by turning it into romance. Like Austen, Charlotte Lennox revels in comedy but is deadly serious about the stakes of marriage for women. It is absurd for Arabella to surround herself with female attendants like a fairy-tale princess, and to accuse her harmless suitor of planning to abduct and 'ravish' her. But in another light – and the light is always shifting – she is quite right to be fearful. For an eighteenth-century woman, marriage was a witch's trick, instantly shrinking a bride's worldly possessions, her body, her children, her very life, to a size that could be held – or crushed – in the palm of her husband's hand. What woman would not take that seriously?

We do not know exactly what her marriage, five years in, had shown Charlotte, but she was writing for her life. Able to read French, Italian, Latin and Danish, she earned money writing translations, which, she told Samuel Johnson in a letter, she found 'a great deal easier than Composition'. She put her language skills to a more ambitious use in her three-volume *Shakespear Illustrated*, a compendium of the romances and chronicles on which the plays were based, with accompanying critical commentary. Pointing out all the places where she thought the playwright had distorted the sources his works were based on and therefore robbed female characters of agency and blunted their spikes, she attacked the revered Bard as a hack and a misogynist. Critics were loud in their outrage and, when she adapted her third novel into a play, the audience booed it into oblivion.

Undeterred, Charlotte worked at a furious pace for the next decade, churning out two novels, a play, multiple volumes of translated essays and even her own magazine, *The Lady's Museum*, in 1760. She wrote everything in it herself, including a defence of women's education, albeit in terms rather more compromised that Christine de Pizan's in the fifteenth century. She advised women to steer clear of 'abstract learning' and 'thorny researches' but embrace the arts and humanities, which would improve their conversation. In 1764, the streak of productivity slowed with the birth of Charlotte and Alexander's daughter Harriot, when Charlotte was in her mid-thirties, followed six years later by their son George. The children's arrival no doubt brought joy, but added new pressure to the strained Lennox marriage.

Charlotte Lennox was not rich or connected enough to burnish her own legacy and preserve her archive. She and Alexander moved seven times in a single decade, skipping out on creditors and landlords, leaving her paper trail patchy and her biography full of gaps. In 1781, Samuel Johnson wrote to a mutual acquaintance asking for help on Charlotte's behalf, reporting that 'She is in great distress; very harshly treated by her husband and oppressed with severe illness.'

After suffering the body blow of her daughter's death at the age of eighteen, Charlotte published her last novel, *Euphemia*, in 1790. It revisited her early years in colonial America to tell the story of a long, unhappy marriage. By now living alone, she became one of very few women to be awarded a small stipend from the Royal Literary Fund, which sustained her for the rest of her life, albeit in poverty and poor health. After glimpsing the dawn of the nineteenth century, she died in 1804 and was buried in a pauper's grave in Westminster.

A quarter-century earlier, in 1778, Charlotte Lennox had been included in painter Richard Samuel's group portrait of the leading intellectual and artistic women of the day. Dressed in classical garb, the women appear as the 'nine muses' in the temple of Apollo. Charlotte plays the lute next to the abolitionist writer Hannah More, and behind the seated Elizabeth Montagu, the hostess of the influential 'Blue Stocking' literary salon. The portrait idealises and celebrates these women while subtly curtailing their impact: as muses they are limited in number, and as goddesses they are set above and apart from the business of art and letters, which men still controlled. And, much as Charlotte might have wanted to spend time in the company of fellow artistic women, she was always hounded by the need for money, and the frustration that literary success did not translate into financial security. Women's roles and limited possibilities preoccupied her, but she was not interested in their moral simplicity or superiority. Her novels, especially *The Female Quixote*, explored women's capacity for heroism within the limits of their power, and how they might, just for a while, bend reality to the wilder shape of their own imaginations.

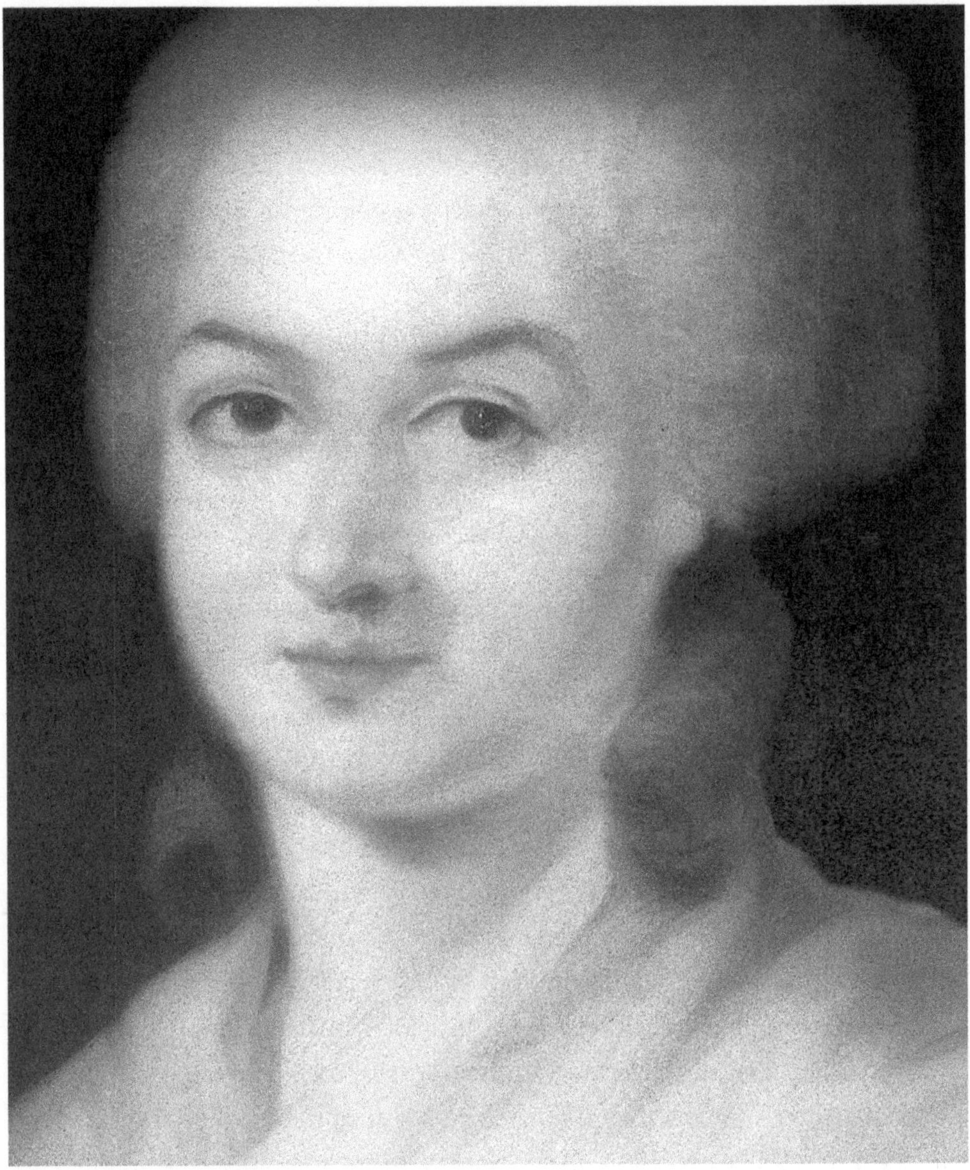

'Women have the right to mount the scaffold, they must also have the right to mount the speaker's rostrum.'

OLYMPE DE GOUGES
(1748–1793)

Telling the story of a writer executed by guillotine means fighting, constantly, against the pull of that ending. It means resisting the temptation to read back from death to see a predestined fate, and keeping alive the possibility that a life might have gone differently, given different choices and different enemies. Yet Olympe de Gouges, born Marie Gouze in the southwestern French town of Montauban in 1748, did not have it in her to be quiet, to behave, to do what others wanted or to compromise with power – even to save her life. Nor was her sex any protection: mere months before Olympe climbed the scaffold, Marie Antoinette became the French Revolution's most iconic victim.

Different choices and alternative endings, however, presuppose multiple possible paths and a world in which a girl could say no to her family's wishes and to men's advances. Marie's choices were no freer and expectations of her no different in the middle of the eighteenth century than they were for her mother, Anne-Olympe, before her, who fell in love as a young girl with her aristocratic neighbour. Jean-Jacques Lefranc, the Marquis de Pompignan, became a prominent poet and playwright, but the difference in their backgrounds meant they could not marry. Marie was most likely conceived during their long affair and both lovers believed the marquis was her father, but Anne went on to marry a butcher named Pierre Gouze. Her daughter's paternity is impossible to verify, but the whisper of illegitimacy instilled in Marie a sense that she was different – born for something more glamorous than the life of a butcher's wife.

As a lower middle-class tradesman's daughter, Marie learned to read and write at the local convent school, which sought to teach girls just enough to become good Catholic wives and mothers. Later her Parisian rivals would sneer that she was illiterate, perhaps because her thick accent and her use of the Occitan dialect marked her as provincial (one goal of the Revolution was to standardise the French language across the country). But she made a rhetorical virtue of her 'natural' learning, claiming it made her a freer thinker.

By sixteen, Marie was well schooled in the extracurricular education routinely imparted to poor and pretty girls. Men paid her attention, which gave her the illusion of power. She began to flout the rules of her petit-bourgeois milieu, grasping instead for the freedom enjoyed by her aristocratic, artistic natural father. She began getting ideas: attending the theatre, reading philosophy and arguing with her friends about the big debates of the day. Like her near-contemporary, Charlotte Lennox, Marie grew up a child of the Enlightenment, a time when rebellious thinkers began to shake loose certainties that had seemed as fixed as night and day: that people were ruled by kings and queens, everyone h̴d a social place dictated by God, and women were born to ̴ure and to serve. They were paying close attention, these girls, and they were quick to notice where the challengers Ordinary people did have the right to read and study, ̴d, but only the men. Citizens did not have to accept a king's divine right to rule, but a husband still held dominion over his wife's body and fortune. It was one thing to debate ideas, but quite another to escape your gendered destiny.

At seventeen, under pressure from her family, Marie was married to Louis Yves Aubry, a local caterer, and before long, gave birth to a son. She doted on the baby, Pierre, and refused to pass him off to a wet nurse, having absorbed the philosopher Jean-Jacques Rousseau's influential ideas about maternal bonding and the importance of breast-feeding. Pierre was barely three months old when the river Tarn burst its banks and flooded the centre of Montauban, a historic disaster in the small city. Although the details are uncertain, it is likely Marie's husband contracted a fatal fever in the wake of the flood, leaving his teenage bride a widow. In that rare position of respectability and independence, she suddenly found herself looking at a different future.

Casting off her married name, plain, provincial Marie Aubry became Olympe de Gouges, a creation of the gods, her own history and the illusion of aristocracy. She and Pierre made their way to Paris, supported by her lover, Jacques Biétrix de Rozières. It is thought that the couple may have had a baby who did not survive infancy, but she refused his offer of marriage, a state that she later called 'the tomb of trust and love'. No, Olympe decided, she would stay among the living, as hard as that might be.

For the next decade, Olympe de Gouges carved out a place in the intellectual culture of the capital with her fingernails. She struggled to balance the need to appear wealthy and leisured with the hard work it took to create that illusion. Backed by Jacques, and determined to conquer the literary world, she moved frequently between various rented apartments, and made wealthy friends, like the salon hostess and artistic patron Madame de Montesson. She used her connection to the Marquis de Pompignan to open doors, dropping the open secret of her illegitimacy into eager ears. Their theatrical worlds overlapped, but he did not acknowledge her in public, nor listen to her pleas to help support her ageing widowed mother. She got her revenge after his death, however, with a fictionalised autobiography that laid bare his sins and his selfishness.

In Paris at the time, there were two major public theatres, the legendary Comédie-Française and the slightly more accessible Comédie-Italienne, as well as a multitude of amateur and private companies of varying quality and prestige. Going to the theatre was almost a job of its own – a social, professional and artistic obligation – and Olympe embraced it energetically, acting in productions at her friends' private theatres and writing her own plays. In 1780, after she had been in Paris for several years, she set up and ran her own amateur theatre as a showcase for her work. It was a bold expression of confidence in her own literary standing. Pierre, who by this time was fourteen, was one of her principal actors. The project ran until 1787, when she closed it down and sold off the sets to recoup some of her investment.

At the same time as she was running her theatre and attempting to get her plays staged in more prestigious venues, Olympe was also making a name for herself as a social commentator. There were innumerable voices competing to be heard in this turbulent pre-Revolutionary decade, in newspapers, on the stage and in the streets. Her friends were writers – journalists and aspiring politicians as well as playwrights – and were engaged in active, sometimes acrimonious debate about the state of the nation and the nature of statehood. Because she found writing difficult, she hired a secretary whenever funds allowed, and dictated her plays, works of philosophy and political arguments to him, which she would pay to have printed and then pasted up on billboards around the city. Her preoccupations were those of her time: social equality, the scourge of poverty and the need for democracy, but increasingly, too, the place of women in society.

As the Revolution approached, Olympe's political writing became more urgent and widely read. Her first political essay to land on a newspaper front page appeared in November 1788, amid the cold and hunger of a harsh winter and a failed harvest. This 'letter to the people', from a *citoyenne* or female citizen, defended the king, who stood accused of callous inaction over the crisis, and protested the rioting that was becoming a more frequent response. More unusually, it called on her fellow citizens to donate to a 'patriotic purse' to help stabilise the situation. The idea of a voluntary tax might have struck some readers as frivolous, especially when Olympe called on rich women to buy fewer hats, but, the following year, it inspired a group of women to donate their jewellery directly to the National Assembly. That was in September 1789, with the Revolution underway. By October, ordinary women gathered in the markets of Paris to march to the palace at Versailles and protest the price of bread.

Yet, to Olympe's frustration, the men leading the charge for equality did not seem to even see these women. Two years after the Marquis de Lafayette's famed 'Declaration of the Rights of Man and the Citizen', she issued a pointed response, the 'Declaration of the Rights of Woman and the Female Citizen (*citoyenne*)', which highlighted the absurdity of a vision of 'universal' rights that only accounted for half the population. Dedicated to 'the most detested of women', Queen Marie Antoinette, it opened with a direct challenge: 'Man, are you capable of being fair?' The declaration followed the seventeen points of Lafayette's original but rewrote them to highlight the rights women still lacked and how they could be punished under laws they had no right to shape or resist. Over and over again, her declaration emphasised that a woman's marital and social status were inextricably linked, which made her private injustices public concerns. No doubt inspired by her own family history, and knowing all too well how mothers suffered under the secrecy and shame of illegitimacy, Olympe insisted that a woman should have the right to name the father of her child and demand financial support. She urged her sisters to recognise and demand their rights as citizens in a society that had long counted on their silence. In a line that would soon take on a chilling new weight, she declared, 'Women have the right to mount the scaffold; they must also have the right to mount the speaker's rostrum.'

It was not just the rights of women that began to preoccupy Olympe at this time. Amid the broader swell of reckoning with political inequality and the increased desperation of the powerless, abolitionist feeling was growing in France. Her countrymen were proud of the absence of slavery on their soil, even declaring that an enslaved person who entered the country would be automatically emancipated. But the colonies told a very different story. For a century, France had competed with Portugal and Britain for the unenviable title of most active slave trading nation, and in total would be responsible for a little over ten per cent of the 12.5 million people uprooted from Africa and forced into bondage between 1551 and 1875. More than four thousand slave ships flew the French flag and launched from French ports, from Le Havre to Marseille. The survivors of those notorious voyages mostly wound up on the French colony of Saint-Domingue, which supplied around half of the sugar and coffee consumed in Europe in the eighteenth century.

Olympe's understanding of the realities of slavery in the French colonies likely had personal roots. It would have come, at least in part, from stories she heard from the Chevalier de Saint-Georges, a protégé of her friend Madame de Montesson, who ran her private theatre. The son of a planter on Martinique and an enslaved woman, he may also have been the inspiration for Olympe's 1784 play *Zamore and Mirza, or The Lucky Shipwreck*, the first French play to feature an enslaved hero. The play also dealt with the inequality of women and the injustice faced by illegitimate children, two other issues close to her heart. She left the specifics of the characters' origins vague – they are described simply as 'dark'. And, although she fought the decision, they were played by white actors at the Comédie-Française.

Zamore and Mirza's journey to the stage was slow. Olympe was triumphant when the Comédie-Française accepted the play for production in 1785. However, for season after season they refused to stage it and, because acceptance meant ownership, its playwright could not produce it elsewhere. Finally, after she took legal action, the theatre begrudgingly produced the play at the very end of 1789, under a new title: *L'Esclavage des Noirs* (Black Slavery). Despite the strong support of abolitionists, it was doomed to failure, in part because the better-financed lobbyists of the slave trade campaigned against the production in print and paid hecklers to disrupt the performances. The play opened the day before New Year's Eve, just as Parisians were leaving town for the holiday. This deliberately bad timing, on top of the protests, sank the play after three nights.

Undoubtedly disappointed and frustrated by her play's reception, Olympe continued to argue in print for a serious reckoning with slavery. In her essay '*Réflexions sur les Hommes Nègres*' (Reflections on Black Men), she explicitly connected the oppressive French monarchy with the slave-holders, arguing that only unjust rulers needed to wield such brutal and extreme forms of power. A just king, by contrast, would quite naturally have 'submissive subjects'. She was never a believer in violent revolution – a restraint that would doom her – but instead believed that fair leadership, within democratic limits, was beneficial for everyone. In those revolutionary years, however, hers was not a message that carried. In Saint-Domingue in 1790 and 1791, inspired by Lafayette's 'Declaration of the Rights of Man and of the Citizen', free colonial subjects and enslaved Africans led by the former slave Toussaint Louverture rose up against the planters, who had grown rich off the labour of around 800,000 brutally subjugated men, women and children. It would be the only colony to seize independence after a slave uprising and would eventually emerge as the nation of Haiti. Olympe de Gouges responded to the uprising by adding a preface to her play *L'Esclavage des Noirs* that urged restraint. She argued that by committing 'barbaric and atrocious torture' in revenge for slavery, the revolutionaries risked erasing the moral distinction between tyrants and the oppressed. However, she found herself accused by the mayor of Paris of having incited the violence in Saint-Domingue and, when her play was staged again at the end of 1792, it ended in a riot.

The guillotine had been in use since that summer and the deposed King Louis XVI was tried and sentenced to death in January. It was not an easy decision, even for those who hated the king – underpinning royal power was the belief that a monarch was essentially immortal, with power transmitted automatically down the line of succession. But banishing or imprisoning the king, rather than killing him, had its own risks. The English experience of regicide followed by restoration in the previous century hung over those who wanted to do away with the monarchy for good. Olympe joined those who argued that the death penalty was a sign of weakness: if the Revolution had truly abolished the monarchy, then killing an ordinary man, the ex-king now called Citizen Louis Capet, was unnecessary. Worse, it implied doubt that the institution had truly been overthrown. Once the king was put to death, and the scale of the killings only increased, she repeated that the execution had been a mistake. Going further, she accused the architects of the Reign of Terror – Robespierre and his followers – of being secret royalists, who had murdered the monarch because they didn't truly believe their fragile republic would last.

In late summer 1793, Olympe posted her last pamphlet, imagining how the country would look from outside if seen by a *'voyageur aérien'* (traveller by air). It would be only too clear to them, she said, that the executions were causing 'incalculable harm' and sowing long-lasting division. Even from high above the ground, it was obvious that no one ought to be killed for his or her political views, and that the country needed a government that would abide by its own laws. 'Blood, alas, has flowed far too freely,' she wrote.

On July 20, Olympe was arrested and accused of royalist sympathies. Her case was not helped by her Declaration's dedication to Marie Antoinette, who also appeared as a character in an unfinished play that was found among her papers. A judge decreed, on the basis of her powerful public arguments, that she could represent herself, and therefore denied her a lawyer. Her friends helped her have the last word, smuggling out her final works *Olympe de au tribunal révolutionnaire* (Olympe de Gouges at the revolutionary tribunal) and *Une patriote persecutée* (A [female] patriot persecuted), in which she defended herself and, again, railed against the Terror.

Found guilty of sedition, Olympe de Gouges was executed on November 3, 1793. The night before, she wrote a letter to her beloved son Pierre, in which she declared herself doubly a victim – first, of her own patriotism or 'my idolatry for the fatherland and for the people', and secondly, of the country's remorseless enemies. But her voice, for women and for equal rights, continued to ring out. In Britain, Mary Wollstonecraft was inspired by the Declaration to issue her own clarion cry, *A Vindication of the Rights of Woman*, which was published the year before Olympe's execution. And at Seneca Falls, New York, half a century later, Elizabeth Cady Stanton modelled her *Declaration of Sentiments* on the United States Declaration of Independence: another woman's red-pen edit of a man's myopic version of freedom.

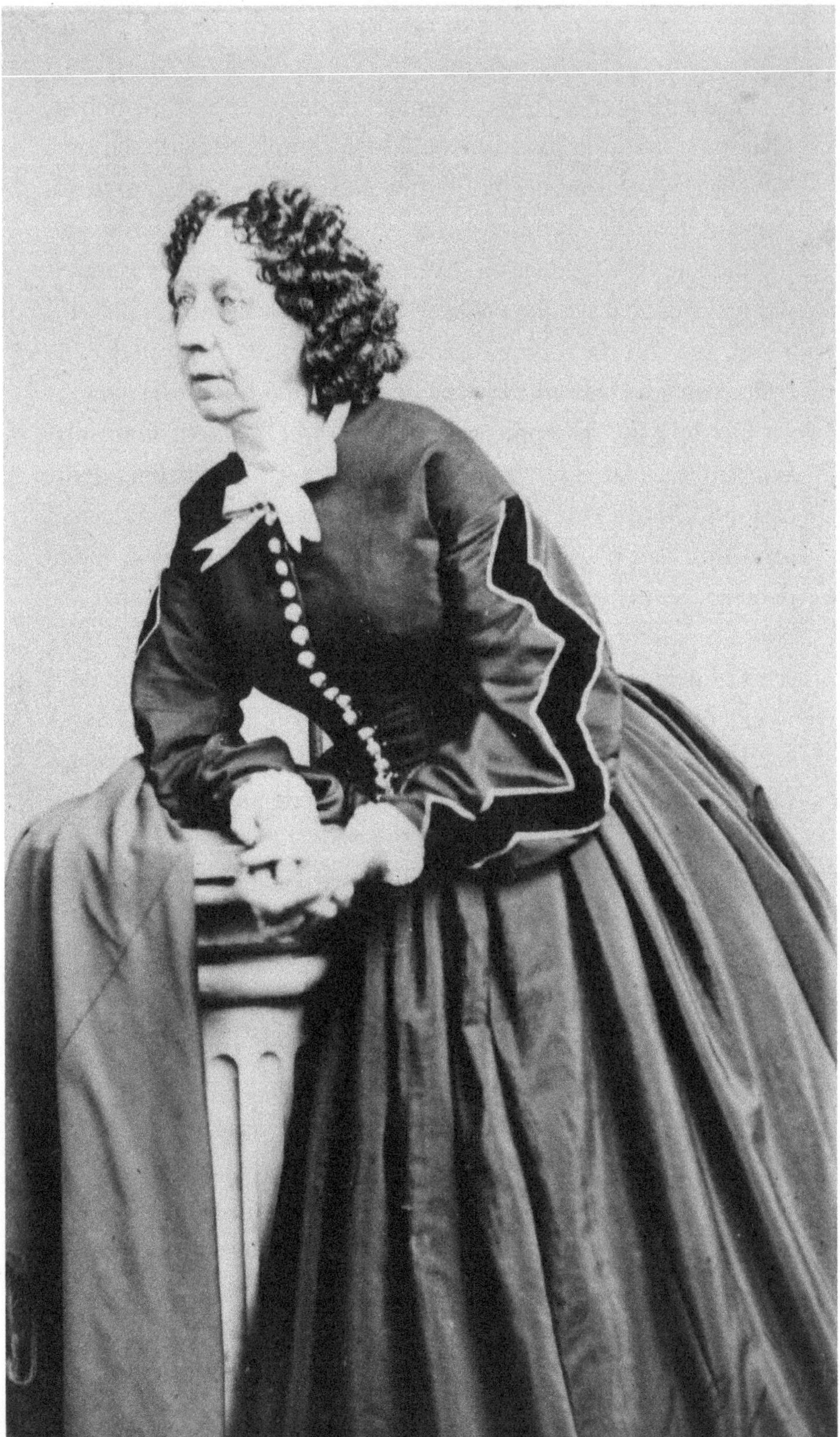

'What a pity when editors review a woman's book, that they so often fall into the error of reviewing the woman instead.'

FANNY FERN
(1811–1872)

In 1854, one of America's most popular newspaper columnists, the pseudonymous Fanny Fern, published *Ruth Hall: A Domestic Tale of the Present Time*, an autobiographical novel so thinly veiled as to be downright shocking in its nakedness. In the preface, Fern announced that her book was 'entirely at variance with all set rules for novel-writing', eschewing an intricate plot, elaborate descriptions and cliffhanging suspense. Instead, the author likened herself to a casual visitor dropping by unannounced with gossip to share – and, clearly, some scores to settle. Fanny Fern's identity had been an increasingly open secret, but now the life of the woman born Sara Payson Willis in Portland, Maine, in 1811, was revealed and therefore forever yoked to that of the novel's long-suffering, noble heroine. Also yoked to the novel, and thoroughly skewered by it, were Willis's family: her monstrous mother-in-law, her mean and hypocritical father and, above them all, her brother, Nathaniel Parker Willis. A famous man of letters and a newspaper proprietor, 'N.P.' was flayed in the pages of the novel via the character of Ruth's brother Hyacinth Ellet – a fop, fortune-hunter and fraud.

Unlike many sentimental fictions of the time, Fern's novel did not claim to impart any simple moral lesson. Instead, the author wanted to 'fan into flame … the faded embers of hope' among readers who felt abandoned and abused – who were, like her heroine, victims of fate rather than of their own failings. The story starts with a lucky young woman: intelligent, beautiful, and about to marry a man she loves. We meet Ruth on the eve of her wedding, reflecting on her unhappy childhood as an awkward, solitary child, who craved true love but was surrounded by people who cared only for flattery. She appears to have triumphed over her past, however, in beginning a marriage that is blissfully happy. It can't even be marred by the obsessive malice of her husband's parents, who are determined to see the worst in her. Their power is limited, however – at least as long as her husband is alive to protect her. Once Ruth is widowed, she becomes vulnerable to the neglect and cruelty of her in-laws and her own relatives. While family members duck and twist to avoid providing for her, she struggles to keep herself and her two young daughters housed and fed, trying all the limited employment options open to a woman. At her lowest ebb, Ruth becomes a freelance journalist.

In the second half of the book, Ruth – and through her, her creator – slowly claws back pride and power, as the sentimental tale transforms itself into a fantasy of vengeance for every downtrodden and underestimated Victorian woman. 'I tell you that placid Ruth is a smouldering volcano,' her mother-in-law observes, reluctantly admitting that she's met her match. One hard-won draft at a time, Ruth ascends to fame and fortune, vanquishes her familial and professional enemies, reclaims the daughter her in-laws tricked her into giving up, and leaves her bleak city lodgings for an idyllic country home – all through the power of her pen.

Fanny Fern's life story tracks closely to Ruth's, but there are a few important differences. Where Ruth has only her obnoxious brother Hyacinth to contend with, Sara Willis was one of nine children. Before she married, she had seen some literary success, publishing articles in her father's newspaper, but she had no intention of continuing. Like Ruth, and millions of other women of her class and generation, she became a wife with the expectation that that would be the end of her public story. In her first marriage, she was as lucky as her heroine, making a happy match with a Boston banker, Charles Eldredge, which produced three daughters. It was a traditional Victorian domestic arrangement, in which she did not need to earn her own living. But after seven tranquil years, a run of tragedies battered her with twice the cruelty she inflicted on her fictional counterpart. Between 1844 and 1846, she lost not only her husband and eldest daughter but also her mother and sister to illness.

Widowhood left Sara Eldredge poor and vulnerable, and she first looked for support via a route Ruth never considers: a second marriage. Here, she was forced to confront the real stakes of the matrimonial gamble, when her second husband, Samuel P. Farrington, turned out to be brutal in his jealousy. The situation became so bad that, after just two years, Sara made the difficult – and rare for the time – decision to leave him. Risking poverty and scandal, she took her daughters and moved into a Boston hotel. After two more years, during which he smeared her reputation and turned her family against her, Farrington divorced her, leaving her bereft of both moral and financial support.

In the novel, Fern vividly portrays Ruth's struggle to find any respectable and sustaining work. Taking in sewing and mending at home requires an abundance of skill and time, and pays a pittance, while the application procedure for a school teaching post is a farce. Her refusal to give up her children to their awful grandparents makes it impossible for her to take work in a factory. Several employers don't believe that Ruth, who both came from and married into well-to-do families, really needs the money. The grim, bustling city quarter where she's living is full of dangers for a pretty widow and her daughters. Out of her boarding-house window, Ruth can see a building with permanently drawn blinds, a stream of male visitors and ghostly female faces at the window. It serves as a warning and spurs her determination.

Writing turns out to be Ruth's salvation, though her brother, despite his literary connections, never helps her career. Similarly, Fanny Fern's famous brother N.P. owned the *Home Journal*, the publication that would evolve into the high society *Town & Country* magazine, the oldest continually published lifestyle magazine in the United States. But even after his sister began to attract a loyal readership, he refused to publish or promote her work.

Ruth accepts that she must begin at the bottom of the ladder, and knocks on the doors of small newspapers until she finds one willing to give her a chance. When her first piece finds a publisher, she's caught between optimism and the realities of the market. 'The remuneration was not what Ruth had hoped, but it was a beginning, a stepping stone.' Fern, likewise, began her career as a contributor to two small Boston papers, the *True Flag* and the *Olive Branch*. Her first article, 'The Governess', appeared in 1851. In contrast to Ruth, whose ambiguous pseudonym 'Floy' let readers speculate over her gender, the writer now known as 'Fanny Fern' left no doubt that she was a woman.

The publishing world in *Ruth Hall* is a male-dominated environment in which talent and inexperience are easily exploited. Low-paid editors and writers grind out content at an exhausting pace to burnish the reputations of journal owners and financiers. Before long, however, Ruth's pseudonymous columns begin to make a splash, and speculation grows about Floy's true identity. An enterprising editor offers her a much-increased salary in exchange for exclusivity and book publishers approach her about collecting her columns in a volume. In real life, the editor who approached Fanny Fern to capitalise on her growing fame was another of her brothers, Richard, who published a New York paper called the *Musical World and Times*. He had no idea that the writer he was trying to poach was his sister, yet he stood by his offer once he found out. Perhaps thinking readers would find that coincidence too great, Fern made Ruth's champion a stranger in the novel, but he nonetheless writes to her to express his 'brotherly' interest in her welfare and addresses her as 'sister'.

In 1853, Fern contracted with a publisher for her first book, a collection of her columns titled *Fern Leaves from Fanny's Portfolio*. Just as Ruth does in her novel (and as Louisa May Alcott did with *Little Women* a few years later), Fern gambled on the success of her book and retained her copyright, choosing to earn ten cents for every copy sold rather than receiving a lump sum. The enormous success of the book – which outsold even the previous year's staggering bestseller, *Uncle Tom's Cabin*, to the tune of some 70,000 copies within the year – enabled her to buy a house in Brooklyn. She published another novel, *Rose Clark*, in 1856, as well as four more collections of columns and two books for children.

As the preface to *Ruth Hall* makes clear, Fern had little interest in shaping her novels to fit lofty artistic standards, and unlike Harriet Beecher Stowe, she was not trying to advance a political cause. She wrote for the moment, and for the world as it was, without much interest in posterity. Fern's columns were frank and conversational. She had a huge range of interests, from prison reform to literature to the importance of breakfast. She's credited with coining the phrase 'the way to a man's heart is through his stomach', and she wrote often about middle-class domesticity, convinced that the apparent trivialities of daily life were more important than they seemed. In an 1869 column, 'Delightful Men', she showed the importance of kindness and consideration within marriage, arguing that the true measure of a man was how he treated his family at home. It was not a man's great deeds but these so-called 'little things', that were, she insisted, 'the hinges of the universe'.

In her columns and fiction, Fern could build whole vivid worlds on these 'little things'. Even in her longer works, the plot is frequently diverted into comic or sentimental vignettes that echo and expand the central preoccupations of the novel. These often illuminate the relationships between parents and children; Fern writes with a mother's attention to the details of young children's bodies and behaviour, from the way they look when sleeping to the particularities of their voices and perceptions. One comic tale in *Ruth Hall* follows Ruth's landlady, who briefly abandons her husband and leaves him with their seven-month-old baby. The father struggles to soothe and feed the infant, until Ruth comes to its rescue, 'loosening the frock-strings and rubbing its little fat shoulders with her velvet palms'. This is the kind of tactile detail that only comes from close observation. By rendering its intimacy so precisely, Fern grounds the vague Victorian fantasy of maternal love in physical reality, through smell and touch, and brings out the truth tucked inside.

Fern was called sentimental, as women writing about family life usually are. Yet there was a core of fury in her work, fuelled by society's hypocritical treatment of women, which idealised them as wives and mothers and yet denied them legal rights and opportunities to support themselves. In *Ruth Hall*, the original sin of all the bad characters is hypocrisy, the capacity to act with outrageous cruelty and still believe in (or at least, declare) their own piety. 'The woman writes as if the devil was in her,' Nathaniel Hawthorne said of Fern, but there was nothing diabolical inside her: just a righteous, clear-eyed woman. She did not strive for a gender-neutral voice, or to 'transcend' her sex, as women writers were so often called upon to do in exchange for critical acclaim. Her energy and inspiration as a writer directly stemmed from her identity as a woman and a mother. And, as a woman in the public eye who wrote about real life, she was in the unique position of being a trusted confidante to thousands of readers she didn't know – a situation that she shared with her character Ruth. In a series of letters supposedly written to 'Floy' by her readers, we hear the voices of desperate women asking for advice, which serves to place Ruth's experiences within a wider chorus of female experience. She also hears from several men proposing marriage, as well as a handful of prototypical mansplainers pointing out errors in her columns.

Written a few years before the Civil War, and set in the antislavery milieu of Boston, *Ruth Hall* nevertheless displays marked condescension towards its few African-American characters, who are all servants in houses of white families. When Ruth's wealthy cousins grudgingly allow her to do her laundry in their house, their maid observes, 'White folks is stony-hearted.' These Black servants speak in strong dialect and in the childlike third person, creating a racist distancing that undercuts the novel's general sympathy for their point of view. A sense of Northern superiority and complacency appears in glimpses of the slaveholding South. For example, Ruth receives a marriage proposal from 'a Southerner who confessed to one hundred negroes', and it's a mark of her brother Hyacinth's cravenness that the word 'slave' is 'tabooed' in his paper, for fear of offending his Southern subscribers. But these are only hints and give no indication of the way the issue would violently split the country within a decade.

After the success of *Ruth Hall*, Fanny Fern's star continued to rise. While Ruth takes her earnings and buys a secluded country house in which to raise her daughters, her creator moved to Brooklyn and immersed herself in New York's booming literary culture. In 1855, the editor of the *New York Ledger* approached her to write a serialised story, offering her twenty-five dollars per instalment, which he raised to fifty, then seventy-five, and finally a hundred before she accepted, making her one of the highest-paid writers in America. She wrote a weekly column for the *Ledger* for the next seventeen years. She became involved in various women's rights causes, and in 1868 – after she was excluded from a dinner held for the visiting Charles Dickens by the New York Press Club – joined fellow writer Jane Cunningham Croly in founding a latter-day Blue Stocking salon, the Sorosis Club, a social and intellectual community for women that soon had chapters all over the country. Fern was one of the first writers to positively review Walt Whitman's *Leaves of Grass*, writing to him privately that she thought it was 'delicious!'

And where Fern left her heroine single, her own romantic life would have one further twist. In the novel, she briefly introduces us to the principled and put-upon Horace Gates, 'a gentlemanly, slender, scholar-like-looking person', who singlehandedly edits Hyacinth's paper. When Hyacinth refuses to publish his sister's columns, along with committing various other offences against common sense and journalistic integrity, Horace begins to make threats of quitting. In life, N.P.'s editor, James Parton, saw the threat through – he resigned his position when Fanny Fern was barred from the pages of the *Home Journal*. Parton went on to become a popular author of biographies of presidents and other important figures, including the two-volume *Eminent Women of the Age*. In 1856, he married the eminent Fern – who at forty-five was eleven years his senior – and the couple lived happily in New York until her death in 1872 (after which, less appealingly, he married Ellen Eldredge, Fern's daughter by her first husband).

On her third marriage, Fern did not take James Parton's name. The woman who had been Sara Willis, then Sara Eldredge, then Sara Farrington officially adopted the only name that was truly hers: Fanny Fern. When she died, that name was all that appeared on her tombstone: the identity she had created for and by herself.

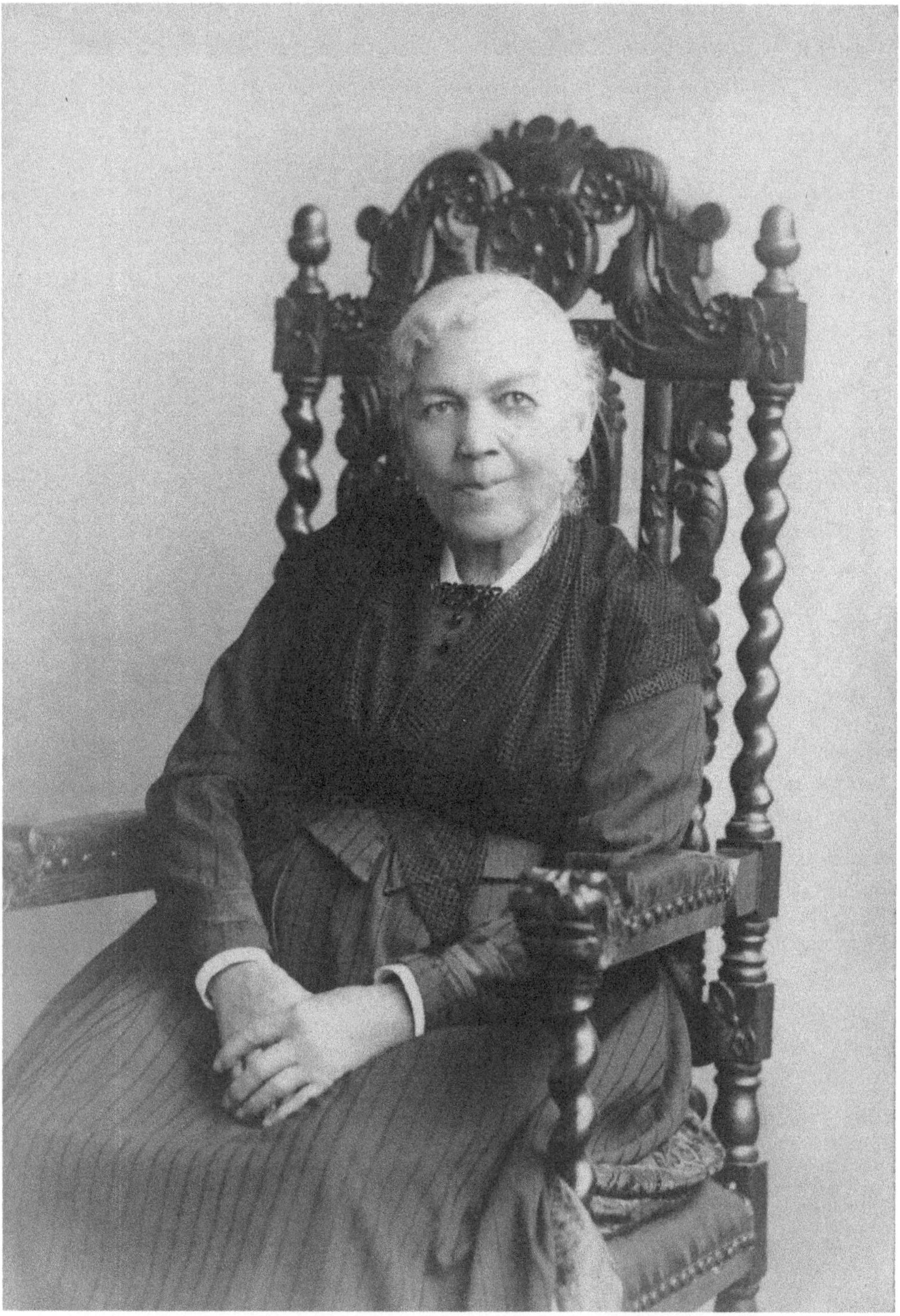

*'Slavery is terrible for men; but
it is far more terrible for women.'*

HARRIET JACOBS
(*c.* 1813–1897)

Harriet Jacobs was six years old when she discovered she was the legal property of another human being. She had lived up to that point in a house with her parents and brother, thanks to her father's skill as a carpenter. Although the money he earned from his work belonged, in law, to his owner, the arrangement created, for a while, the illusion of a stable, self-sufficient family unit. This was bolstered by the love and protection of her grandmother, who had been able to save enough money to buy her own freedom and secure a home of her own nearby. The mirage wavered as the children grew up and vanished for good when their mother died and they learned the truth. Harriet moved into the home of her legal owner, who taught her to sew and, unusually but not (at the time) illegally, to read and write. At twelve, when this woman died, Harriet passed as inheritance into the family of one Dr James Norcom. On paper she belonged to his three-year-old daughter. In reality, he claimed full control over Harriet's existence.

Once she turned fifteen – 'a sad epoch in the life of a slave girl', as she later wrote – Harriet's life became a relentless struggle to maintain her bodily autonomy. Long before desperation made her a fugitive, she was harassed and hounded by Norcom, whose 'restless, craving, vicious nature roved about day and night, seeking whom to devour'. He whispered 'filthy' words to her and made promises and threats that 'scathed ear and brain like fire'. Yet he did not overpower her physically, preferring to win her compliance even if, under the circumstances, there could be no true consent. Harriet steadfastly refused. 'My master had power and law on his side; I had a determined will,' she wrote. 'There is might in each.'

In her remarkable autobiography, *Incidents in the Life of a Slave Girl*, Harriet's alter ego Linda Brent also pitches her mighty will against a malevolent but ultimately pathetic antagonist, Dr Flint. She comes to realise that he is a mere puppet of 'that demon, Slavery' and that this diabolical force distorts the lives and souls of everyone in the United States: white, Black, rich, poor, North, South, enslaved and, nominally, free. When Linda falls in love with a free Black man, who wants to buy her freedom and marry her, Flint refuses to sell and threatens her lover's life. Fearing for everyone's safety, she breaks off the relationship. All that is left is to find the least 'degrading' path toward the inevitable for an enslaved young woman: increasing her owner's property value through the forced production of children.

In Harriet's case, this took the shape of a white man named Samuel Sawyer, who was almost twice her age but, unlike James Norcom, unmarried. Portrayed as the character of Mr Sands in the book, he showed interest in her and a modicum of respect. She did not hate him and, most importantly, he did not own her. And so, he became the father of her son Joseph, born in 1829 when Harriet was sixteen, and then four years later of her daughter Louisa. Sawyer's being single meant she was not betraying another woman or the sanctity of marriage, that holy Christian institution from which she, as an enslaved person, was legally excluded. 'Pity me, and pardon me, O virtuous reader!' Jacobs begs, as she tells this story, which lays bare the centrality of forced birth within the American system of slavery and the difficulty of describing it honestly. Not a violation of the natural order but the fulfilment of capitalist logic, the rape of enslaved women was seen as 'legitimate use of property' for two and a half centuries. After Linda gives birth, Dr Flint, who is both her doctor and her legal owner, 'did not fail to remind me that my child was an addition to his stock of slaves.' But at least he was not also their father.

For Jacobs, the sexual corruption of slavery leaked poison throughout the slaveholding society. It perverted the moral development of children, both white and Black, who learned far too early, and in the worst possible ways, about sex and adult relationships. 'The slaveholder's sons are, of course, vitiated, even while boys, by the unclean influences everywhere around them,' she wrote. These boys grew up knowing that their fathers were free to do as they liked to the women (and men) they owned, and that they, too, would be similarly licensed. Less commonly, but by the same logic, the white daughters and wives of slaveholders could force themselves on enslaved men who could not refuse. And sometimes pregnancy was the result. 'In such cases the infant is smothered, or sent where it is never seen by any who know its history,' Jacobs tells us, revealing the sharp contrast to the 'unblushing' acceptance of children born to enslaved women, as long as they stayed silent. 'My master was, to my knowledge, the father of eleven slaves,' she writes. 'But did the mothers dare to tell who was the father of their children?'

For this conspiracy of silence, Jacobs lays blame at the feet of the slaveholders and also their wives, who too often, and quite openly, directed their anger and jealousy at the women, rather than their husbands. An enslaved girl 'will learn, before she is twelve years old, why it is that her mistress hates such and such a one among the slaves'. Mrs Flint, in the book, is the much younger second wife of the 'hoary-headed miscreant' Dr Flint. Linda pities her, but her sympathy is tempered by the wife's treatment of her female slaves: instead of using what power she has to shield them, she instead makes them the objects of her suspicion, jealousy, and surveillance. She forces Linda to sleep in an adjoining room and watches over her as she sleeps. 'You can imagine, better than I can describe, what an unpleasant sensation it must produce to wake up in the dead of night and find a jealous woman bending over you.'

Becoming a mother does not shield Linda from her owner's advances; rather, her children become a new weapon for him. 'Sometimes, when my master found that I still refused to accept what he called his kind offers, he would threaten to sell my child. "Perhaps that will humble you," said he.' Flint offers to house Linda and her children in an isolated cottage, in exchange for putting her body up for his use. After construction of the cottage has begun, over her protests, she accepts the compromise of moving out of town to Flint's son's plantation. She appeals to the father of her children to purchase them, which he does, on the promise of freeing them, which he does not. Linda goes to the plantation, where she begins to weigh the immensely risky prospect of running away.

Going north, however, would mean separation from her children, perhaps forever. So Linda, like Harriet, hatches a plan to hide out in a tiny attic above a storage shed behind her grandmother's house and finds a paradoxical freedom in extreme confinement. The space is too small to allow her to stand or even sit comfortably; it has no window, just a tiny hole she is able to carve out for light and air, and only the flimsiest of coverings from the elements. Occasionally, after dark, she can let herself down into the shed to stretch her body, catch a glimpse of her children and hear their voices, although they believe she has escaped north. The predatory Dr Flint is agonisingly close by but, with the help of her family, she writes him letters to convince him she is beyond his clutches, and he makes several trips to New York to try to track her down. She is eventually able to send her nine-year-old daughter to the North. She takes an enormous risk to spend a night with her before she leaves, in a moving scene of parting in which she has to trust the child with the enormity of her secret.

Harriet Jacobs survived, undetected, in her tiny prison for almost seven years. The experience damaged her physically and threatened to break her mentally, before she was finally able to seize the chance to venture north by boat. She arrived in New York in 1842, where she was reunited with her daughter. But now, in addition to the ongoing daily risk of betrayal and recapture, she had to earn a living in a place where Black women's employment options were almost entirely limited to domestic service. In a twist of fate, she found a position in the home of Fanny Fern's brother, the illustrious writer and editor Nathaniel Parker 'N.P.' Willis. Her daughter, Louisa, would, in due course, find work in Fern's household as a nanny.

After Willis's English wife died giving birth to their daughter in 1845, Harriet travelled with the newborn baby and her grieving father to visit his late wife's family. In Britain, she met with prominent abolitionists and experienced palpable relief from the daily weight of racism. 'I was treated according to my deportment, without reference to my complexion,' she wrote, drawing a distinction between behaviour and outward appearance, one that she had never experienced before. Optimistically, or perhaps strategically, her book offers a rosy vision of race relations in Victorian England: 'During all that time, I never saw the slightest symptom of prejudice against color.'

Back in America, the Fugitive Slave Law of 1850 made life infinitely more precarious for those who had fled in search of freedom in the North. The law flung a net across the entire country and turned humans into bounty. When Harriet returned with the Willis family after almost a year in England, New York was no longer a safe haven. 'What a disgrace to a city calling itself free,' she exclaimed. Even after her tormentor died, she was a target: she was still the legal property of Norcom's daughter and as the family finances were rocky, she was a valuable asset. As she weighed the odds of another escape, this time to California where her brother had settled, her employer's second wife, a wealthy abolitionist named Cornelia Grinnell Willis, negotiated with Norcom's son-in-law to buy Harriet's freedom. The successful outcome lifted the immediate burden for Harriet but lit her up with rage. '"The bill of sale!" Those words struck me like a blow. So I was sold at last! A human being sold in the free city of New York!' With bitter irony, her book subverts the expected denouement of a nineteenth-century novel: 'Reader, my story ends with freedom; not in the usual way, with marriage.' It's a more revealing line than it seems: like a Victorian marriage, Harriet's 'freedom' is a negotiated financial settlement, dependent on the goodwill of someone more powerful and incurring a weight of obligation.

In writing her story, however, Jacobs laid claim to her own power, exhibiting a freedom of mind that could not be bought, sold, cajoled or captured. She waited until 1853, when her beloved grandmother Molly Horniblow passed away, to begin sketching out the scenes of her life, using time that she squirrelled away from her round-the-clock duties in the Willis home. She took the manuscript to London in an effort to find a publisher and support from abolitionists there, which she knew would increase its chances in the American literary marketplace. She found a publisher, but the firm went bankrupt during the printing. Jacobs was able to buy the printing plates, however, and publish the book herself, becoming the first formerly enslaved woman to publish a full autobiography 'written by herself'. It appeared in January 1861, on the eve of the Civil War that would, on paper at least, put an end to slavery.

Incidents in the Life of a Slave Girl is a bold, poised and incendiary story – a grenade tossed into the mid-Victorian library. Jacobs addresses a female reader, knowing exactly who she is and which stories have shaped her. She knows that her reader is deeply invested in the nineteenth-century cult of true womanhood and believes women to be angels of domesticity and guardians of sexual purity, who show their worth in service and submissiveness to men. Her favourite stories describe virtue tested and rewarded, celebrate the joys of motherhood, and offer softening sympathy for loss. She comes to *Incidents*, most likely, having read Harriet Beecher Stowe's *Uncle Tom's Cabin*, published a decade earlier, a novel whose influence was so seismic that Abraham Lincoln allegedly greeted its author as 'the little woman who wrote the book that made this great war'. But when an abolitionist friend wrote to Stowe to share Jacobs's story and ask her advice about publishing it, Stowe addressed her reply to Nathaniel Willis, thus revealing private details of Harriet's past to her employer. When Jacobs herself wrote to Stowe, the author never responded.

Incidents shared in the collective howl of protest against the inhuman institution of slavery, yet it refused to utilise certain tropes intended to elicit sympathy from or flatter a white readership. Motherhood does not turn white women into the defenders of their enslaved sisters, nor do sympathetic feelings bend their actions toward justice. There are no white saviours in this story, only a handful of unreliable allies. And there are no moral quibbles or qualms about the urgency of ending slavery. Linda Brent is never in any doubt that she is a human being with a fundamental right to freedom, her country's defining mythology.

'"Give me liberty, or give me death," was my motto,' she declares in *Incidents*, seizing on the rallying cry of the American Revolution, stirringly delivered in 1775 by Virginia governor Patrick Henry (who, like most of the Founding Fathers renowned for their rhetoric of liberty, owned dozens of slaves).

Jacobs's story also departed in several important ways from her book's most famous precursor, the 1845 *Narrative of the Life of Frederick Douglass*. In this masculine tale the narrator, feeling isolated even from his fellow slaves, sets out alone to fight for his freedom, and ultimately voices compassion and forgiveness for his enslavers. Linda's escape is quite different: there is no dramatic solo flight, no exertion of physical power, just the bowing of the body to suffering and a desperate confinement. She does not separate herself from her family and friends, but remains utterly dependent on their support, secrecy and care, and tightly bound to her place of origin by her children. And she does not forgive her enslaver, even in death: 'The man was odious to me while he lived, and his memory is odious now.'

After publishing her story, Harriet Jacobs devoted her life to supporting enslaved and newly emancipated African Americans. Beginning in 1863, she worked with her daughter Louisa, by then thirty years old, to provide education and medical care to Black communities, first in the South and then, after a flare-up of post-war violence in Savannah, Georgia, in the North. She and Louisa ran well respected boarding houses in Cambridge, Massachusetts (where they catered to Harvard University circles) and in Washington D.C. But it was impossible to catch up to the enormous financial advantages of white America. Despite working until her late seventies and enduring illness and exhaustion, Harriet could never amass the capital to secure the 'hearthstone of her own' that she dreamed of – let alone the income that might have allowed her to work less and write more.

During her lifetime, Jacobs's authorship and ownership of *Incidents in the Life of a Slave Girl* went uncontested, but it is a troubling sign of the instability of Black and female literary legacies that her authorship later fell into doubt. Because she had changed the names of the central characters, and because elements of the story were so sensational and disturbing, some later readers insisted that the book had to be fiction, written to inspire abolitionists rather than reflect slavery's realities. For many decades, the book was called a novel and attributed to its editor, the white abolitionist Lydia Maria Child. It was not until the late 1980s that historian Jean Fagan Yellin's archival research reinstated Jacobs's story within the documentary record of slavery, and brought women's experiences within it to the fore.

The literary devices and narrative choices that made her book plausible as fiction resoundingly demonstrate that Harriet Jacobs was an artist as well as a survivor. The confident personality of the narrator and her fiery commitment to her own humanity elevate it above straightforward testimony. It is a story, gripping and vibrant, that bears out the words of the Reverend Francis Grimké, in his eulogy for Jacobs after her death in 1897: 'She was no reed shaken by the wind, vacillating, easily moved from a position. She did her own thinking.'

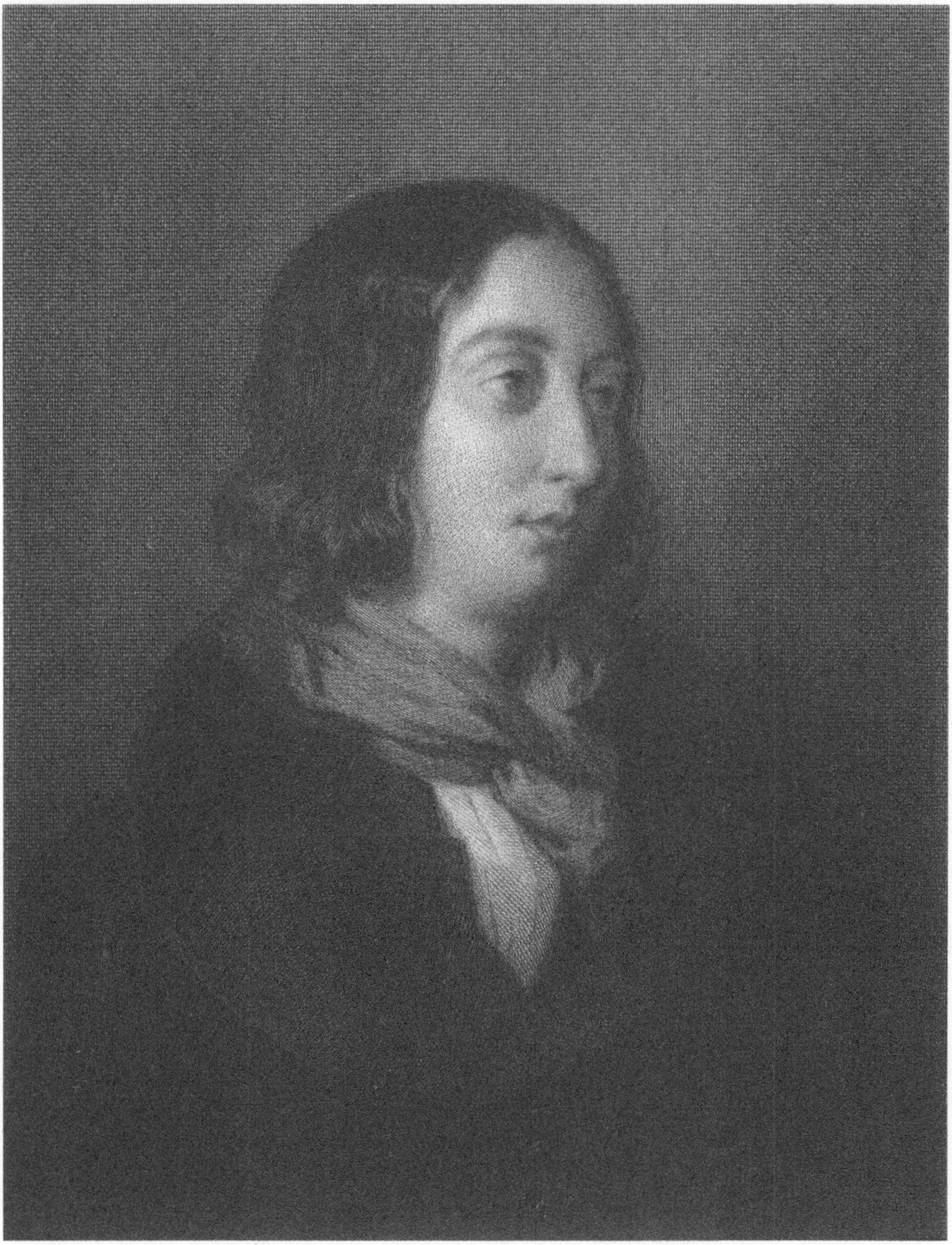

*'It seems to me that we change from day to day and
that after some years we are a new being.'*

GEORGE SAND
(1804–1876)

In her native France, the protean George Sand needs no introduction: she is a titan of nineteenth-century letters and a national monument, alongside the men who were her friends and lovers (Balzac, Flaubert, Chopin – the list is long). But monumentality feels inappropriate for a character who changed dramatically with the years and times. Hers was a life of abundance – or excess, depending on where and by whom the boundary is drawn. She outlived most women of her time and, into her seventies, defied her doctors to continue to take regular dips in the Indre river near her country estate. She was an involved mother and grandmother, a keen traveller, a painter and a gardener – when she made jam, which she loved to do, it was in overwhelming quantities.

But it is in her writing that the excess is most visible. Different critics give different estimates – sixty, seventy, eighty or ninety novels and novellas, buttressed by plays and articles, cultural criticism, essays, poetry, an autobiography and letters. Pages upon pages, numbering into the tens of thousands: it's safe to say no one has read it all. Even Sand herself lost track, apologising to her editors for sending manuscripts whose contents she couldn't recall. Her methods of writing became part of her mythology: she wrote at night, fuelled by chocolate and cigarettes, at a desk where a pet cricket kept her company. At least twenty pages per night, every night, whether she went to bed alone or with a lover. Sometimes she would finish one book and start another the same night. She wrote through bodily pain, cramps in her limbs and stomach, failing eyesight, migraines and depression. In all possible senses of the phrase, she wrote for her life. Balzac's productivity (and coffee consumption) are legendary but Sand's, somehow, seems too much – it demands an answer. What was she pursuing? And what was she neglecting, by writing so much?

'I came into the world on July 5, 1804; my father was playing the violin and my mother wore a pretty pink dress,' Sand wrote, in a description longer on atmosphere than accuracy – her actual birthday was July 1. Her version of events evokes a world of comfort, ease and fashion, and elides the tensions that would soon split the family apart. The baby was named Amantine Aurore Lucile Dupin, after her paternal grandmother Marie-Aurore, who held the purse strings. She was always known as Aurore and was the only one of her parents' children to grow up legitimate, and by the narrowest of margins: they had married just a month before she was born. When Marie-Aurore found out, she tried strenuously to get the union annulled, hoping to make baby and mother disappear and free her only son, Maurice, for a more appropriate marriage. But he was not much interested in behaving appropriately. He'd already had two children – one of whom was a boy named Hippolyte, conceived during an affair with a family servant, who grew up as part of the family. Sand's mother, Sophie-Victoire Delaborde, was, in her daughter's words, a member of the 'transient bohemian underworld'. Her father owned a billiard parlour and hawked goldfinches and canaries on the banks of the Seine, while Sophie most likely supported herself through sex work. She was five years older than Maurice, who was just twenty-two when they married.

Legitimacy was a cause for which Marie-Aurore had fought long and hard. She was herself a 'natural' (that is, illegitimate) daughter of Maurice de Saxe, a nobleman and military commander, who was in turn the son of Augustus II, King of Poland, by his mistress, a Swedish-German countess also named Aurore. 'The blood of kings was mixed in my veins with that of the poor and lowly,' George Sand would write. But blood was nothing without paperwork. In her teens, Marie-Aurore successfully petitioned the French government to amend her birth certificate to reflect her noble paternity, and she fought for a further two decades to lay her hands on the financial support she was owed as a result. Through such determination, ambitious offspring born on the wrong side of the blanket could claim their rights and secure a lineage. Marie-Aurore married twice, although neither husband lasted long. She emerged from the Revolution somewhat battle-scarred, but with a country estate, a pampered son and her name.

When Aurore was four years old, just a week after the death of her infant brother, the hapless Maurice was killed in a horse-riding accident. Over the next few months, his mother and his widow negotiated a deal that would see Sophie head back to Paris, leaving Marie-Aurore in charge of her little granddaughter and namesake. The girl who would become George Sand grew up in the country, learning that there were children, there was family, there were names and there was inheritance, but the supposedly straight lines connecting those elements could be erased and redrawn at will. Even the story of her own parentage – of her noble(ish) father and her lowly mother, joined in hasty union – was possibly invented. Both her mother and her grandmother later dropped hints that Maurice was not her real father after all, throwing her connection to the 'blood of kings' into doubt. This uncertainty of parentage, of identity, haunted Sand's life, and drove her to endless pursuit of the unanswerable question: 'Who am I?'

When Sand was seventeen, her grandmother died, bequeathing her the country estate at Nohant, in the old province of Berry in central France. This was an inheritance more solid than blood or a name, and she would spend her life deeply rooted there, even as she established herself as a writer in Paris. The following year, she married forty-two-year-old François-Casimir Dudevant, yet another illegitimate son of a nobleman. He gave Sand two children – Maurice and Solange – and a less than rosy view of marriage, which she considered a backward, oppressive institution. She was already chafing against its constraints by the time Solange was born – possibly the child of her lover, rather than her husband. The inheritance of doubt over her identity and the pain of uncertain belonging reverberated in her daughter's life, which became a bleak echo of her mother's. Solange failed to escape her bad marriage or find success as a writer, and her two children did not survive past early childhood.

To write or to mother? It felt impossible to do both. In the early days of 1831, when Aurore Dudevant was twenty-seven and her children eight and three, she broke out and moved to Paris. Her unfaithful husband had betrayed her again, this time by trying to draw up a will that would have robbed her, materially, of her ever-precarious inheritance. With her lover, a writer named Jules Sandeau, Aurore co-authored a novel under the shared pseudonym J. Sand, and soon adapted the name for herself. She also jettisoned the ambiguous initial for the name that, thirty years later, another woman in the throes of romantic and literary rebellion, the Englishwoman Mary Ann Evans, would adopt for herself when she became George Eliot. Thus disguised, George Sand launched herself into literary Paris. Her first solo-authored novel, and still one of her best known, *Indiana*, appeared in April 1832.

Sand's penchant for dressing in masculine clothing and her choice of a male pseudonym offer clues to her gender identity and to how she understood herself and wished to be understood by the world. But they are not definitive: there were many reasons a woman might wish to fling a trousered leg across the gender binary and, although it was somewhat scandalous for women in her era to dress in men's clothing, it was not unheard of. Heavy skirts and layers of petticoats made it almost impossible to move freely or to walk the mucky streets in comfort, let alone ride a horse. Men's clothing (then as now) was warmer, more robust and far less decorative, and therefore expensive, than the wardrobe of an upper-class woman. As a child, Sand had often been dressed as a boy by her grandmother, for reasons of practicality and economy. Yet ideology does not succumb to practicality that easily. A few years before Sand's birth, the French authorities placed an irritating and humiliating bureaucratic hurdle in the paths of women who wished to dress as men in public, by forcing them to first apply for a permit. Sand ignored this edict, but she was protected from reprimand first by her social standing, and then by her notoriety. The freedom she claimed, to stride into masculine spaces that were off-limits in her routinely sex-segregated world, became part of her mythology, along with other gender transgressions like smoking tobacco. Yet at other times and in other places (especially at her country house), the writer embraced her femininity. The collection of her personal effects donated by her granddaughter to the city of Paris included a sparkling array of jewellery. According to her friend Victor Hugo, Sand could not 'determine whether she is male or female'. He added, 'it is not my place to decide whether she is my sister or my brother.'

In the five years between leaving Nohant and officially separating from Dudevant, Sand embarked on a series of romances with the men in her orbit – novelists, politicians, actors, musicians and playwrights – while she gathered around her an illustrious circle of friends. But she also had at least one important romance with a woman, an actress named Marie Dorval. Like so many of her predecessors, Sand found that writing for the theatre paid better than novels, and it was, increasingly, a world suffused with glamour and celebrity. In 1833, she wrote a fan letter to Dorval, which led to an intense relationship, marked by passionate correspondence and later recollections from Sand, who declared, 'Only those who know how differently we were made can realise how utterly I was in thrall to her...' Watching Marie on stage, Sand said, felt like recognition, as though the actress was somehow channelling and expressing Sand's own thoughts and feelings. Their relationship was the subject of gossip and speculation in the tight-knit world of the theatre, further fuelled by Sand's increasingly notoriety, and societal assumptions about the sexual proclivities of women who dressed and acted like men. But whatever its precise contours, their partnership was deeply rooted in friendship and artistic respect. In 1840, the women worked together to produce *Cosima*, a play intended to showcase Marie's talents, which unfortunately met with poor reviews and a premature closure. The sparkling years of an actress's career tend to be brief, and in the mid-1840s Marie was forced to return to the gruelling life of a touring performer. She was barely fifty when that life finally wore her out, but Sand remained a loyal friend, and financially supported her family after Marie's death.

In the late 1830s, while still close with Marie, Sand began one of her most enduring relationships, with the composer Frédéric Chopin, who for several years spent his summers at Nohant. Here he wrote several of his best known works in the peaceful and luxurious surroundings of Sand's country estate. But the couple fell out a few years before Chopin's death in 1849, in part because of tensions with Sand's now adult children. Her son resented the composer's interloping presence, while Chopin upset Sand by continuing to be friendly with Solange after she had fallen out with her mother. The situation was not helped by the popularity of Sand's novel *Lucrezia Floriani*, in which a central character, an ailing prince, was widely read as an unflattering portrait of her lover. Sand burned many of their letters after Chopin's death, consigning the details of their relationship and its rupture to the flames.

Although she is now best known as a novelist, Sand was enmeshed in the world of journalism from the beginning of her career, when she celebrated the freedom of the press in the preface to her novel *Indiana*. The petty injuries and brief suffering caused by mistakes and misjudgements, she wrote, were nothing when set against the 'infinite benefits' that independent journalism offered the world. Less loftily, journalism supported her: many of her novels were serialised in newspapers and, early in her career, she wrote an anonymous column, '*Bigarrures*', in the *Figaro*, a title that evoked its variety of subject matter. As with Fanny Fern across the Atlantic a few years later, the identity of the writer behind the popular column became a source of rampant speculation. But Sand did not remain anonymous for long. In the 1830s she became a shorthand, much parodied image of the modern, independent woman: five feet tall, athletic, chain-smoking, cross-dressing and fearless. In 1841 Sand, with friends, launched her own paper, *La Revue indépendante*, and began to write more frequently about the plight of ordinary people and the status of women, advocating for educational reform and better schooling – especially for girls growing up in the countryside. When the American feminist and journalist Margaret Fuller visited her in 1846, she stressed Sand's 'simple and ladylike dignity', in contrast to all the mocking caricatures, and praised her 'energy and courage' as a woman forging a solitary path in a man's world.

When the 1848 revolution sparked to life, Sand threw herself into the republican cause, pausing her other publishing endeavours in order to take a more active political role, writing pamphlets and launching a short-lived journal, *The Cause of the People*. But in the wake of that heady political moment, and disappointed by the compromises that resulted, Sand withdrew somewhat from her outspoken public platform. In the 1850s she published letters, travel journalism, art and literary criticism, and began to serialise her autobiography *Histoire de ma vie*. More novels and essays followed, including tales for children. After Chopin's death, and despite a chequered and dramatic romantic history, she found a lasting and stable relationship with Alexandre Manceau, a graphic artist and playwright who was several years younger than her. Invited by his friend, her son Maurice, to spend Christmas with the family in Nohant, Alexandre soon became her lover, secretary and close companion for the next fifteen years, before his death from tuberculosis. In her own final years, Sand returned to Nohant, where she died in 1876 and was buried in the private cemetery.

After her death, George Sand's reputation went through almost as many twists as her career and her personal life. Men turned on her, attacking the spectacle she had presented of a liberated woman, and her unapologetic claiming of her own freedom: Friedrich Nietzsche called her an 'involuntary argument ... against emancipation and feminine autonomy'. But for later feminists, too, she made an uneasy heroine. She fought for herself alone, rather than making common cause with other women, and despite her own transgressions of the gender binary, she maintained a belief in its power, arguing that 'men and women can have different functions without this giving women inferior status'. In the 1920s, after American women had won the vote and largely retreated from organised fights for their rights, the feminist leader Marie Jenney Howe published a biography of George Sand and a translation of her *Intimate Journal*. She was fascinated by the writer's personality and inner life, rather than her politics. In English today, there are more biographies of Sand in print than translations of her writing.

In France, she remains both inside and outside the canon. A proposal in 2003 to move her remains to the Panthéon in Paris prompted an eruption of the old argument about whether women's recognition as artists depends on their inclusion in such male-dominated bastions of greatness. There was fierce resistance to moving Sand: her Nohant cemetery seemed a more appropriate resting place, as it was where all the drama of her lineage and inheritance ceded their power to who she actually was. At Nohant, she studied the land and its human, animal and plant life. She learned about herbal remedies and acted as the village doctor. She drew and painted the landscape and placed it, in wisps of disguise, into her novels. The estate made room for her contradictions as a woman politically committed to republicanism who nevertheless prized this symbol of aristocracy above all else. Then again, hers was an unusual sort of aristocracy: a blended, matriarchal family that absorbed illegitimate children, cousins, friends and lovers in defiance of patriarchal strictures. Nohant became a bohemian enclave dedicated to the arts, especially music and theatre. And it was where Sand developed her truest vision of autonomy. There, she wrote, she needed no one's help 'to kill anyone for me, pick a bouquet of flowers, correct a proof or go to the theatre. I'll go there on my own, like a man, by my own choice; when I want flowers, I'll walk by myself to the Alps.'

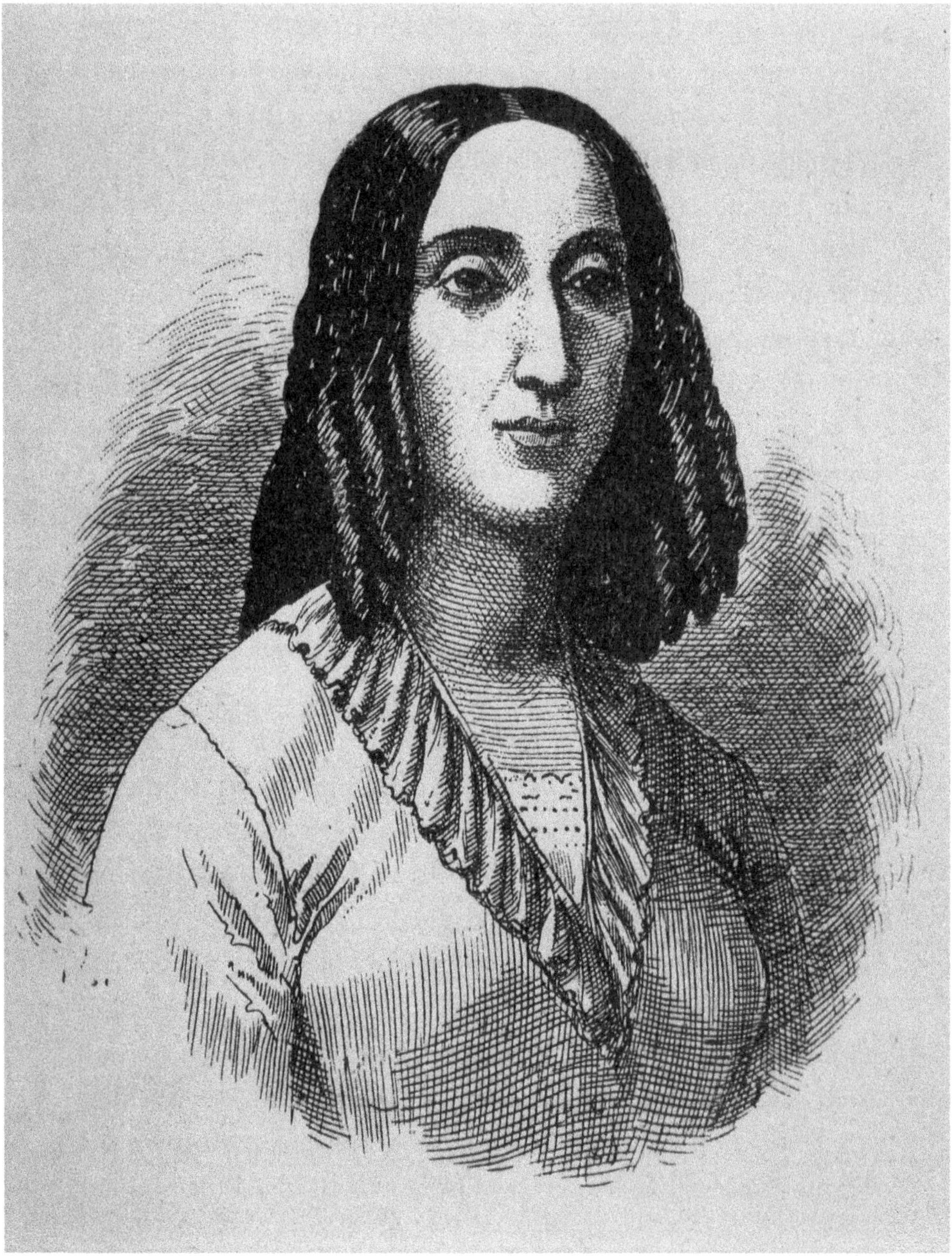

'Do you know anything which is so sought after and yet so sad as travelling?'

JUANA MANUELA GORRITI
(1816–1892)

In 1818, eight years after Argentina broke free of Spanish rule, Juana Manuela Gorriti was born in the northern province of Salta. She was the seventh of eight children in a family of wealthy landowners and politicians; her father, José Ignacio de Gorriti, had fought in the war of independence and signed the founding declaration of the new nation. Juana Manuela briefly attended a convent school as a child, but most of her education happened at home, on the family estate in Horcones, which boasted an enormous library. Her study of European classics blended with the indigenous languages she spoke, Quechua and Aymara, and the stories shared by the staff on the estate, which were rich in local folklore and mythology. She and her siblings were especially entranced by tales of Inca treasures lost in the Spanish conquest. These conflicting yet tightly entwined inheritances would provide her first grounding in national identity, and her first experience of its rupture.

After independence, Argentina witnessed violent power struggles as the liberal Unitarian party, supported by Juana Manuela's father, challenged the dominance of the dictatorial Juan Manuel de Rosas. In 1831, when Juana Manuela was thirteen, her family was forced to flee into exile in Bolivia, forfeiting their family wealth and status. It was the first of many displacements over the course of her life, and four decades would pass before she was officially able to return to her native country. As she wrote in one of her last published collections, 'Destiny, for its capriciousness, determined, from the cradle and during the best years of my youth, that an absorbing, bitter, destructive force would surround me – politics.'

The young girl grew up quickly. Just before she turned fifteen, two years after leaving Argentina, Juana Manuela married a captain in the Bolivian army, Manuel Isidoro Belzú. Despite an impoverished background, he was rising rapidly through the ranks, thanks to his bravery in combat and a friendship with the general who served as Bolivia's president. The couple had two daughters together, Edelmira and Mercedes, but the marriage began to crumble under the pressure of the intense power struggles among senior army officers and, most likely, infidelities on both sides. By the early 1840s, Juana Manuela had begun writing and publishing short stories that traded in melodrama, intrigue and political violence, of which she had firsthand knowledge. In 1841, she disguised herself as a man to slip back over the Argentinian border and visit the family estate in Salta, which was being raided by her father's political enemies: she turned the escapade into the story 'Gubi Amaya'.

Life as a woman in politics was no more stable in Bolivia than Argentina. After Belzú's political enemies forced the family to flee again, Juana Manuela settled in Lima, Peru, where she would spend the next forty years, on and off, becoming a central figure in the city's blossoming literary and cultural scene. While her husband seized the presidency in Bolivia in a coup d'état in 1848, Juana Manuela Gorriti was busy establishing herself as a writer and cultural figure in Lima. The city was booming with creative energy – with new theatres, salons, journals and newspapers springing up regularly. Amid this ferment, Gorriti hosted regular weekly *tertulias*, or literary salons, to which she invited leading artists, musicians and intellectuals to discuss the cultural issues of the day, especially the roles and rights of women. Although men did participate, women were at the centre of the salon's life – just as they were for their counterparts in London, Paris, New York and elsewhere in the nineteenth and twentieth centuries.

At her salons, Juana Manuela Gorriti and her intellectual women friends hashed out their version of feminism as an elastic blend of what was and what could be. In mid-nineteenth-century Lima, they had a formidable enemy in the Catholic church, and a social structure that wanted to confine women to domestic invisibility. Women were valued for their role as mothers – literally and symbolically – rather than for their individual contributions to public life. Education for women was a passion for these progressive women. Many of them, including Gorriti, established and taught in schools for girls. Their feminism still hewed closely to the moral values of the new nation, rather than challenging its foundations, so they generally did not champion populist causes or labour rights, or fight for women to have a bigger political role. Instead, they pushed for intellectual emancipation, through books and writing.

Juana Manuela had two more children during this period – a daughter, Clorinda, who died in infancy, and a son, Julio – but she neither married their father nor revealed his identity. Like other women throughout this book, she faced the challenge of balancing art and motherhood, as well as the judgement of conservative authorities who disliked her subversive thinking. Within her circle, other women confronted the same pressures. Her friend Manuela Villarán de Plasencia contributed to the rich body of poems by women who were mothers, to which Lucille Clifton would add a century later in America. Manuela's poem describes trying to write in snatched moments of peace: 'I fly to my desk. And then a cry I hear/It's my youngest child who demands my care./I run to calm her, a pen in my hand.' Another friend and regular salon guest, Clorinda Matto de Turner, who edited a weekly illustrated paper, faced sterner opposition when she published a story that imagined a romantic relationship between Jesus and Mary Magdalene. The church's protests pressured her until she quit her editorial job, and she was eventually forced into exile.

Alongside her friends, Juana Manuela published articles and stories in Lima's many literary journals, although some of the details are disputed. Her novella *La Quena*, possibly written when she was just eighteen, first appeared in print in Lima in 1851. The title refers to a kind of reed flute played by indigenous musicians, and the story unfolds themes that were of enduring interest to her: impossible love across the barriers of race and class, a turbulent political backdrop and plot twists including mistaken identity and sudden violence. In the opening scene, the heroine's lover reveals in a secret nighttime tryst that he is the 'son of an Indian woman', torn from his mother's arms by his father to be educated in Spain. His indigenous origins are linked to dispossession and the legends of secret, buried Inca gold: 'The man who loves you is an unfortunate soul who does not possess anything in this world, though his feet tread upon the treasures that his forefathers confided to the depths of the earth to keep them from the sanguinary greed of their tyrants.'

Gorriti's early stories are filled with motion and drama, as characters try to outrun the destiny revealed in dreams. They clearly show the influence of her childhood interest in folklore and indigenous culture, and often feature elements of the supernatural, acknowledging how the nation's violent past endures into the present, especially for bereaved women. Her story 'The Dead Man's Fiancée', for instance, unfolds a *Romeo and Juliet*-style romance between a young soldier and his lover,

Vital, the daughter of the general of the opposing army. After a bloody, decisive battle, the story focuses on the loss and grief of wives and mothers amid the victory celebrations of men: 'In the country house next to the ceibo tree grove, locked up in her white virginal alcove, on her knees, pale and shaking, Avendaño's daughter begged the Mother of God for her husband, while her father celebrated with his men the triumph of their cause with an endless feast.' Grief induces a hallucination that her husband is still alive, until an order that the women must bury the dead, lying in the town square, reveals her loss. 'From that day on, Vital turned into an unreal being who slid among the living like a ghost.' In that supernatural state she lingers between life and death, and 'the inhabitants of the neighbouring fields still find her on summer nights, in the moonlight, under the fragrant foliage of the orange trees, wandering, pale but serene' – her black hair and smooth skin unmarked by time even thirty years later. Stories filled with ghosts, hallucinations and doubles – Gorriti's characters frequently appear in disguise, often cross-dressing – are ways of reckoning with what might have been, with alternative pasts. The child wrenched out of her homeland becomes the woman who is repeatedly forced into exile, and finds herself haunted by the path not taken and the life twisted out of its expected shape.

Despite her claim of hating the 'bitter, destructive force' of politics, it formed an important element of Gorriti's fiction. Although she was born several years after the end of the Argentine war of independence, she returns again and again to that backdrop for her stories, as well as to the years of the Rosas dictatorship – formative and dramatic political moments that shaped her early life. The victory and declaration of independence remained a wellspring of hope for her native Argentina, despite the violence and terror that followed. The constant revisiting of that history allowed Gorriti to imagine the future that she wanted and to call into being a world that lived up to the promise of independence.

In Bolivia, Juana Manuela's estranged husband, Belzú, had become a populist dictator since rising to power in 1848. He held on until 1855, surviving an assassination attempt. In 1855, he stood down and named his daughter Edelmira's husband as his successor, but his son-in-law lasted just two years before being overthrown in yet another coup and assassinated in 1861. Belzú himself was murdered by his political opponents in 1865, while Juana Manuela was visiting Edelmira in La Paz. She had had little contact with her husband for twenty years, but some tie of political ambition and sympathy endured between the couple, despite their very separate lives. She spoke at his funeral – a vast and furious gathering of his supporters, mainly women, who called for his killers to be brought to justice. Alarmed at the size of the crowd, the new Bolivian government who had been responsible for his assassination quickly drove his widow out of the country.

Back in Peru, territorial violence engulfed her life. The port of Lima was under fire by the Spanish navy and Juana Manuela volunteered as a nurse and helped evacuate the wounded. Amid the fighting, yellow fever ran rampant, and she continued to nurse the sick and wounded, recording her experiences in a series of stories and eyewitness articles. Ten years later, in 1876, the Peruvian government would bestow on her a top military honour in recognition of her work as a medical volunteer. By then, however, she had already begun the slow journey of returning to her native land. In 1865, a major two-volume collection of her stories and novellas, *Sueños y Realidades* (Dreams and Realities) had been published in Buenos Aires, and she was now hailed as an Argentinean literary celebrity.

In 1875, Gorriti – who was always in need of cash – returned to Argentina with the help of the country's First Lady and secured a monthly pension for the descendants of those who had fought in Argentina's war of independence. She threw herself into the task of connecting with other women writers and editors in Buenos Aires, and launched her own periodical, a journal of politics and culture called *La Alborada del Plata* (Argentina Dawn), which advocated strongly for women's rights and education, as well as the need for Latin American countries to develop their own native literary traditions out of the shadow of Europe. She launched a new version of her famed salon in her adopted city, and published a new collection of fiction and biography, *Panoramas de la vida* (Views of life), which capped the dramatic years of her marriage with a notably flattering portrait of her ex-husband. She would spend the next few years moving back and forth between Argentina and Peru. At the end of the decade she tried to reach her daughter, Mercedes, who had fallen ill in Peru. As so often over the course of her life, war – this time between Peru and Chile – threw up a barrier and prevented her free movement. She could not reach Mercedes before she died. In 1885, in her late sixties, she settled permanently in Argentina.

In her later years, Juana Manuela began to reflect more positively on the way that her life of border crossings, expulsions and returns had forged in her a cosmopolitan outlook. She cultivated readers across the Americas and Europe – in her lifetime, she was the most widely read woman writer in Latin America – and she embraced the role that modern cities like Lima and Buenos Aires played in cultivating cultural exchange. The network she developed through her weekly salons was, likewise, an international and transcultural one. In 1889, she even brought together more than a hundred women writers across Latin America to create a cookbook – *La Cocina Ecléctica* (Eclectic Cuisine) – that celebrated the continent's multiplicity of food traditions, both native and imported. The project demonstrated how the feminised and domestic arena of the kitchen could be a valuable venue for understanding across cultures.

Her final writings returned her to her origins. For the first time since she had left it as a child, she travelled back to her childhood home, to reminisce on what it was and how it had changed. Her 1889 novel *La Tierra Natal* (Our Native Land) lays bare the incompatibility of modernity and memory: 'There was a hotel, carriages, beautiful buildings of modern construction with all the comfort of our present existence, but alas! Nothing from other times, nothing except the old church … neglected and broken down.' In this church, where she was baptised, she finds traces of the old world, but they are decrepit and forgotten. The encounter with ruins is a common trope in her writing, a way of combining nostalgia and humility in the face of the overblown claims of progress. In an autobiographical narrative, *Lo íntimo* (The Intimate), which she completed less than two weeks before her death in 1892, she describes the return to Horcones, 'now a mound of ruins inhabited only by jackals and snakes'. Nature has taken over, and the once impressive buildings have become symbols of the fragility of human achievement. 'What remains of your former splendour?' she asks. 'Your walls have decayed, the pillars of your arches have crumbled as if once erected upon an abyss.' Although her early childhood might have felt like an era of lost tranquillity, the ruins of her childhood home were a reminder that everything solid will decay.

Few writers felt more acutely than Gorriti how reversals of fortune could uproot a life. Her later stories reflected her need for money, as she took on more commercial and contemporary themes. But she also began to engage directly with the crisis of the lost past and the uncertain future. She wrote about the California gold rush and the economic dominance of the United States – a place, she wrote in *Lo íntimo*, that was 'endowed with a superlative national ego'. She filled her stories with descriptions of cities and modern technology – the roar of factories and trains, the glare of electric light, the array of new things to buy – and contrasted these conveniences and temptations with a lost rural past, now vanished into myth. But that past is not stable or secure. It is populated by ghosts, and by people on the run who speak many overlapping languages, and whose stories are never easy to separate into truth or fiction, victim or oppressor, colonised or coloniser. Gorriti's literary works reflect the challenge of the post-colonial Americas in trying to balance what each nation had been – if it were even possible to recover any pre-conquest purity of myth and identity – with what it was going to become. What kind of future would be built on top of the ruins?

Edith Eaton

Sui Sin Far

1900

'Individuality is more than nationality'

SUI SIN FAR/EDITH MAUDE EATON
(1865–1914)

As a child, Edith Maude Eaton felt like a creature in a zoo, and not a fierce one. Born in 1865 in the north of England to an English father and a Chinese mother, her family then moved to Montreal, where white people stared at her and her troupe of black-haired siblings (she was one of fourteen) as though they were 'strange animals in a menagerie'. Her brothers and sisters squared up against this hostile curiosity, but Edith, to her great shame, shrank from the fight. 'I have no organic disease,' she recalled years later, 'but the strength of my feelings seems to take from me the strength of my body.' Instead, the injustice of racial prejudice raged inside her: a storm in the body rather than out in the world.

Edith's father and mother met in Shanghai, where Edward Eaton had been sent in pursuit of silks for his family's textile business. He brought home, instead, a Chinese wife known as Grace, and a son, Edith's elder brother Charlie. The highly coloured family legend held that Grace was the daughter of a noble family – Edith wrote that she was 'stolen from her home' as a child and forced to work in a circus, until she was rescued by

British missionaries and taken to England to be educated. She had returned to Shanghai to study when she met Edward, an aspiring artist. Edith saw her parents as wildly romantic figures, creative wanderers who remained committed to one another and their big, unorthodox family, despite their constant battles against racism and encroaching poverty.

As she grew up, sensitive Edith sought refuge in the library, where she found books that presented China as a complex and ancient civilisation – a heritage in which she could take pride, rather than a source of shame she needed to tear out. 'At eighteen years of age,' she later recalled, 'what troubles me is not that I am what I am, but that others are ignorant of my superiority.' But no amount of teenage arrogance could turn the tide of anti-Chinese prejudice in North America. The mid-century gold rush had brought speculators from all over the world to the West Coast, including thousands from China, who were systematically disadvantaged even in that freewheeling arena. Many Chinese men found work on the expanding railroads, breaking their backs to build the hardest sections over the highest ground. Even the lowest wages in America were worth a lot more back home, so despite the dangers and deprivation, more people made the journey, and Chinese communities took root in a number of North American cities. These Chinatowns were densely populated, closed-off areas and sites of fear and fascination for the white neighbours who skirted their perimeters and peered through the cracks.

Racist rhetoric stoked white America's fear of the 'aliens' flocking to its coastal cities, culminating in the 1882 Chinese Exclusion Act, the first U.S. immigration law explicitly to name and shame an entire nation. The act banned Chinese workers from becoming U.S. citizens and, going a cruel step further, barred them bringing their wives and families over. In Canada, where immigration was somewhat easier, a network of smugglers helped Chinese people slip into the United States – a murky but profitable business in which Edith Eaton's father was almost certainly involved.

Her family always needed money, so Edith, in her late teens, learned shorthand and found work as a journalist for local newspapers. At this moment of explosive urban growth, innumerable new publications were springing up to cater to specific demographics, while papers aimed at the mass market, claiming objectivity and neutrality, needed reporters who could traverse ethnic and cultural borders. Women like Edith were especially useful in gaining access to communities whose members might be wary of answering a white man's questions. So Edith reported on the Chinese community in Montreal and, perhaps in an effort to exorcise those incidents in her childhood where she had failed to stand up for her siblings or herself, she made a point of defending Chinese people, taking up their battles with the authorities and counteracting negative stereotypes. In her mostly unsigned journalism, Edith strove to give a thorough and thoughtful picture of Chinese immigrant life, although she was constrained by the demands and expectations of her white audience who were steeped in prejudice and eager for tales of the exotic. She wrote in English and her physical appearance allowed her to pass for white, but she had an outsider's perspective, alert always to stereotypes and prejudice, and fighting them in her own way. She was a literary smuggler, trafficking in secret knowledge.

Broadening her horizons beyond Montreal, Edith lived for a time in Jamaica, working as a journalist 'under a tropic sky', where she was accepted as white by the island's fashionable elites. The experience forged in her a sense of racial solidarity with the 'reputed descendants of Ham' – that is, the island's Black population. 'Occasionally an Englishman will warn me against the "brown boys" of the island,' she wrote, 'little dreaming that I too am one of the "brown people" of the earth.'

But that identification was tenuous, and ahead of its time. Edith found herself trapped between cultures in a way that neither of her parents could understand. 'He is English, she is Chinese. I am different to both of them – a stranger, though their own child,' she wrote. The Chinese communities she wrote about did not welcome her, despite her preference for Chinese men, whom she declared to be superior to whites 'in mind and heart qualities'. As she put it, 'the Americanised Chinamen actually laugh in my face when I tell them I am of their race.' She never travelled to China, and it's usually assumed that she could not speak Chinese, beyond a few phrases – although she apparently studied the language, and knew enough to interview people in Chinese and to read and translate Chinese folk tales. Despite her strong cultural sympathy, Edith lived in the overlapping, liminal space she designated as 'Eurasian', and spent her life struggling to understand and articulate that identity as a cultural go-between, an inadequate interpreter and a mystery to herself and others.

Although she paid the rent by working as a stenographer, before the turn of the century Edith began to experience more success as a writer, submitting fiction to American periodicals and her work being accepted by bigger publications like *Ladies' Home Journal* and *Century*. Around this time, she began to use the pen name Sui Sin Far (sometimes spelled Sui Seen Far or Sui Sin Fah), a family nickname meaning 'lotus flower'. As researchers today continue to unearth her work from a scattered archive, it's clear how versatile she was – writing travel journalism, middlebrow women's fiction and more daring stories set in bohemian milieus. She explored, and sometimes appropriated, cultural identities far beyond her own.

Her increasing success as a writer enabled her move to San Francisco, home to one of North America's largest Chinatowns, around 1898. Here, she found a community more integrated into the dominant white culture, with young Chinese men striving to get ahead in business rather than manual labour, and middle-class women trying to distance themselves from poorer immigrants who brought with them the language, superstitions and prejudices of the old country. The clash between cultures, and between tradition and modernity, form the thread of her only published book, the story collection *Mrs Spring Fragrance*, which appeared in 1912, two years before the author's death at the age of forty-nine. It came packaged in a red cover adorned with stylised gold lilies and 'oriental' lettering – a design that carried on through on its pages. It was a beautiful, exotic object created to capture the white reader's eye by harnessing the trend for Chinoiserie fabrics and motifs in clothing, interiors, and objects. To Sui Sin Far, there was no doubt some irony to the presentation of her stories in this elegant, superficial wrapping. She would sardonically comment on advice she had been given to trade on her nationality: 'I should dress in Chinese costume, carry a fan in my hand, wear a pair of scarlet beaded slippers, live in New York, and come of high birth', as well as constantly quote Confucius. The stories within her book's pages, however, were much less decorative and one-dimensional.

The book is divided into two sections, with stories aimed at adult readers in the first half, and the second made up of shorter pieces for children that draw on Chinese fables and folk tales. The more substantial stories explore the relationships between mostly middle-class white and Asian characters in Seattle and San Francisco. The titular Mrs Spring Fragrance appears in several stories, and is a well liked, coolheaded observer of American customs, operating in an old-fashioned, Jane Austenesque world where neighbours gossip and conspire to get young people married, where letters pass between friends and the problems caused by men are solved and soothed by subterfuge and scheming between women. There's a sly, subversive humour to Mrs Spring

Fragrance's musing and meddling. In a knowing jab at ethnographic jingoism, we see her in 'The Inferior Woman' considering writing a book about Americans for Chinese readers, finding that 'the American people were so interesting and mysterious'.

But the veneer of middle-class tranquillity is as delicate as Mrs Spring Fragrance's decorative parasol, and violence stalks these tales of superficial assimilation. In a dark period of anti-Chinese sentiment, the stories return insistently to the profound and sometimes tragic disconnect between the dreams of the immigrant, the promise of America and its reality. The tone is one of cool irony, the rage banked deep. One can't help think of the child, Edith Eaton, refusing to fight her tormentors.

In the title story, Mrs Spring Fragrance visits her cousin in San Francisco and writes to her husband to report on her activities, which include attending a lecture with a white woman friend about America's benevolence toward China. In the spirit of the lecture her letter, dripping with irony, encourages her husband to overlook the daily slights of racism, and to counsel his brother, detained by the U.S. immigration authorities, to be thankful for his good fortune in 'being protected under the wing of the Eagle, the Emblem of Liberty'. An even more chilling irony drives 'In the Land of the Free', a tale in which U.S. officials at the dock in San Francisco separate a two-year-old boy, born in China and arriving for the first time with his mother, from his immigrant parents. Unable to believe that any law 'would keep a child from its mother', the parents engage a shady white lawyer to 'hurry the government' to return their son, a process that nevertheless takes almost a year. When the family is finally reunited, the boy no longer recognises his parents and has forgotten his Chinese name. It is perhaps no accident that the then astronomical sum the lawyer extracts from the parents in this story, five hundred dollars, is exactly the same figure the Canadian government had, in 1896, proposed levying as a 'head tax' on Chinese immigrants. An irate Edith Eaton, who had lived most of her life in Montreal, published 'A Plea for the Chinaman' in the *Montreal Daily Star*, in which she insisted that 'every just person must feel his or her sense of justice outraged by the attacks which are being made by public men on the Chinese who come to this country.' Almost a century later, when a group of Chinese Canadians lobbied the government for reparations for this tax on their ancestors, they brandished copies of her article.

Sui Sin Far's stories also engaged with another unavoidable cultural question of her era: the place of women in society and the compromises they faced in trying to balance family and financial independence. In an autobiographical essay, she mentions a fellow Eurasian woman who decides to marry her white suitor not because she loves him, but 'because the world is so cruel and sneering to a single woman'. In her fiction, she was fascinated by the ways that gender shaped cultural assimilation, and the different compromises men and women were willing and able to make in adapting to a new life in a new country. Her male protagonists, in particular, cast off Chinese traditions in exchange for the capitalist fantasy of equal advancement for equal work, only to find that the game is rigged against immigrants from the start. Several of her stories feature white women who are committed to advancing women's rights according to their own definition and beliefs. Sui Sin Far was ahead of her time in recognising – again through a veil of irony – the shortcomings of a particular kind of ardent, narcissistic white feminism that seeks to impose its own values, seeing them as universal, and to claim to speak for all women, without any effort at dialogue or understanding of difference.

The darkest story in the collection, 'The Wisdom of the New Life', brings these currents into a tragic convergence. The protagonist is a striving Chinese man who arrives in the United States having married a fellow countrywoman whom he does not know. When she arrives to join him, she resists any integration into the new culture, holding firm to values that make no longer make sense to her husband. She refuses to educate their young son in Western ways, cut his hair or dress him like an American boy. Deeply suspicious of her husband's friendship with one well intentioned white woman, who hopes to befriend and liberate the Chinese wife, she kills their child – a horrific act of revenge on her husband, and the ultimate blow against the project of cultural assimilation.

In another story, 'The Story of One White Woman Who Married a Chinese', Sui Sin Far inverts the expectations of a title that might have appeared as a cautionary headline in a contemporary newspaper. Instead, the heroine is a working-class white woman, Minnie, abandoned by her cruel white husband and rescued by a kind, caring merchant named Liu Kanghi. 'I can lean upon and trust in him,' Minnie says of her Chinese husband. 'I feel him behind me, protecting and caring for me, and that, to an ordinary woman like myself, means more than anything else.' The story ends tragically, with Liu Kanghi's murder at the hands of Minnie's violent ex-husband – perhaps representing a capitulation to the entrenched cultural taboo against mixed-race marriages. It also trades on the stereotype of Chinese men as less virile yet, within these constraints, it manages to make a hero of the murdered man and to lay bare the toxicity of white conventions of masculinity. As Eaton wrote to an editor a few years before her book was published, she was deliberate in her efforts to use fiction to achieve anti-racist ends, 'to break down prejudice, and to cause the American heart to soften and the American mind to broaden towards the Chinese people now living in America – the humble, kindly, moral, unassuming Chinese people of America'.

Anti-Chinese prejudice in the late nineteenth century stood in stark contrast to the concurrent Western fetish for all things

Japanese. Japan – seen as wealthy, cultured, and, crucially, self-contained – had just reopened to the West after two hundred years of isolation. Edith recalled a dinner party in a midwestern American town at which her fellow guests, not knowing her heritage, aired their racist opinions of Chinese people, but were careful to observe that 'the Japanese are different altogether'. Elsewhere in the same autobiographical essay, she tells the story of a Chinese woman who breaks off her engagement to a white American when he suggests, 'Wouldn't it be just a little pleasanter for us if, after we are married, we allowed it to be presumed that you were – er – Japanese?' (That woman, it seems likely, was Edith herself.) So it is not altogether surprising that Edith's sister, Winnifred, who was ten years younger, embraced the vogue by adopting the pen name Onoto Watanna and passing herself off as an authority on the country, despite having never visited, nor having any Japanese ancestry or knowledge of the language. She became the successful author of popular novels that flirted with the exotic and forbidden, although they stopped short of the transgression of interracial romance.

Edith's path as Sui Sin Far was less commercial, but truer to her own roots and background – although she, too, wrote some stories, mostly for children, from a Japanese perspective. Her writing tackles a huge range of issues that arise from her status as in between cultures, and does not offer easy answers or flat stereotypes. She veers between pride in her identity and deep-rooted shame, and righteous anger at how she and other Chinese and mixed-race immigrants in the West were treated. In a culture of rigid racial hierarchies, she was one of the people whose very existence challenged the categories that underpinned white supremacy. She strove to see and celebrate the individual within, and see beyond, his or her racial markers.

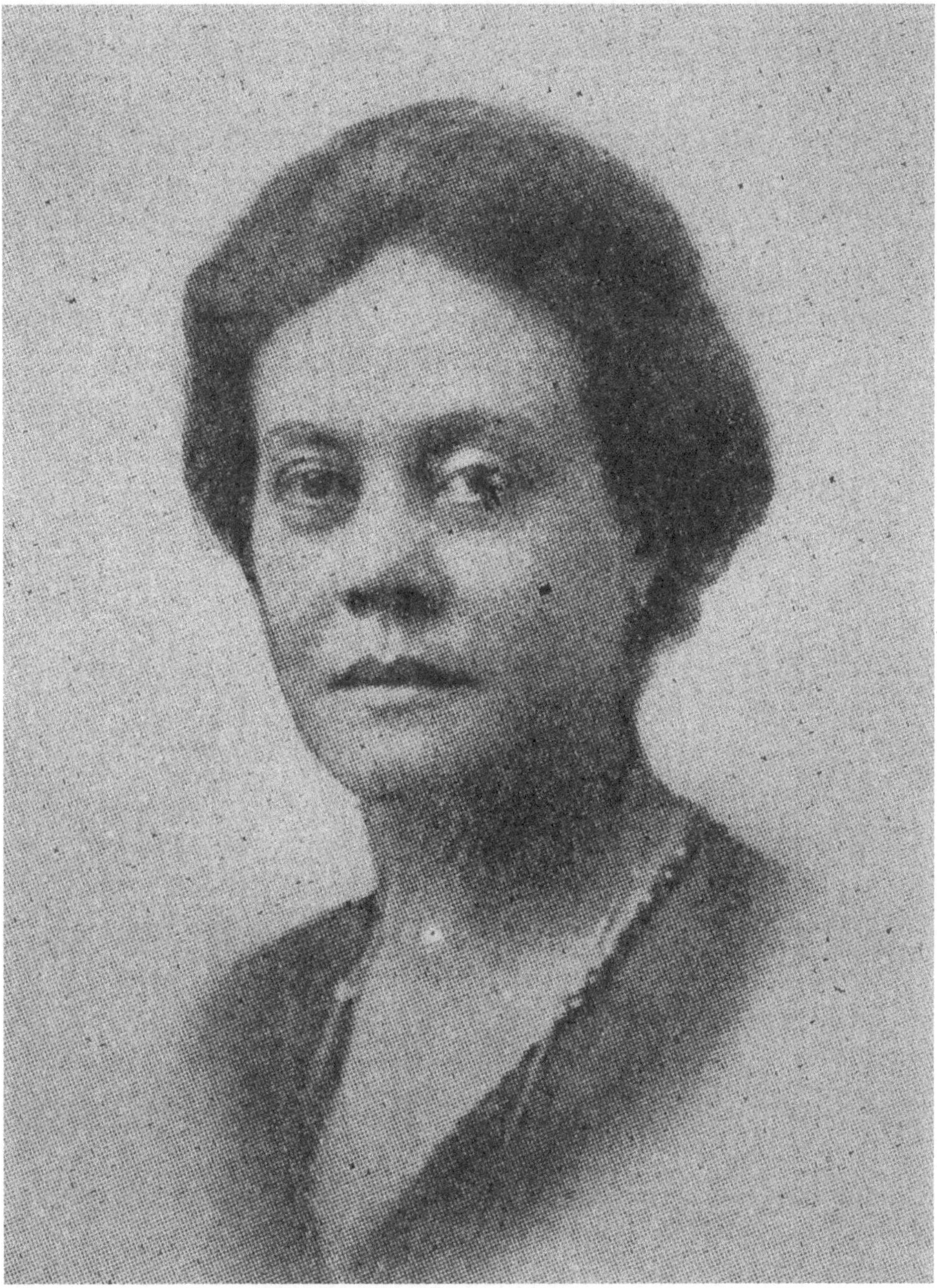

'To an independent spirit there is a certain sense of humiliation and wounded pride in asking for money, be it five cents or five hundred dollars. The working woman knows no such pang; she has but to question her account and all is over ... There is an independent, happy, free-and-easy swing about the motion of her life.'

ALICE DUNBAR-NELSON
(1875–1935)

In Dayton, Ohio in April 1895, an up-and-coming young Black poet named Paul Laurence Dunbar happened to pick up a copy of *The Woman's Era*, a new monthly newspaper written and edited exclusively by African-American women. In its pages, he found himself captivated by a poem attributed to Alice Ruth Moore, the paper's New Orleans correspondent – or, more accurately, by its accompanying photograph, which portrayed a strikingly beautiful young woman with deep, soulful, downcast eyes and abundant, stylishly arranged, dark hair. He immediately sent a letter to the poet at her home on Palmyra Street in New Orleans to express his admiration, launching an intense epistolary courtship that lasted two years. Six months into their correspondence, Paul was declaring, 'I love you and have loved you since the first time I saw your picture.' He imagined her beauty matched by the feminine accomplishments appropriate to an upper-class young woman of the day – 'Do you recite? Do you sing? Don't you dance divinely?' – and exclaimed that she was 'the sudden realization of an ideal!'

The poetic couple, who would marry in 1898, modelled themselves self-consciously after Robert and Elizabeth Barrett

Browning, another pair of lovers and writers whose romance began by letter – Paul referred to 'This Mr and Mrs Browning affair of ours'. Alice, for her part, enjoyed her role as muse, colleague and practical support: 'We worked together, read together, and I flattered myself that I helped him in his work,' she recalled. 'I was his amanuensis and secretary, and he was good enough to write poem after poem "for me," he said.' But in its time and place, their relationship was more remarkable than the Brownings'. At the tail end of the nineteenth century, in a deeply segregated country, the Dunbars came to embody an aspirational ideal of educated, cultured Black Americans, who were allowed access to white-controlled halls of fame and power as long as they were willing to remain flattened and fixed in the role of representatives of their race.

Such a role did not allow much space for passion and disorder. But after Alice and Paul met in person, the refinements of their written courtship were scrawled over with violence. In November 1897, in what Paul described as 'one damned night of folly', he raped Alice, leaving her with internal injuries. Five months later, the couple eloped. The marriage lasted four years, but ended as violently as it had begun, with a drunken beating. Alice left, and never returned. Paul tried to woo her back with letters, but she answered only once, with a single word delivered by telegram: *No*. He returned to live with his mother in Dayton, and they did not see each other again.

When Paul died of tuberculosis in February 1906, at the age of thirty-three, Alice found out by reading a notice in the newspaper. In the years that followed, despite their estrangement, she worked hard to keep his reputation and his work alive. She read his poetry in public and, in 1920, edited *The Dunbar Speaker and Entertainer*, a hefty anthology of 'the best prose and poetic selections by and about the Negro race', which included many selections by Paul, but also Alice's own poetry and pieces by writers from James Weldon Johnson to Abraham Lincoln. The 'caucasian' contributors were denoted by an asterisk. Although the volume nominally honoured her husband, it was Alice's portrait, rather than Paul's, that adorned the book as a frontispiece. Thanks largely to her efforts, Paul's reputation continued to burn brightly well into the 1920s, when his poetic style and voice began to sound old-fashioned amid the confident, modern chorus of the Harlem Renaissance. That light of her husband's legacy kept Alice in view, as his widow, but always in shadow – even though she outlived Paul by three decades and married twice more.

The sheer variety of names Alice adopted to publish her work – Alice Ruth Moore, Alice Dunbar, Alice Moore Dunbar, Mrs Paul Dunbar, Alice Ruth Moore Dunbar, Aliceruth Dunbar-Nelson, and Alice Dunbar-Nelson – suggests the difficulty she faced in reconciling her marital identity with the declaration of herself as an author. Her ambivalence was widely shared at the turn of the twentieth century. The term 'New Woman' roared into vogue and is generally credited to a British writer, Sarah Grand, who coined it in 1894 just as Alice was poised to publish her first book. New Women, also known as 'Bachelor Girls', were flocking to cities across Europe and North America in pursuit of jobs in department stores, offices and factories. Despite being paid much less than men, they embraced the independence that wages brought. Would this spell the end of marriage, and therefore morality, the social order, the whole human race? Before long, everyone had an opinion. Alice Dunbar-Nelson's 1895 story 'The Woman' opens with a debate at a literary society 'upon the question, whether woman's chances for matrimony are increased or decreased when she becomes man's equal as a wage earner?' In the narrator's own head, the question is more emphatic, and simpler: 'Why *should* well-salaried women marry?' Her answer is a list of the advantages a working woman enjoys, which all come back to the simple freedom to spend her money and her time as she wishes. At the very end, however, she concludes rather weakly, 'It is not marriage I decry, for I don't think any really sane person would do this.' She instead argues that women should marry later, after working for a while, so that their choice of spouse can be made from a position of maturity and self-knowledge. Finally, she reassures the reader that even a New Woman, when she chooses her mate, will 'sink as gracefully into his manly embrace' as any other bride. 'It comes natural, you see.'

Perhaps Alice's ambivalence about her name was simply a reflection of this conflict between the 'natural' and the 'New'. But it also indicates a more personal uncertainty about her identity. For a writer who otherwise documented her life meticulously, she was notably silent about her early life. In one letter to Paul, her distress is palpable when he presses on the sore point of her origins: 'Dearest – dearest – I hate to write this – How often, oh how painfully often, when scarce meaning [to] you have thrust my parentage in my face.' Both children of the post-Civil War era, Paul and Alice grew up watching the gains of emancipation steadily rolled back, and the ideal of an integrated society trampled in favour of the 'separate but equal' doctrine of racial division (one which lawyer and poet Pauli Murray would later help overturn). Campaigns like the one to capitalise the 'N' of 'Negro' were emblematic of late nineteenth-century efforts by elite African Americans to lend dignity to members of their race while tacitly accepting their second-class status.

But the binary did not hold everywhere. Alice Ruth Moore was born on July 19, 1875, in New Orleans, Louisiana, where the city's Black population had historically been divided between enslaved 'Negroes' and free *gens de couleur*, light-skinned Creoles of French or Spanish descent, who were a powerful and elite social group. This was the identity Alice claimed for herself, and the figure who dominates her early short stories. She likened the 'true Creole' to 'the famous gumbo of the state, a little of everything, making a whole dilightfully [sic] flavored, quite distinctive, and wholly unique'. This status carried little weight outside New Orleans, where the colour line was brutally policed, but its existence shaped Alice's unusual understanding of race as complex, unpredictable and even, if one chose, malleable.

Her story 'The Stones of the Village', dramatises the bullying and exclusion that her light-skinned hero endures from both the Black and white boys of his village, and the moral corruption that stems from his decision to pass as white. This initiates a Dickensian journey from his grandmother's village to a job working for an elderly book dealer in New Orleans, and then – via a legacy in the old man's will – to college, law school, marriage to a white woman and a position as a respected judge. Throughout his career, his fear of being exposed drives him to overt and virulent racist treatment of 'Negroes'. Eventually he learns that an up-and-coming Black lawyer knows his true identity but agrees to keep it quiet in exchange for fair treatment in court. The choice *not* to pass, however, carried its own complications which Alice explored in her unpublished story 'Brass Ankles Speaks'. The narrator describes herself as 'white enough to pass for white, but with a darker family background, a real love for the mother race, and no desire to be numbered among the white race'. Her anger throughout the story, which hews close to Alice's own experience, is directed mainly at darker-skinned Black people who tease and ostracise her, resenting both her ability to pass and her decision not to.

Alice Moore's light skin did not mean that she hailed from upper-class Creole society, even if she implied as much. Although the evidence is not conclusive, she was more likely descended from enslaved 'Negro' women – which hints at why the question of her parentage was so painful. Her father's identity is uncertain, but he was not part of her life, and likely not married to her mother, Patsy Wright. Patsy and her mother, Mary, belonged to the enormous Black female labour force of domestic servants, often washer-women and menders of clothing, whose work in the homes of white families put them at routine risk of sexual exploitation. Together, Mary and Patsy worked to shield Alice and her sister, Leila, from this work and to give them an education that might boost their class status and prospects in work and marriage. Alice was first sent away as a young teenager to Southern University in Baton Rouge, and graduated from New Orleans' prestigious women-only Straight University (now Dillard) in 1892 with a teaching qualification. Teaching offered a route into elite society for African-American women, who dominated the profession. In Washington D.C., a few years before Alice moved there with Paul, more than eighty per cent of the city's Black schoolteachers were women.

Alice's first book was published three years later, when she was barely twenty years old. *Violets and Other Tales* was a collection of poetry, stories, sketches and essays rooted in New Orleans Creole society – 'pieces of exquisite art', as Paul, who was courting Alice when the book was being published, described them. Its reception in the press is a reminder of how absolute the division was at this time between works by Black and white artists. In the African-American press, the book and its author were effusively praised, as much for what they represented – the 'best of the race' – as for the specifics of the work. *The Daily Picayune*, the city's white-run paper, on the other hand, denounced it as 'slop'. Interestingly, Alice used the same pejorative years later when reassessing her early collection, which is undeniably sentimental in keeping with the style of its era. But its themes and setting – New Orleans – would linger into her next collection, *The Goodness of St. Roque, and Other*

Stories (1897), even though she left the city for good the following year, following the artist's well-trodden path to New York City.

In New York, her life and writing became more political, via her involvement with the Black women's clubs that fought for women's suffrage and racial justice across the country. She worked with the writer and activist Victoria Earle Matthews at the White Rose Mission on East 86th Street in Manhattan, which offered housing, training and social activities to Black girls newly arrived in the city, with the intention of keeping them out of sex work. She continued to write, working on an unpublished collection of stories about the new community in which she found herself.

In 1902, when her marriage to Paul Dunbar ended, Alice moved to Wilmington, Delaware, and began to work as a teacher at Howard High School, maintaining her activism and writing alongside. She wrote about women's suffrage for *The Crisis*, the preeminent chronicle of African-American life in the early twentieth century, established in 1910 with a fourfold mission of news reporting, reviewing, publishing new literature and providing commentary on 'the race problem'. She also became a field organiser for the campaign for suffrage in Pennsylvania. In 1916, a few years after her short-lived second marriage to a fellow teacher, she forged a happy partnership with her third husband Robert J. Nelson, a journalist and politician. Together they edited and published a progressive newspaper, the *Wilmington Advocate*, and Alice joined the increasingly fervent campaign to make lynching a federal crime. Four years later, in an atmosphere of intense paranoia about the spread of socialism, the high school fired her for her radical views.

Teaching was not just a job – it offered Alice both a creative outlet and a form of political engagement: she wrote plays for her students to perform, and believed passionately in the transformative power of the classroom for Black children. Like Jessie Redmon Fauset a few years later, she wanted them to be able to read stories about children like themselves, and in her essay 'Negro Literature for Negro Pupils' lamented that 'for two generations we have given brown and black children a blonde ideal of beauty to worship, a milk-white literature to assimilate, and a pearly Paradise to anticipate, in which their dark faces would be hopelessly out of place.' She also recorded less lofty reactions to the daily grind of the classroom in her diary: 'Exhausted?' she burst out one day in 1897. 'I feel like a dishrag. Sixty-two untamed odoriferous kids all day ... Fiends, just fiends pure and simple.'

In the frank, uninhibited space of her diary, she also detailed the romantic relationships she had with women, including the considerably older school principal at Howard, Edwina B. Kruse, the Los Angeles-based activist Fay Jackson Robinson and the artist Helene Ricks London. The entries are sometimes tortured, but often frank and celebratory. In private, clearly, Alice was not afraid to cast off the constraints of respectability. In 1928, she described an evening with a group of women who were, like herself, married clubwomen: 'We want to make whoopee ... Life is glorious. Good homemade white grape wine. We really make whoopee ... Such a glorious moonlight night.'

In the 1920s, Alice Dunbar-Nelson found herself swept up in the cultural and political explosion of the Harlem Renaissance. Her poetry, much of it written earlier, was rediscovered through its appearance in journals like *The Crisis* and the 1927 collection *Ebony and Topaz*, and she was friends with most of the leading lights of the era, especially W.E.B. Du Bois and the poet Georgia Douglas Johnson. Nevertheless, she remained wary of artistic judgements that depended too heavily on race. She worried that Jessie Redmon Fauset's celebrated novel *Plum Bun*, for example, was being heaped with 'injudicious laudation' just because the author was Black. As an artist herself, she wanted a bigger frame, and was determined to lay claim to a white literary canon that was as much her heritage as any other. She wrote a scholarly dissertation on William Wordsworth, and found she shared his love of nature. One of her best known poems contrasts a violet growing wild with one sold in florists' shops in the city. The flower in the urban setting calls to mind everything that is decadent and artificial about that environment: 'bows and pins, and perfumed papers fine;/And garish lights, and mincing little fops/And cabarets and songs, and deadening wine.' By contrast, wild violets 'that spring beneath your feet' connect the speaker with the wholesome joys of nature and her 'soul's forgotten gleam'.

The 1920s also saw Dunbar-Nelson find her voice more and more as a journalist. She wrote a newspaper column, '*Une Femme Dit*' ('A Woman Says'), in the spirit of Charlotte Lennox and Fanny Fern. She was an in-demand speaker and recognised the importance of maintaining a public profile against the twin forces of gendered and racial erasure. But her appearances, like her writing, were often uncredited, unpaid, or both. 'Damn bad luck I have with my pen,' she wrote in her diary. 'Some fate has decreed I shall never make money by it.' Even when she knew this was not her fault – 'the depression hit my royalties!' she lamented in 1931 – she also blamed herself for her inability to find a stable footing. After that 'whang of a year', as the Great Depression bit, Alice and her husband Robert ('Bobbo' as she called him) saw their luck turn. He was appointed to a government job with the state's boxing commission, and they moved to Philadelphia the following year. The fresh start was sadly short-lived, as Alice, sick with heart disease, passed away in 1935 at the age of sixty, leaving a reputation still mostly overshadowed by the precocious success she found in her early twenties. Nevertheless, she deserves recognition for her writing beyond her youthful years, when she found her voice as a mature commentator and activist for her race, despite the ambivalences of her origins – and, indeed, enriched by them.

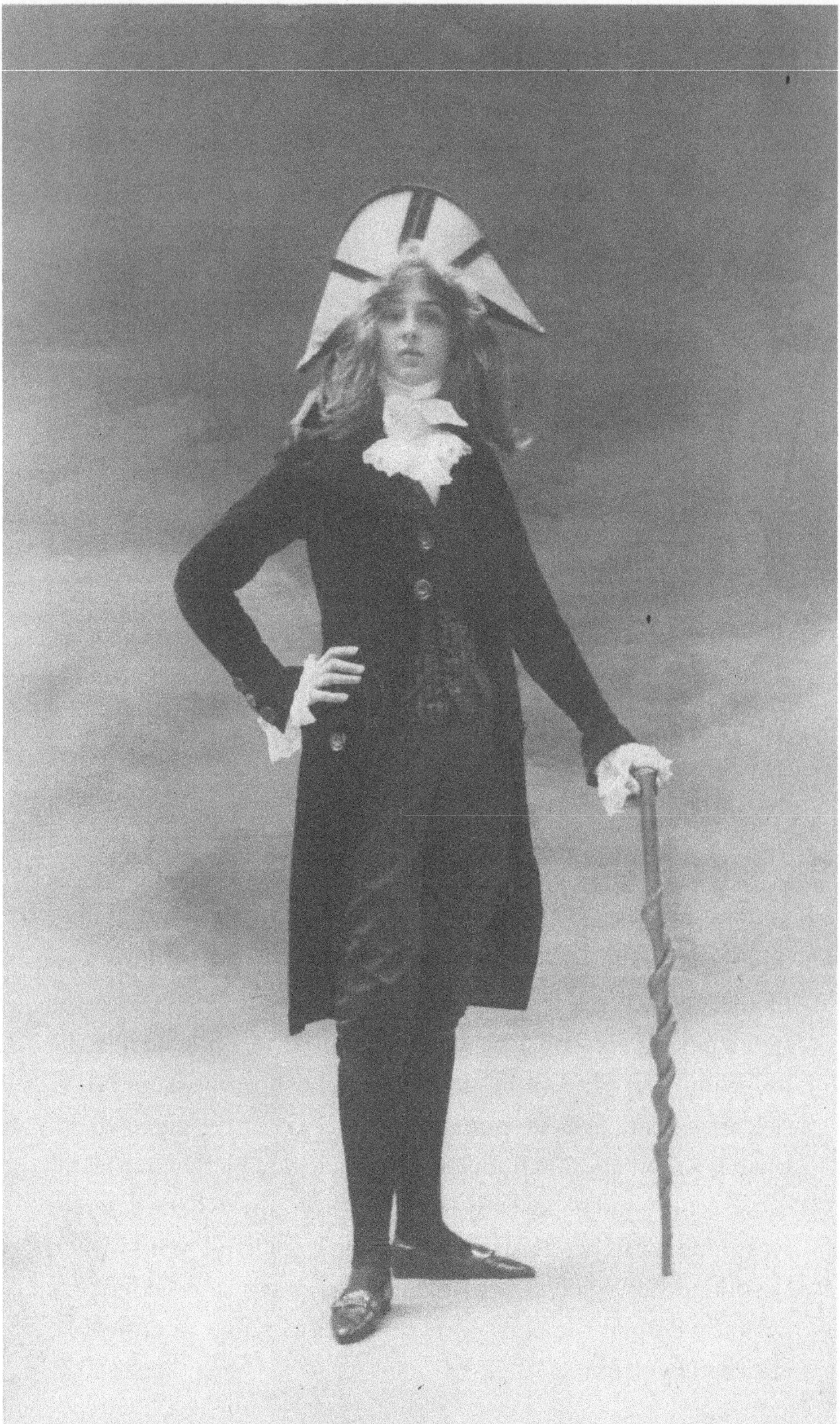

'The Amazon smiles above the ruins.'

RENÉE VIVIEN
(1877–1909)

The poet named herself. Renée Vivien, an androgynous French sobriquet drawn from words meaning 'rebirth' and 'life' together. She was a symbolist – one of the last; an heiress; an expatriate; a lover of women and a translator of Sappho. After one heartbreak too many, she sank, destroying herself by the age of thirty-two. Everything, in this small summary of her life, feels too much – too heavily symbolic – like a turn-of-the-century case study in poetic despair. It makes her a myth, as she longed to be.

But all myths have human beginnings. Renée Vivien was born in London in 1877 and named, far more prosaically, Pauline Mary Tarn. Swaddled in Gilded Age wealth, she was the daughter of a British property investor and an American mother, and spent her early childhood in Paris, in a luxurious family apartment at 23 Avenue du Bois de Boulogne (now Avenue Foch) in the elegant sixteenth arrondissement. Pauline befriended two sisters, Violet and Mary Shillito, who also lived in the building and whose parents owned a chain of department stores in Chicago. When she was nine years old her father died – a loss that would reverberate throughout Pauline's life – and she and her younger sister were yanked back to London, away from friends and the home and language Pauline considered her own. In her grief and loneliness, she turned to music and books. A talented pianist who loved Chopin, she kept passionate journals, read voraciously, and began to imagine her future as a poet. Her relationship with her mother, however, was cold and distant. In her teens Pauline began using chloral hydrate, a powerful sedative, to treat insomnia. In a plot twist that could have played out in a late-Victorian melodrama, her mother tried to use this damage to her daughter's mental health to have Pauline committed to an insane asylum, which would have invalidated her claim to her inheritance, landing the entire fortune on her mother instead. Her gambit failed, and Pauline was made a ward of court until she came of age at twenty-one.

As soon as she could, Pauline returned to Paris, setting up home on her own, at a *pension* on Rue Crevaux, around the corner from her childhood home. Wealthy, unchaperoned and now free to do as she pleased, she rechristened herself Renée Vivien, and set about establishing herself as a poet. She resumed her intimate friendship with Violet Shillito, although in secret, as Violet's conservative parents were shocked by Renée's independence. Two months apart in age, the girls' relationship developed into a particularly intense but platonic romance. 'Ignorance kept our two mouths, too ingenuous, away from each other,' Renée would later write. The network of phenomenally rich Anglo-American expats in Paris was small. Through the Shillito sisters, Renée met Natalie Barney, who had been Violet's neighbour when they were girls in Cincinnati. Although these eligible young women were bred to be trophy wives, they had no inclination for men or marriage. Natalie was already the veteran of several stormy love affairs with women, and when Violet introduced her two friends at a matinée at the theatre, Natalie was initially unimpressed by Renée, judging her 'charming but too banal to hold my interest'. Renée remembered the meeting in sharply contrasting terms, describing 'the thrill which went through me when my eyes met hers of mortal steel, those eyes sharp and blue as a blade'.

Renée's version of the meeting, it turned out, was prophetic. 'I had the strange feeling that this woman was telling me my destiny, that her face was the formidable face of my future.' And so it proved. After the theatre, the women went riding in the Bois de Boulogne, and Renée read Natalie one of her passionate poems, which worked to belatedly stir her interest. The Shillito sisters decamped for the winter with their family to the south of France, but Renée and Natalie, then twenty-two and twenty-three, remained in Paris and began to see each other more frequently. One night, Natalie came to visit Renée at home. She found her room filled with candles and an abundance of white lilies, the flower Renée associated with Natalie. To Natalie, the more experienced lover, the scene evoked a 'passionate, virginal chapel'. Renée played Chopin and recited a poem for Natalie. Then, after pulling her to her feet, Natalie kissed her. The two 'young poetesses', Natalie wrote, 'came together and began to love'.

Natalie Barney was a jolt of fire to Renée's creative brain as well as to her body and heart. Renée wrote exclusively in French, and began to chronicle her passions for women in language that was daringly explicit – 'The Touch', from 1903, contains the lines 'My fingers climb,/Trembling, provocative, the line of your haunches./My ingenious fingers wait when they have found/The petal flesh beneath the robe they part.' Both Renée and Natalie styled themselves as modern devotees of Sappho, and studied Ancient Greek to feel closer to her. They would both go on to write plays about their idol. Together they read, wrote, and dissected poetry for tireless hours, and each encouraged the other to ever bolder creative feats. At a time when women's poetry was treated dismissively, and when lesbianism was beginning to be examined and classified as a mental disorder, their bold proclamations of literary prowess and sexual pleasure still feel revolutionary. Both would publish their first poetry collections within two years of meeting. Renée wrote hundreds of poems to Natalie. Natalie, who did not believe in editing her own words, was also a prolific yet uneven writer across multiple genres. But it was Renée who showed the discipline, perseverance and talent to assume the stature of the modern Sappho.

Despite her often suggestive verses, the sexual side of Renée's relationship with Natalie seems to have been less than fulfilling for either partner. Renée's love was all-consuming, but in Natalie's eyes she remained stubbornly virginal. Her morbid fascination with death and decay, which manifested in an atmosphere of decadence that hung over her poetry, contrasted with Natalie's embrace of all things carnal and life-giving. Renée's first sexual encounter with Natalie is painfully easy to read as a young girl's overheated fantasy of what romance should look like. Natalie's memoirs later recounted her inability to overcome Renée's 'physical inertia' and acknowledged that all her caresses failed at 'unveiling the woman who slept within the virgin'. She recognised, at least with the distance of decades, that Renée was stimulated primarily by poetry and that while 'her soul vibrated passionately to our union', her body did not. For Renée, the poetry was enough, and she did not understand why Natalie needed more. Her passionate possessiveness did not permit Natalie's arguments that they might be happier in an open relationship – a partnership of the soul that would give Natalie licence to pursue sexual affairs elsewhere, which she did anyway, with gusto.

Unsurprisingly, this stormy creative and romantic partnership left little breathing space for other relationships, even Renée's deep and longstanding friendship with Violet Shillito. In the spring of 1901, Violet's sister wrote to Renée to ask her to come urgently to Cannes, where Violet was dangerously ill with typhoid fever. Renée raced south, but was in the midst of finishing her first book of poetry, *Études et Préludes*, so made a return trip to Paris to deliver the manuscript. She arrived back in Cannes just in time to hear the devastating news of Violet's death, on April 8, just two days after her twenty-fourth birthday. Violet's namesake flower and its blue-purple colour marked Renée's poetry for the rest of her life, so much that one of her literary nicknames was the 'Muse of the violets'.

A few days after Violet's death, Renée had the quite different, but still destabilising experience of seeing her first collection of poetry published to considerable acclaim. Written in classical French alexandrines, it was saturated in her romance with Natalie, full of songs and sonnets praising her lover's beauty and body, and liberally laced with invocations to Sappho – 'Prolong the night, Goddess who set us aflame!' But under the ambiguous authorship of 'R. Vivien', the collection was assumed, beyond the poet's inner circle, to be the work of a man. The daring truth was veiled by the conventions of love poetry that stretched back to Christine de Pizan.

By that summer, the cataclysm of Violet's death, and Natalie's ongoing infidelities, led Renée to break with her lover. When Natalie left with her family for the chic resort of Bar Harbor, Maine, passionate letters flew across the Atlantic, begging, resisting, regretting, and rehashing the past. 'It was crazy to let her go, but it would have been worse to follow,' Renée wrote to a mutual friend, aware that Natalie's presence was addictive to her, and that the physical separation might help her keep to her decision to end the relationship. After she returned to Paris, Natalie did not make it easy for Renée to forget her. When her letters didn't work to win Renée back, she galloped on horseback up and down her street dressed in an eye-catching Amazonian get-up and enlisted the world-renowned opera singer Emma Calvé to serenade her.

Renée moved into a new apartment at 23 Avenue du Bois de Boulogne, the building where she had lived as a child and become friends with Violet, and where her own family still had a home. Her ground-floor spread would eventually be furnished with antiques, statues and objets d'art picked up on her travels to Egypt, China and the Middle East, including shrines to the Buddha and Sappho, and 'iridescent glassware from Ceylon'. The apartment opened onto a Japanese garden – all the rage during the Belle Époque – and the air was filled to choking with flowers and incense. Friends who visited her begged to open the windows, but increasingly Renée preferred to live in heavy-scented gloom.

After her split with Natalie, Renée began a relationship with Baroness Hélène van Zuylen, a daughter of the Rothschilds, who was fourteen years older and a married mother of two. Natalie petulantly called the rather dumpy Hélène 'the brioche' and fumed in frustration at having been left for someone less attractive. But, although Renée sometimes characterised Hélène as an oppressor who kept her on a tight leash, she also offered the poet a sense of security and a motherly protectiveness she deeply craved. In the title poem of her 1906 collection *À l'heure des mains jointes* (At the time of joined hands), Renée wrote, 'Your fingers have knotted around my rough heart.' She describes how 'fatigued from the rough sea/I bless the anchor at the port where my skiff is docked': imagining her lover as a literal safe harbour. The two travelled widely together and collaborated on poetry and novels, published under the pseudonym Paule Riversdale, evoking Renée's birth name (Paule, like Pauline, is a French feminine form of Paul) and her surname, Tarn, also a river in southern France. It's likely that Renée was responsible for all, or most, of the text of these works.

In 1904, in the midst of her relationship with Hélène, Renée and Natalie rekindled their romance after three years apart.

Visiting Bayreuth for the Wagner music festival, Renée wrote to let Natalie know she was alone. Natalie quickly travelled to join her in Bavaria and read to her from the draft of *Je Me Souviens* (I Remember), a long poem composed in an effort to win Renée back. They met up again in Vienna and took the Orient Express to Constantinople (now Istanbul), where Renée went off briefly to meet Kérimé Turkhan Pacha, a French-educated Muslim woman with whom she had been exchanging passionate letters. Kérimé was married to a high-ranking Ottoman diplomat and lived in veiled seclusion in the city. Their largely epistolary relationship continued for several years, punctuated occasionally by clandestine meetings, and it inspired a number of Orientalist poems by Renée, who addressed her lover as *'ma Sultane'*.

From the mainland, Renée and Natalie sailed together to the island of Lesbos, then a Turkish territory. Sappho's island had loomed large in their shared poetic mythology, and now in a pair of rented villas set in gardens abundant with jasmine, peaches, figs and roses, with a staircase leading down to the sea, they had found their Eden. According to Natalie, they were even able to resolve their sexual difficulties and truly join together at last. Exhilarated, they dreamed of staying for ever and of forming a commune with other women poets, although Natalie was careful to stipulate that she should be allowed to leave whenever she craved society and other women. But she promised always to return.

The fantasy held for a few summer weeks, until a letter from Hélène recalled Renée to duty, or perhaps reality, and the memory of how things had ended with Natalie before. With the excuse that she needed to end things in person, Renée went to Constantinople to meet her lover while Natalie returned to France, where she had set up an artistic, Greek-inspired salon in a house in Neuilly, on the banks of the Seine just outside Paris. She waited for Renée – and waited. Eventually, she realised she had lost out to the baroness. Unwilling to be cast as the femme fatale who had driven away her more innocent lover, Natalie moved on quickly. But, although they would never be lovers again, Renée and Natalie could never truly escape each other. The circle of elite literary lesbians in Paris was hardly large, and Natalie reigned at its centre, a notorious figure for decades to come.

Writing her memoirs toward the end of her life, it made sense for Natalie to cast her poet-lover as always, in some sense, suicidal – in love with death to the extent that her demise was pre-written. 'She could not be saved,' Natalie wrote. 'Everything turned to dust and ashes in her hands.' Certainly the romance with mortality is there in Renée's poetry from the start, as indelible as the women and the violets – *Cendres et Poussières* (Ashes and Dust) was the title of her second poetry collection. But her life was not 'a long suicide' so much as a determined, if unwinnable, struggle for art and joy, for recapturing the spirit of Sappho in the modern world.

After the final break with Natalie, Renée continued to visit Lesbos, often with Hélène, where they stayed in that same lush, flower-bedecked villa. They also spent several winters in Egypt. In 1907, after Hélène broke off their relationship, Renée travelled even further afield, visiting Japan and Hawaii with her mother.

The following year, her Turkish lover, Kérimé, also ended their affair. While visiting her sister in London, Renée drank laudanum and lay down grasping a bouquet of violets. The attempt at a symbolically picturesque suicide failed, but chronically weakened her body: by the following summer, she was walking with a cane. She died in November 1909, aged thirty-two.

A memorable glimpse of Renée appears in the writings of Colette, the writer who was Renée's friend and neighbour and also, briefly, a lover of Natalie's. In *The Pure and the Impure*, her loosely autobiographical collection of portraits of men and women in the throes of desire, Colette vividly describes Renée's struggles with alcoholism and anorexia, claiming that the poet used perfumed water to rinse her mouth to disguise the smell of drink. Natalie protested the details, and also the exposure – Renée was the only character in the book who appeared under her real name. But it was true that, towards the end of her life, Renée was deeply addicted to alcohol and sedatives, especially chloral hydrate, which she had continued to use since her teens to help her sleep.

In France, the country she embraced as her home, Renée Vivien's poetic stature is higher than it is in the English-speaking world. She is known as the 'modern Sappho', and is credited as the first Francophone woman poet to write openly about her love of women. She is also the second woman, after the seventeenth-century scholar Anne Dacier, to translate Sappho into French. In 1935, the Renée Vivien Prize (*Prix Renée Vivien*) was created in her honour. Under the patronage first of Hélène and then, after her death and the interruption of the war, of Natalie Barney, the prize was awarded to women poets. Since 1994, poets of any nationality or sex writing in French are eligible. A square in the Marais district of Paris is also named for her.

Renée Vivien is buried in Passy cemetery in Paris, next to her father. Hélène built a small chapel with a stained-glass window above her grave and its interior walls are inscribed with Renée's poetry. On the exterior, in French, is her faded epitaph, which she wrote for herself. In Natalie's translation, it carries the hallmarks of her verse – a measured, traditional meter barely containing the intensity of feeling and ending with the lines: 'My ravished soul, from mortal breath/Appeased, forgets all former strife/Pardoned the crime of crimes – called Life.'

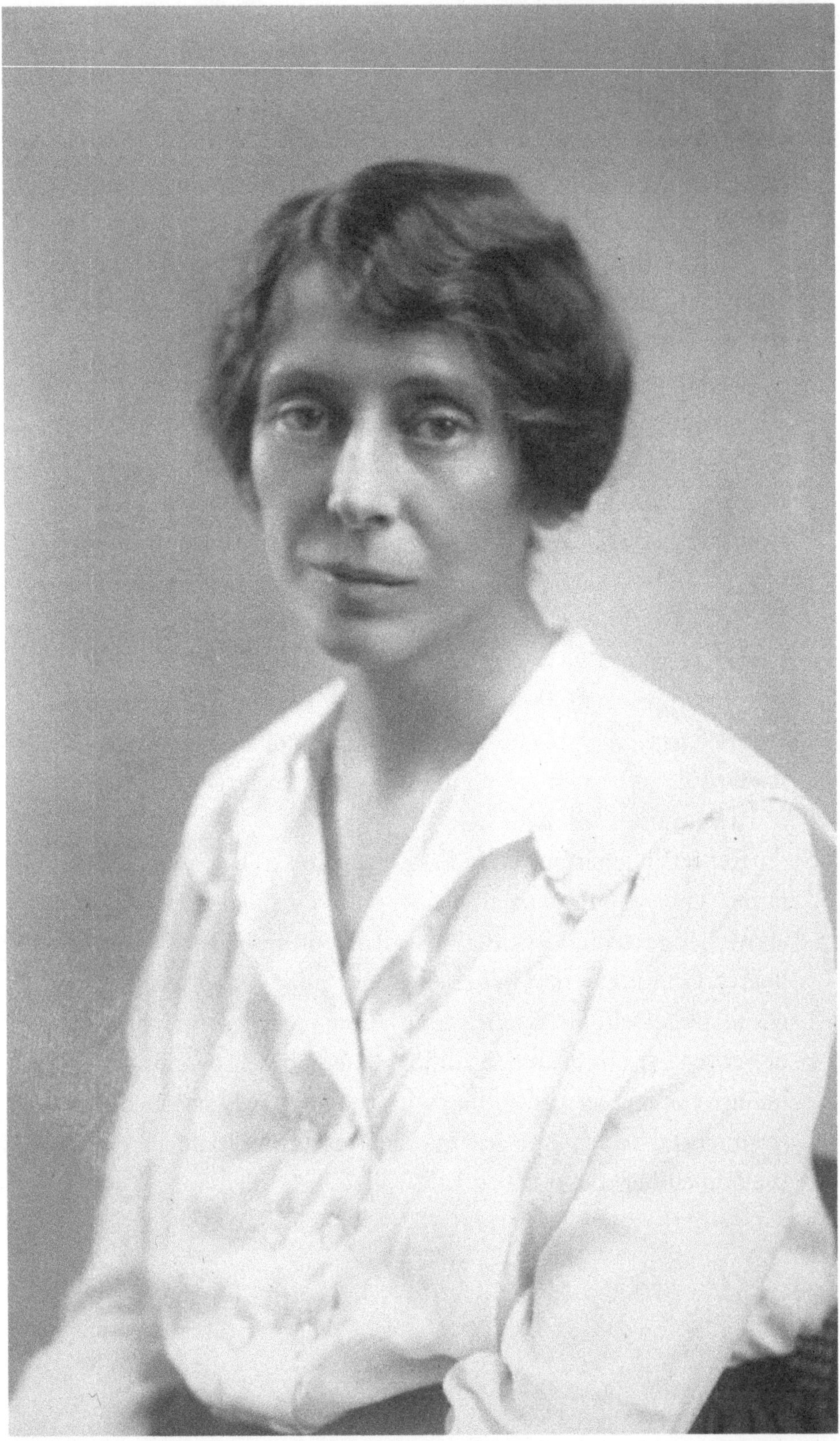

'I am part of the avant-garde. I have overstepped the bounds!'

MARY HEATON VORSE
(1874–1966)

Mary Heaton Vorse, a prolific novelist, journalist and labour activist, spent most of her long life trying to escape her upper-middle-class origins. Camilla, the heroine of her 1918 novel *I've Come To Stay*, refers to bourgeois values as life's 'blue serge lining' – a practical fabric that protected the inside of coats and suits, it represents in the novel the constraining conformity of class. Forming a barrier between the self and the world, the lining gets, not quite under the wearer's skin but right next to it, holding her upright and inhibiting her imagination and her freedom. Camilla is constantly on the run from it. She embraces the pretensions of bohemian Greenwich Village in New York – anarchist friends, artistic aspirations, a Polish violinist lover and nights spent in smoky bars – and repeatedly rejects her neighbour and suitor, the equally middle-class Ambrose Ingraham, out of fear that he will wrap her up in blue serge once again and strangle her with it. Subtitled *A Love Comedy of Bohemia*, the novel is more of an archaeological find than a timeless classic. Yet its ironic depiction of young people trying to outrun their conventional destiny reflects the central conflict of its author's life, and that of her generation of American 'New Women'.

Mary Heaton was born rich and rebellious in 1874, and spent most of her childhood in Amherst, Massachusetts, a place that was, by contrast, rural and religious. She was close to her bookish father, Hiram, and idolised her distant mother, Ellen, who paid more attention to her five older children from her first marriage. Mary watched her intelligent, energetic mother struggle to fill her days with meaningful activity. Other women of her era and class threw themselves into social reform and the fight for women's suffrage, but Ellen believed too many people already had the vote, and that a woman's place was in the home. This did not preclude plenty of European travel and culture in order to burnish her daughters' marriage prospects, and so Mary had a rich, if haphazard education, bolstered by voracious private reading. Although she belonged to a generation of women who were breaking down the doors to academia and the professions, she had no interest in submitting to the rules of a women's college. She longed for greater freedom, and begged to be allowed to go to Paris to study art.

Her mother insisted on coming with her, somewhat curtailing the nineteen-year-old's freedom to indulge in the temptations of the Left Bank, but Mary managed to embark on her first serious romance there with a domineering fellow art student. Although she didn't consider herself especially beautiful – photographs show a thin woman with a strong, straight nose, a wide mouth, and pouched, piercing eyes – Mary nevertheless exuded confidence and rarely had trouble attracting men. Her lover praised her intelligence and independence yet undermined the praise by constantly pointing out her social and physical limitations as a woman. It was a dynamic that would mark Mary's subsequent relationships and come to life over and over again in her fiction: a young heroine enthralled by male strength but chafing against male dominance.

Upon her return to America, Mary convinced her parents to let her go to New York to continue her art studies, adopting the persona of the 'Bachelor Girl'. This mid-1890s phenomenon, a more rebellious version of the already mythologised 'New Woman', was discussed at the time with an eager censoriousness, while the girls themselves enjoyed a brief respite from family obligations. 'I am part of the avant-garde. I have overstepped the bounds!' Mary wrote exultantly. Having decided rather late that she could not paint, she attached herself to the city's male-dominated literary scene, which mostly involved drinking and pontificating in downtown cafes. Then, in 1898, she met and secretly married Albert White Vorse, a Harvard-educated son of a Massachusetts minister, who was trying, as earnestly as she was, to reinvent himself as a bohemian. Despite his pretensions to modern broadmindedness, Bert was delighted to discover that, despite her Paris sojourn, he had been the one to take her virginity (and further noting how she 'hesitated' to have sex until he 'pushed' her). Their letters make clear Mary's deeply conflicted desires for both marriage and independence.

Although she had published her first short story in a local newspaper at the age of sixteen, and was now regularly publishing book reviews, Mary and Bert both believed that her writing was merely something to fill her time and not a career. But before long it became obvious that she was the talent of the two of them. Mary became the breadwinner in their house as well as managing its upkeep. Perhaps they might have navigated this uneven division of labour, but then there was a baby, and then there was Bert's cheating. In 1903, in the first of many attempts at a fresh start, the couple decamped to France, where Mary started writing fiction. 'I reel off stuff like a regular phonograph,' she wrote – painfully aware that Bert, at the same time, was a stuck record.

By her mid-thirties, Mary's literary star was rising as her marriage crumbled. The couple now had two children, a boy and a girl. In 1924, she would write an essay, 'Why I Have Failed as a Mother', that articulated the impossible struggle between motherhood and work. She admitted that the fault lay not just in the obligation to earn money, though she certainly felt that. No, her real failure, as she saw it, was the very thing that was supposed to undergird male success: 'I grew ambitious.' She wrote that she dreaded leaving her desk to tend to her children and their needs: 'They seem to me like a nestful of birds, their yellow beaks forever agape for me to fill.' Yet her intense love for her children, which was woven throughout her fiction, was as much of a drive as the work.

Between 1906 and 1911, Vorse sold story after story about domestic relationships and family life – popular fiction that was lucrative enough to support her family. Her fiction was aimed at a middle-class female audience, but it resonated with men trying to figure out their own roles in a changing society. The marital ideal was shifting away from the traditional dynamic of dominance and submission, toward a union of friendly equals. Yet gender roles, deeply ingrained, could not be shaken loose as easily as that. Her novels from this period – *The Breaking-in of a Yachtsman's Wife*, *Autobiography of an Elderly Woman* and *The Heart's Country* – often blame men for failing to understand women, but she also criticises women for embracing their own subservience, whether to husbands or children. Mothers who sacrifice their own needs for their families – as explored in her 1907 story 'The Quiet Woman' – end up breeding 'beautiful soulless monstrosities', as selfish and tyrannical as their mothers are selfless. Yet Vorse also paid a rare degree of attention to parental love. Her 1911 novel *The Very Little Person* brings to life a father's bewildered affection for his infant daughter, emphasising how absurdly little middle-class men were expected to know about children and about women's maternal experiences. A subtle rivalry lingers between the parents in the story, John and Constance. When his wife reports on their daughter's first smile, John feels 'secretly hurt that the baby hadn't smiled at him, and to hide this feeling, pretended a disbelief'. The book's ending hovers in that gap between them, with John triumphant that his daughter has said her first word, and thus 'she isn't a baby any more, she is a grown-up little girl'. He is oblivious to the heartbreak this causes his wife.

The Very Little Person is rooted in a close and tender observation of Mary's own daughter, conceived partly in an effort to save her marriage. Mary had tried to reconcile herself to Bert's cheating by treating him with the patience of a mother nursing a sick child. (She would scrutinise that 'maternal instinct' of women toward adult men in *I've Come To Stay*, published in 1918.) But the marriage was all but over by the time Bert died suddenly of a cerebral haemorrhage, alone in a hotel on Staten Island in 1910. The next day, Mary's mother died of heart failure.

It is hardly surprising that the direction of Mary's life and writing changed after this brutal sequence of events. Yet it was the 1912 textile workers' strike in Lawrence, Massachusetts, that she would name in her 1934 autobiography as the turning point for her. For the rest of her life, until her death in 1966 at the age of ninety-two, workers' battles for fair treatment would be her primary focus. 'We knew now where we belonged,' she wrote about the strike; 'on the side of the workers, and not with the comfortable people among whom we were born.'

The conditions for workers at Lawrence are still shocking to read about today. At the turn of the century, labourers in the mills – many of them teenagers – scraped by on two or three dollars a week, most of which went to paying their rent in overcrowded slum districts. Women were subject to routine sexual exploitation by their bosses, and death from accidents or lung diseases were everyday occurrences. Thirty-six out of every hundred men and women who worked the mills died before the age of twenty-five. In early 1912, the state attempted to enforce a law limiting the hours of women workers and those under eighteen to fifty-four hours a week. In response, the mill owners slashed everyone's hours and their salaries, and were accused of speeding up output. The result was a citywide strike.

Vorse's report on 'The Trouble at Lawrence' ran in *Harper's*, where she was one of the few left-leaning writers the magazine would publish. She also wrote for liberal publications like *The Nation* and *The New Republic*, and was a contributor and editor at the Greenwich Village socialist monthly *The Masses*, but this piece was aimed at a wider audience. It opened with a focus on a group of workers' children, who had been prevented by local authorities from leaving Lawrence to stay with relatives in other cities – a relief effort spearheaded by birth control crusader Margaret Sanger. The 'forcible detention' of children was a rare event, Vorse wrote, that Americans all over the country would surely rise up to protest against. She went on to describe the killing of a nineteen-year-old Syrian striker by a member of the militia formed by the Lawrence factory owners to put down the strike, and the reaction of his community. Stepping into that closed-off world, she describes it for her readers almost as a tour guide might, noting both the beauty of the Syrian women and the presence of posters that had lured the immigrants from Damascus with the promise of good jobs. Although the strikers were 'of warring nations and warring creeds' (Lawrence's workforce included at least twenty-five nationalities), Vorse wrote that they had come together spontaneously in protest. The experience of striking opened the workers' eyes to a life and a world beyond home and the mill. She said hopefully, 'A strike like this makes people think.'

Mary travelled to Lawrence with Joe O'Brien, a reporter she'd met the year before. Three months later, they married. He was a gregarious, joyful partner who loved family life, and they soon had a son together – a brother for Mary's two older children. She continued to write 'lollypops' – what she called her lucrative women's stories. And she continued to spend summers at her home in Provincetown, a place that was an anchor throughout her life, and that she gradually turned into the summer 'colony' of her Greenwich Village friends. In 1915, those friends entertained themselves by writing and performing each other's satirical, self-consciously modern plays. Their summer venture evolved into the influential avant-garde theatre group they called the Provincetown Players, which would give the playwright Eugene O'Neill his start, and highlight the work of Mary's close friend, the writer Susan Glaspell. But throughout this social and energetic time, Joe was plagued by an illness that turned out to be stomach cancer, and after just three years of marriage Mary was widowed again. The tragic bad luck of her romantic partnerships continued: during her subsequent relationship with the political cartoonist Robert Minor, she suffered a devastating second-trimester miscarriage, and spent several years afterwards addicted to the morphine she was given for the pain.

Yet throughout her life, she displayed a remarkable resilience, energy and commitment to her work. She travelled to protests and war zones, covering events with a focus on the human story. Through her friendships with labour activists and her reporting, she paid particular attention to the intersecting challenges of being female and working-class. She was also the rare journalist who actively participated in strikes and worked with unions, which enabled her to bring readers an insider's perspective. And, despite ill health and her advancing age, she remained committed to reporting from the ground, and highlighting the experiences of ordinary people. During the Second World War, she was one of the oldest official American foreign correspondents – she was seventy-one when the war ended – and she remained politically active up until her death at the age of ninety-two.

In addition to her novels and journalism, Vorse published two volumes of humorous, sharp-eyed autobiography: *A Footnote to Folly* in 1935, and *Time and the Town* in 1942 – the latter a 'chronicle' of her beloved Provincetown, where she lived on and off for many years. Her fiction hints at the compromises and costs of rebellion for middle-class women of her era, but her autobiographical writing lays bare what it really meant to break out and blaze her own trail. Vorse wrote for the world in which she lived, with an immediacy that cares little for posterity. To read her now feels as disorienting as time travel, as it plunges us into a world that resembles ours but for which we lack crucial maps and signposts. Nevertheless, her values hold strong. Throughout her long flight from the stifling Amherst mansion of her childhood, Mary Heaton Vorse cherished freedom and the people who would fight for it, a value that to her was not an abstraction but a deeply human impulse.

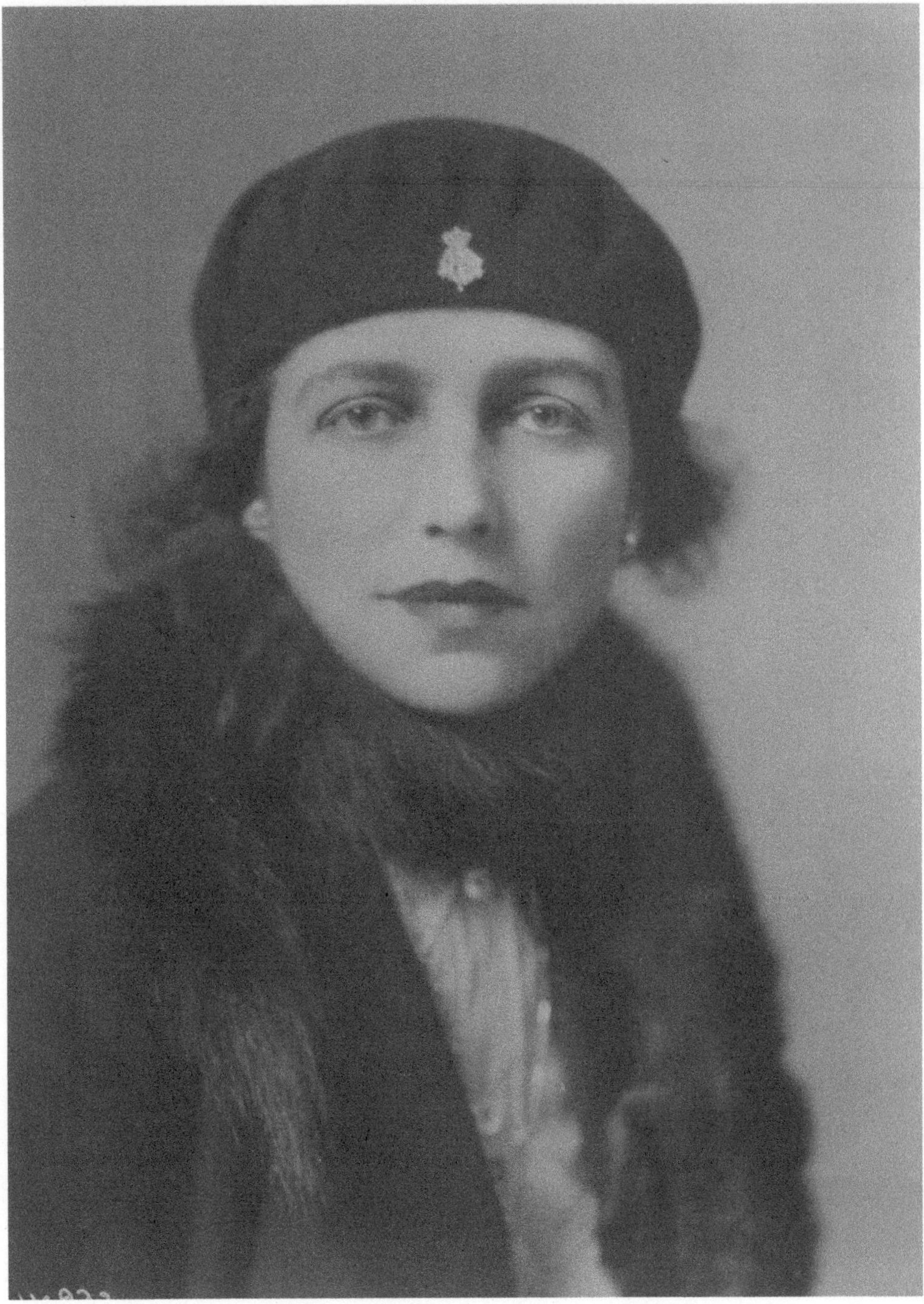

'There are no men here, so why should I be a woman?'

MARY BORDEN
(1886–1968)

Mary Borden's story demonstrates the capacity of the unimaginable and the ordinary to coexist in a single life: one that may be stretched to the limits of endurance at some points, and at others, bounce back to a comfortable, tidy sphere. The extent to which that stretching will leave scars, and where they will be, is impossible to predict.

Born into serious Gilded Age money in Chicago in 1886, Mary Borden – like her almost-contemporaries Mina Loy and Jessie Redmon Fauset – belonged to the generation that came of age around the turn of the twentieth century, began marching in the vanguard of a new century with all its promise, only to crash, as young adults, into the historical roadblock of the First World War. But that's not really the right image. It wasn't a barrier into which they slipped and stumbled, but the all-consuming mud. As Mary described it:

> 'The pale yellow glistening mud that covers the naked hills like satin,

The grey gleaming silvery mud that is spread like enamel over the valleys,
The frothing, squirting, spurting liquid mud that gurgles along the road-beds,
The thick elastic mud that is kneaded and pounded and squeezed under the hoofs of horses.
The invincible, inexhaustible mud of the War Zone.'

Everyone who was there on the Western Front remembered the mud. For some low-ranking soldiers it wasn't much of a change from the labour and muck of farming, mining and the industrial grind. For an American heiress, it was a new world.

How did she get there? May, as her friends and family knew her, graduated in 1907 from the elite New York women's college Vassar, where she excelled in drama and debating. Her father had died the previous year, leaving her a fortune, which she wanted to use for socially responsible ends. She left America for Japan, then travelled to India, donating money to missionary settlements and educational institutions – but her trip was not entirely altruistic. May's mother had converted to a devout evangelical Christianity some years earlier, and her daughter was desperate to escape the intensity of her faith and the stifling atmosphere it created at home.

In India, May met and married her first husband, George Douglas Turner, a Scot who worked as a missionary. The couple settled in Lahore and had two daughters, Joyce and Comfort, but a similar suffocation to the one she'd felt at home with her mother soon set in. The family moved to London where, despite the consuming presence of young children, May threw herself into literature and politics – the twin poles that would, from that moment on, direct her life. She joined the increasingly militant movement agitating for votes for women, and in 1913 was arrested and held for five days after throwing a stone through the window of the Treasury building. The previous year, under the pseudonym Bridget Maclagen, May had published her first novel, the semi-autobiographical *Mistress of Kingdoms*. She had also begun mixing in the city's avant-garde literary and artistic circles, befriending the likes of George Bernard Shaw, Ezra Pound, E.M. Forster, and the painter, writer and all-round cultural provocateur Wyndham Lewis, who briefly became her lover. He and other members of the scene appreciated her talent, but also the generous financial support that flowed from her deep American pockets.

When the First World War broke out in September 1914, twenty-eight-year-old May was pregnant again. Her third daughter, Mary, would be born later that autumn. Instead of going safely home to Chicago, however, she committed to the war effort, serving first as a Red Cross volunteer and then as a nurse, despite having no prior medical experience. By the summer of 1915, she had set up her own frontline hospital for French soldiers, paying for its equipment and staff from her own pocket. It was successful, insofar as that meant anything under the hellish conditions, in having one of the lowest mortality rates on the Western Front. In late 1916, as fighting shifted to the Somme, May set up a new hospital, which became the largest in the area. In what little snatches of free time she had, she began recording the scenes and emotions of a nurse's world, with a view to turning them into a novel. But the writing that emerged was far stranger and more disturbing than fiction.

First published in 1929, several years after it was written and subsequently suppressed by military censors, Borden's extraordinary memoir *The Forbidden Zone* attempts to record, in stories and fragments, the paralysing shock of the experience of war. Like most British memoirists of the First World War who came from her social rung, Borden lacked any real experience of physical hardship or deprivation, although she was older and worldlier than volunteer nurse Vera Brittain, author of the doorstopper memoir *Testament of Youth*, to whom the details of the male anatomy came as a complete surprise. Borden's war memoir is quite unlike Brittain's, or those of soldiers like Robert Graves and Siegfried Sassoon, who told a realistic, conventional tale of the journey from innocence to experience. *The Forbidden Zone* is all-consuming, like its subject, offering none of the comfort of chronological structure. 'I have lived here ever since I can remember,' its unnamed narrator tells us. 'It had no beginning, it will have no end. War, the Alpha and the Omega, world without end – I don't mind it. I am used to it. I fit into it. It provides me with everything that I need, an occupation, a shelter, companions, a jug and a basin.'

Although Mary Borden's name is on the title page, there's nothing in the book to identify her as its narrative voice. We don't know where this narrator comes from, what she's learned, whom she loves or where she's going. She is absolutely isolated. Not only does the nurse have no regiment to support her – no big-shouldered comrades to carry her to safety – but she shares her work only with 'the old ones': the silent and private orderlies who don't speak her language. The 'forbidden zone' of the title is neither home nor battlefield, female nor male, peaceful nor violent. It is the ragged edge, the mud and the unsealable leaking wound.

'There was a man stretched on the table,' she writes in the story 'Blind'. 'His brain came off in my hands when I lifted the bandage from his head. When the dresser came back I said: "His brain came off on the bandage." "Where have you put it?" "I put it in the pail under the table." "It's only one half of his brain," he said, looking into the man's skull. "The rest is here." I left him to finish the dressing and went about my own business. I had much to do.' This is one of the book's more gruesome scenes, but the tone is like this throughout: wooden, denuded and cold as the draughty hospital huts where the wounded are lined up on their stretchers. The nurse is sometimes 'I' and sometimes 'she'. Later in this same story, when a moment of human contact upsets her perfect routine, she literally breaks down: 'My body rattled and jerked like a machine out of order.' The men around her are disturbed and sympathetic, but can only offer small, physical comforts: 'Then one of them timidly stuck a grizzled head round the corner of the screen. He held his tin cup in his hands. It was full of hot coffee. He held it out, offering it to me. He didn't know of anything else that he could do for me.'

It's a moment of humanity – a connection that doesn't live in language but in shared, wordless actions to satisfy bodily needs – and hints at a world of kindness and empathy that has no more substance, here in this war zone, than an echo. It is hard to know whether this tenacious humanity is hopeful or futile because the story ends there, and there's no way to connect this nurse to any of her later incarnations throughout the book. Is this one character, or many? Has she learned, grown, changed?

No authorial voice intervenes to help us: the strength and the challenge of the book lies in its resistance to moralising. The narrator's observations are delivered in a blend of Old Testament cadence and infantile simplicity; she watches like a child and a god. 'There is a captive balloon in the sky, just over there. It looks like an oyster floating in the sky. They say that a man lives in the balloon,' one narrator tells us. Elsewhere she notes that 'There was no sign of horror in the heavens or upon the earth.' But horror lives in the war's consequences, even for those who do not see them coming. Watching a young nurse sitting with her permanently wounded sweetheart on a beach, the narrator gives voice to the hopelessness of their situation. 'He was rotting and he was tied to her perfection ... his one delight would be to give in to the temptation to make her suffer.' By his side, the woman is equally trapped: 'I must love him, now more than ever, but where is he?'

The relationship between the forbidden zone and the war zone is one of complicity: healing is temporary, and men are patched up only in order to go back into danger. An anguished awareness of this structure threads the stories together and generates their characteristic detachment. The nurse is a cog in the war machine, not a ministering angel. In the tale filled with the most guilt at this complicity, 'Conspiracy', the nurse describes in a deadened, passive voice the true nature of her task. She patches, cleans and mends bodies and sends them back where they came from, in order that they may be damaged all over again. 'Just as you send your clothes to the laundry and mend them when they come back, so we send our men to the trenches and mend them when they come back again. You send your socks and your shirts again and again to the laundry, and you sew up the tears and clip the ravelled edges again and again just as many times as they will stand it. And then you throw them away. And we send our men to the war again and again, just as long as they will stand it; just until they are dead, and then we throw them into the ground.'

The image of the laundry, its caring and mending function twisted into complicity with violence, is reflected in a later image of the nurse presiding over a gleaming parody of a kitchen, replete with boiling pans of syringes. Domestic spaces and domestic arts appear in a distorting mirror – women cannot be women here, but can only parody and mimic their supposedly sacred role of caring for the home. 'There are no men here, so why should I be a woman?' the narrator demands. 'There are heads and knees and mangled testicles.' Like domesticity, sexuality is meaningless in the forbidden zone; people are broken machines and maimed animals, not lovers. The long association of nursing with sexual healing is displaced on to a feminised abstraction – Pain – who is 'insatiable, greedy, vilely amorous, lustful, obscene – she lusts for the broken bodies we have here ... plying her traffic in the hut next to me.' Pain creeps into bed with the wounded men, coming between Life ('the sick animal') and Death ('the angel of Peace'). The description of Pain's lust goes on and on and is as excessive as the lust itself. Although its tone is restrained, this isn't a book of moderation. It doesn't moderate reality with a romance between the beautiful nurse and her stoical patient, like its blockbuster contemporaries *All Quiet on the Western Front* and *A Farewell to Arms*. Instead, it's a bracing reminder that war is not a story but a series of hideous, senseless pictures. Although possibly influenced by the avant-garde artists she knew in London before the war, the intensity and resistance to narrative comforts are all the author's own.

Yet in Borden's own life, there was a story. Amid the intensity, horror and isolation of the experience she describes, amid the mud and machine-gun fire, Mary met the love of her life, Brigadier General Edward Louis Spears, and began an affair with him in the spring of 1917. Spears was a dashing, complex figure. Born in Paris a few months after Mary, to English parents – with, on his mother's side, Jewish ancestry – he anglicised his birth name from Spiers after the war. Louis, as he was known, spoke French fluently, a rare advantage during a war in which the Allied generals prided themselves on their incomprehension of each other's languages as an expression of patriotism. As a liaison between the leaders of two armies – the British and the French – whose mutual distrust and dislike ran deep, Spears rose quickly through the ranks and befriended several other iconoclastic figures, including Winston Churchill. He and May married in January 1918, as soon as Turner granted her a divorce, although he battled her ruthlessly for custody of their three young daughters. During the Paris Peace Conference, Spears played a central role as a negotiator, and the couple's home became a gathering place for diplomats and artists alike.

Once the peace treaties were signed and the couple moved back to England, May Borden's life reformed itself into a more comfortable, if not complacent shape. Throughout the interwar years, she was a prolific and prominent writer, who counted many of the period's leading authors, including Noël Coward and Freya Stark, among her friends. The war underpinned her most important work, but it did not remain her only subject. Indeed, her novels dealt frequently with more private battles: infidelity, pre-marital sex and divorce. Her own experience had shown her that the line between personal and public battles was not clear. In her 1937 novel *Action for Slander*, which was made into a popular film, the tangles of infidelity turn into a legal drama that ruins a man's reputation and threatens his life. May also clashed with the Catholic church over her novel *Mary of Nazareth*, an attempt to create a realistic fictional portrait of the mother of Jesus. She remained involved in politics, especially campaigns to advance women's rights, and she supported her husband's bids for political office. He was elected twice and served first as a Liberal and later as a Conservative, although he faced ingrained antisemitic suspicion from the latter party. Despite her up-close experience of the horrors of the First World War, May and her husband vociferously denounced the Conservative government's appeasement of Hitler and Mussolini in the late 1930s.

When the Second World War began with a chilling familiarity, Mary once again used her money and hard-won experience to help the wounded for whom the war soon ceased to be a question of politics. She set up a mobile hospital in Lorraine, France, while her husband operated as his friend Winston Churchill's liaison to the French government under Charles de Gaulle. When France fell to the Nazis, Louis spirited de Gaulle to England in his plane from Bordeaux, and back in Britain, he worked to support Free French efforts against the Vichy regime. Working with the wife of a prominent industrialist, May set up an ambulance unit, operating in Europe and the Middle East, where Louis continued his government liaison work and was appointed as the first British minister to Syria and Lebanon. May balanced her social role as a diplomat's wife with her ongoing work running her ambulance unit.

After the war, she recorded its history, along with what she saw as the failures of the French government's resistance to the Nazis, in her memoir *Journey Down a Blind Alley*. Nothing in this later book, however, matched the shock to literary language and human comprehension that *The Forbidden Zone* had represented a quarter of a century earlier.

Mary Borden continued to write, publishing five more novels through the 1950s, and maintained her political interests and activities. Upon a return to her native America, she campaigned and wrote speeches for Adlai Stevenson, who twice challenged the Republican incumbent Dwight Eisenhower for the U.S. presidency and was the former husband of her niece Ellen. And despite its beginnings in the throes of international conflict, her second marriage was long and happy, weathering even the illness and early death of their son, Michael, and enduring until May's death in 1968. Somehow, their love for each other stretched enough to accommodate Louis's decades-long relationship with his secretary Nancy, whom he married shortly after his wife's death. Years earlier, in 1924, May had confided to the *New York Times* that the secret to successful English marriages lay in the equality between men and women, which she compared favourably to America's gender divisions. 'A wife to an Englishman is a pal,' she claimed. 'The Englishwomen do everything the men do.' Hardly a universal truth, perhaps, but one that goes some way to explain the forthright resilience of a woman who lived, wrote and spoke without regret.

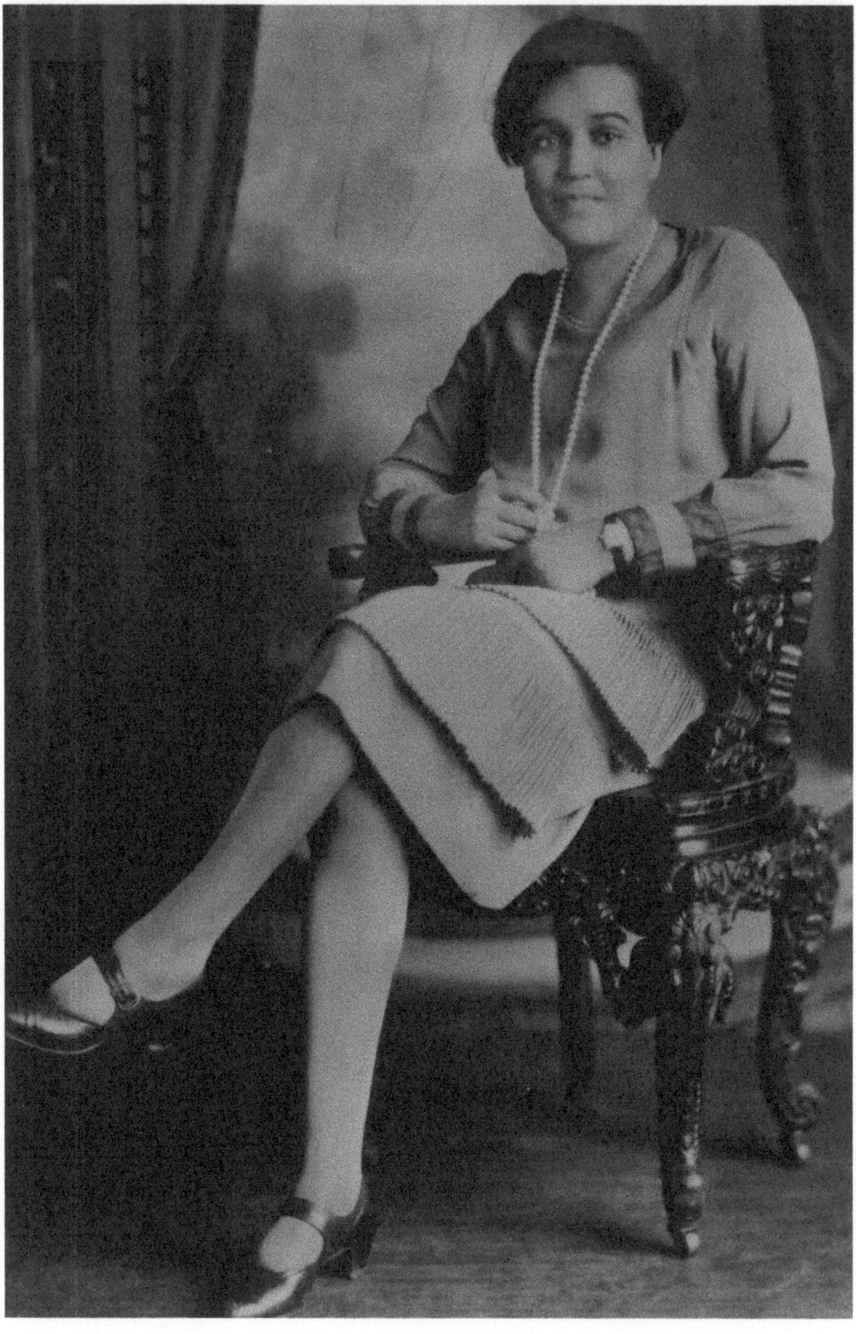

'The world's ours as much as it is theirs.'

JESSIE REDMON FAUSET
(1882–1961)

In 1934, the prominent African-American poet and critic William Stanley Braithwaite described novelist Jessie Redmon Fauset as 'the black Jane Austen'. It was a tempered piece of praise, which celebrated Fauset's talent for social comedy but hinted that her characters were overprivileged and their dramas trivial. Later critics were less subtle, claiming outright that Fauset was a conservative whose novels pandered to white America by mimicking its elitist prejudices. Neither the praise nor the criticism is entirely just: her irony is less deft than Austen's, yet the injustices of the world she depicts are abundantly clear. And triviality, as so many of the writers in this book could attest, is hardly a neutral accusation, but one based on the assumption that women's lives, loves and labours are not worth talking about.

As a writer, Jessie Redmon Fauset was ambivalent about fame – the 'being-talked-about' on which a literary legacy relies. In her translation of a poem by the Haitian writer Massillon Coicou, published in 1922, she anticipates, and even yearns for, posthumous 'Oblivion – the shroud and envelope of happiness'. For many decades after she retired from literary life, Fauset found herself wrapped in that oblivion. Yet, at the peak of her career, she was a powerful figure in a pivotal moment of Black creativity, when what began as the 'New Negro Movement' flowered into the Harlem Renaissance. Since 1912, Fauset had been publishing poems and short stories in *The Crisis*, the pre-eminent magazine covering all aspects of African-American life, which also welcomed writers like Alice Dunbar-Nelson. In 1919, the magazine's co-founder and editor, W.E.B. Du Bois, invited her to New York to join its staff as literary editor. In this role, she encouraged, published and mentored male poets and writers – including Jean Toomer, Langston Hughes and Claude McKay – who would form a new Black canon.

It was a powerful role, and one in which Fauset had to balance her own taste with the attitudes of the writers she published. Holding an idealistic belief in the power of literature to transcend the barriers between people, she praised writing that was not overtly political. At the same time, however, she passionately championed and promoted artists who were more revolutionary than she was. The apartment she shared with her sister, Helen Lanning, on West 142nd Street in Harlem became a meeting place for artists, writers and intellectuals, who regarded her as an old-fashioned, elegant presence, who was nonetheless more approachable than the aloof Du Bois. 'All the radicals liked her,' recalled the poet Claude McKay in his autobiography, 'although in her social viewpoint she was away over on the other side of the fence.'

Fauset's four novels explore people and communities who were socially conservative and old-fashioned, at least in contrast with jazz age New York City. The tight-knit, upper-middle-class African Americans who populate her stories maintain their precarious position by conforming as closely as possible to white moral standards. The plots frequently follow talented young Black women torn, as their creator was, between artistic ambition and the comforting obscurity of domestic life. Her first novel, *There Is Confusion*, sets out her abiding theme, as the young heroine, Joanna Marshall, climbs onto her father's lap and begs for a story "bout somebody great'. Joel Marshall is the successful owner of a catering company, but this is not what 'great' means either to him or his young daughter. Wealthy as he is, Joel's aspirations point towards political leadership, yet have been thwarted by his race. The novel goes on to follow Joanna's own pursuit of greatness which, like her father's, is incomplete, uncertain and ultimately abandoned. Although there are no white characters of any significance in the book, the Black protagonists struggle to breathe inside the ever-present and poisonous smog of a white prejudice that speaks in a collective voice: 'Those Marshall children, you know those colored children that always dress so well and as though they had someone to take care of them. Pretty nice looking children too, if only they weren't colored.'

There is no healthy way to live in such a world. Joanna is frequently unsympathetic to others in her assurance of her own and her family's superiority, and her high-handed treatment of those she thinks are beneath her brings to mind Jane Austen's famously unlikeable Emma Woodhouse. She is a talented singer and dancer, but there are no strains of jazz in this novel published in 1924. Her success is entirely in the hands of white gatekeepers: 'America doesn't want to see a colored dancer in the role of a *première danseuse*.' Bolstered by her talent, her family and her own single-mindedness, it takes a while for Joanna to fully accept the insurmountable barrier of race. Her highest triumph comes when, wearing a mask, she dances the role of 'America' in a performance called the 'Dance of the Nations', in New York's bohemian Greenwich Village. A Black dancer is permitted to represent America only for this one brief, exceptional moment and in this exceptional place, but that realisation does nothing to awaken in her a larger sense of racial solidarity or political action. Greatness, for Joanna, remains a solitary pursuit.

Jessie Redmon Fauset's own life reflected the compromised nature of greatness for an intelligent African-American girl at the turn of the twentieth century. The daughter of a minister, Jessie was born in New Jersey in 1882, at the height of the post-Civil War 'Jim Crow' era that overtly segregated all aspects of daily life in the South and placed more subtle, but no less pervasive, restrictions on Black freedom in the North. She was raised in Philadelphia, in a highly class-conscious world similar to the one she evokes in her novels, where quiet Sundays and family Bibles were the structuring staples of a life lived with your head down and your chin up. Respectability is an edifice built on the sandy base of white acceptance, and any hint of misbehaviour or protest threatened its foundations. Academically gifted, young Jessie became the first woman of her race to graduate from Cornell University in upstate New York, a significant achievement accompanied by high honours. Yet she only ended up there after she had been forced to leave Bryn Mawr, the prestigious women's college closer to her home in Philadelphia, which had admitted her without realising she was Black. Under the leadership of a prominent women's rights activist, Bryn Mawr nevertheless operated strict quotas for Jewish and African-American students, which remained in place until the 1960s. Jessie went on to obtain a Master's degree from the University of Pennsylvania, and to study at the Sorbonne in Paris. Even with this pedigree, she had to move from Philadelphia to Baltimore in order to find a high school that would hire her to teach.

In her fiction and essays, Fauset gives a thorough accounting of the toll taken by the relentless indignities and exclusions that are a feature of daily life for a Black woman. Her 1922 article

'Some Notes on Color' describes these instances of everyday racism, which make up the background hum of humiliation and anxiety for the characters in her novels. In the essay, she frames a response to an unnamed 'distinguished novelist' who asserts that 'the race problem' is antithetical to 'art'. Fauset is politely incredulous: 'It's life, it's colored life. Being colored is being a problem.' Her essay is measured and modulated; but at times the sentences run on in frustration: 'Either we are inartistic or we are picturesque and always the inference is implied that we live objectively with one eye on the attitude of the white world as though it were the audience and we the players whose hope and design is to please.' She recounts the 'inhibition of natural liberties' engendered by a constant awareness of being watched and judged. On the crowded subway a seat becomes vacant and a man looks around for a woman to offer it to. 'I am the nearest one. "But oh," says his glance, "you're colored. I'm not expected to give it to you." And down he plumps.' A slow waitress at a diner might be a sign of the establishment's deliberate racism, or simply an inattentive server, and there's no way to find out: 'The uncertainty beclouds my afternoon.' It is up to the Black woman on the receiving end to ensure that the uncertainty and the unpleasantness don't ruin her day. Fauset admits that these slights and doubts are small in themselves, what we might today called micro-aggressions, but argues that they form part of a larger abdication by white America of its purported values of liberty and democracy: 'I do not have to fear lynching, or burning or dispossession. No, only the reflex of those things.' Her novels are full of individual performers and performances, but always layered atop is this unasked-for and unending role of representing the Black race to white eyes.

There Is Confusion weaves the story of Joanna together with those of her poorer friends, who see the obstacles of class and race more clearly – though they are no more successful in overcoming them. Joanna's lover, Peter Bye, is the descendant of enslaved people and is overt about his hatred of white people: 'he did not believe that any of them were kind or just or even human.' The novel is torn, however, between presenting Peter's bitterness as an obstacle to his success and therefore a flaw to be overcome, and supporting his clear-eyed assessment of the structural racism that is so deeply ingrained that other characters fail to see it. While he is working as a musician to put himself through medical school, employers demand that his band be heard and not seen; on one occasion, a white woman requests that they conceal themselves behind a floral display. Peter's bandmate tells him he plans to leave for South America where, he says, Black people are treated better. 'What business has any one "treating" us, anyway?' Peter demands in response. 'The world's ours as much as it is theirs. And I don't want to leave America. It's mine, my people helped make it.' As they pass 'the famous Bye orchards', Peter points to them as evidence of his connection to his land. There are the trees that his ancestors helped cultivate. His friend is surprised, and asks, 'How'd they come to lose them?' Of course, Peter corrects him, 'They never owned them. The black Byes were slaves of the white Byes.' Peter later enlists to fight in the First World War and, in a melodramatic twist, the youngest son of the slave-owning Bye family is shot and dies in Peter's arms. There is a strong physical resemblance between the two young men, making their blood relationship obvious long before the dead soldier's elderly relative, now the last of the white Byes, admits the truth. As any reader of Harriet Jacobs knows well, under slavery, family trees are full of tangled branches. Once Peter and Joanna finally marry, this man tries to reconcile with them by offering an inheritance for their son. 'They come too late,' says Peter, although he says it 'gently'. Instead, the couple return to the Marshall family home, where Joanna renounces her ambition for 'greatness' in favour of 'happiness'. This belated switch – in the very last line – suggests that Fauset could never quite imagine a combination of public fame and private joy for her female protagonists. Or at least, not in America.

When she came of age in 1900, fully ninety per cent of working African-American women were employed in domestic or personal service. By depicting female protagonists who were artists and businesspeople, Fauset cracked a window of opportunity into the gloom of 'the help'. In her second novel, *Plum Bun*, she created a protagonist, Angela Murray, who chooses to pass as white in order to pursue her dreams of being an artist, at the cost of renouncing her darker-skinned sister, mother and the larger Black community. Her sister, Virginia, embraces that community, with its belief in tradition, domesticity and religion, while the radically individualistic Angela transforms herself into 'Angèle Mory' and tries, like Jay Gatsby, to transcend her heritage through sheer force of will. But her relationship with an upper-class white man, tentatively balanced on the deception of her passing as white, collapses when she realises that his interest in her is superficial. She's merely a sweet, sexual treat – as the title of the novel implies – not a marriage prospect. When she reveals her true identity and her lover abandons her, Angela's artist friends urge her to go to Paris. There, in an atmosphere more tolerant to her race and more welcoming to artists, she falls in love with and marries a fellow mixed-race American artist.

In 1929, the same year *Plum Bun* appeared, Fauset's contemporary Nella Larsen published *Passing*, which has a similar plot, revolving around sisters whom an accident of genetic inheritance has placed on different sides of the colour line. Larsen's novel hewed more closely to the 'tragic mulatto' theme common in literature of the era, which suggested that 'passing' between racial categories was no kind of freedom, and that the sacrifices made to do so could be disastrous. Fauset's novels end not in tragedy but romantic fulfilment which can feel abrupt, even forced – declaring, at the last minute, a private solution to the structural, intractable 'race problem' that has been so richly elucidated beforehand. Her subsequent novels, published in the early 1930s – *The Chinaberry Tree* and *Comedy, American Style* – continued to focus on what one reviewer called 'amber-tinted, well-to-do, refined Negroes'. A minority within a minority, her characters remain obsessed equally with skin colour and class. The relatively privileged worlds she depicted, and the kind of racism her characters experienced – subtle and debilitating, rather than overt and devastating – were out of step with the growing political urgency spurred by the Great Depression. Critical judgements from the 1930s on asserted that Fauset's parlour performances were little more than literary attempts at passing, and that Black literature should turn away from the white gaze to speak to the shared realities of Black life.

Yet Fauset herself was not apolitical, at least in the 1920s. In 1921, she attended the second Pan-African Congress, a global effort to chart a path out of colonial rule, and she returned from Europe inspired by the vision of international racial unity. Yet her ideas for improving the lot of African Americans were gradual rather than revolutionary. She saw hope in education and in giving the next generation the role models that Joanna Marshall lacked. To that end, she and Du Bois collaborated on *The Brownie's Book*, a richly illustrated and playful monthly magazine for 'the children of the sun', that debuted in 1920 and showcased inspirational stories and poetry. It arrived in the wake of the 'Red Summer' of 1919 – a nationwide scourge of racist violence and lynchings that accompanied Black soldiers' return from the First World War, and which was meticulously, furiously documented in *The Crisis*.

Both Fauset and Du Bois were convinced it would help meet the urgent need to give Black children something to celebrate and aspire to. Fauset wrote a poem dedicating the magazine 'To Children, who with eager look/Scanned vainly library shelf and nook, For History or Song or Story/That told of Colored Peoples' glory...' Although the magazine only lasted a year, Fauset went on to write short biographies for young readers celebrating African-American political and cultural figures, intending to collect them into a book. That project did not materialise, but the ethos behind it was in keeping with the idea, influential in early twentieth-century America, that a small faction of educated, accomplished African-Americans known as the 'Talented Tenth' could serve both as inspiration to their own people and as proof to whites of the potential of the race. Achievement (on white terms) would demonstrate Black people's humanity, and, in theory, trickle down into better treatment for all. It would take decades before another generation began to insist, and fight for, the belief that humanity came first.

After her tenure at *The Crisis* ended, Fauset tried to find work in white publishing houses, offering to work from home if her colour should be a problem in the offices. However, following the publication of *Comedy, American Style* in 1933, she retired from literary life. She had married an insurance broker, Herbert Harris, in 1929, at the age of forty-seven, and seems to have renounced her own literary ambitions for domestic life. The couple lived in New Jersey until her husband's death, when Fauset moved back to her family home in Philadelphia. She died there in 1961, as obscure as she could wish. But she left a vital legacy: shaping the lasting literary impact of the Harlem Renaissance as an editor and, in her own novels, providing an atmospheric, flawed and spirited portrait of a vanished era in American history.

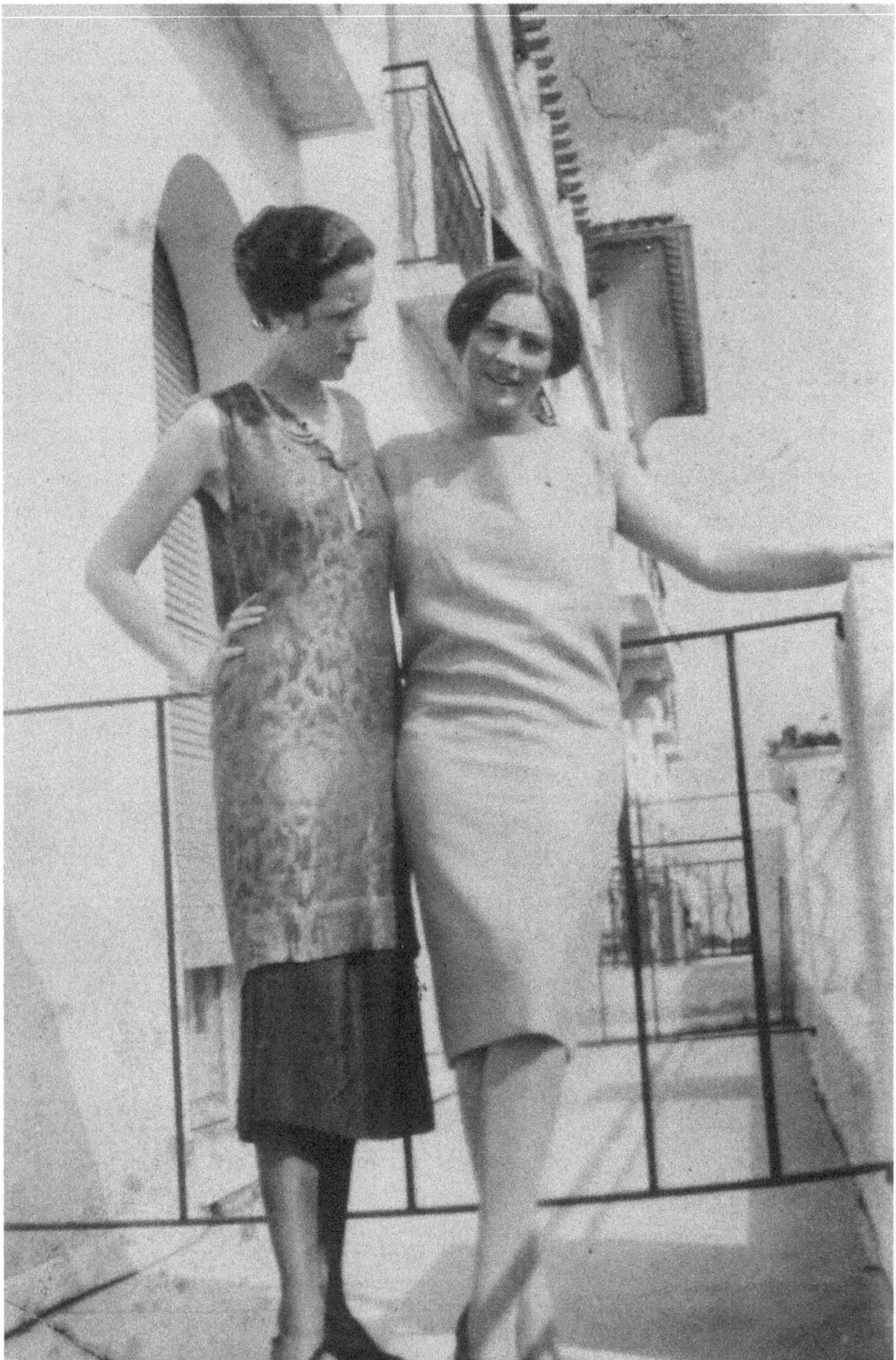

> *'The woman*
> *As usual*
> *Is smiling as bravely*
> *As it is given to her to be brave.'*

MINA LOY
(1882–1966)

Mina Loy is a modernist's modernist – the archetypal forgotten-and-rediscovered and celebrated-yet-misunderstood figure of the global artistic scene of the early twentieth century. But when it comes to literary canons, there is such a thing as *too* modern, and Loy's reputation has suffered through her being too completely what a modernist was supposed to be: irreverent, restless, self-inventing and untethered by worldly concerns – the great illusion of the movement. She was a poet who wrote about sex and bodies and male egos, meaning that she often offended the important (and self-important) men who wanted to be her lover but balked at becoming her subject. A half-Jewish beauty from London, she made a talent of being on 'the scene' wherever it moved – travelling from Europe to America and back and then once again to America. Poet, painter, muse, designer, mother: Loy was 'a binarist's nightmare' and a rollicking good time.

She was not supposed to be everything she became. Born Mina Löwy in 1882 in Hampstead, London, she was the eldest of the three daughters of a Jewish Hungarian immigrant who became a tailor and a strait-laced Protestant Englishwoman who prized middle-class respectability above all. It was not a happy marriage, as the pervasive antisemitism in England at the time only widened the couple's ideological divide. Years later, Mina would dissect their cultural and religious mismatch in her long poem, 'Anglo-Mongrels and the Rose'.

As their eldest daughter grew ever more wild and wayward, her parents blamed each other. Nevertheless, Mina convinced them to let her go to art school – although they drew the line at the progressive, daring Slade School of Fine Art – and enrolled at the local St John's Wood Art School. Stylistically, she was attracted to the Pre-Raphaelites and interested in the 'applied' arts, craft and design: feminised forms of creative expression often sneeringly subordinated to 'fine' art. After art school, she furthered her studies in Munich, where she lodged with a baron and baroness who did not chaperone her as carefully as her parents seem to have believed they would. After that adventure, as she put it, 'I went home to England and stayed there for a few minutes,' before hightailing it to Paris as the new century began.

Mina was always an arresting presence. Her talent for fashion was unmissable in her long, draped robes and tunics of wine-red velvet, set off by centre-parted hair, long earrings and bold hats. In Paris, she studied under Whistler at the Académie Colarossi, and met an English fellow student, Stephen Haweis, a talented photographer who pinned down her youthful loveliness on film and got her pregnant in short order. As the son of a pastor, Haweis met with Mina's parents' approval (both of his parents had died while he was young), and they agreed to the hasty marriage. Five months after the wedding, at the age of twenty-one, Mina gave birth to their daughter Oda Janet. Stephen wasn't faithful, and her 1914 poem 'Parturition' roars with rage at the 'irresponsibility of the male', who is carrying on his affairs and 'running upstairs to a woman's apartment' while the poem's speaker is in labour, 'climbing a distorted mountain of agony'. A still greater pain was to come, when Oda Janet died of meningitis two days after her first birthday. Mina sat up all night after her daughter's death, making a painting she called *The Wooden Madonna*, which depicts a mother in anguish, kneeling over her dead child and raising her fists to the vacant, smiling figure of the Virgin Mary. She sought treatment for her 'neurasthenia', or what we might now call trauma, and embarked at some point on an affair with her doctor, Henri Joël Le Savoureux, which led to a second pregnancy. The doctor was, unfortunately, engaged to be married. Mina tried offering Stephen half the allowance she received from her father, which was conditional on her remaining married, if he would agree to a secret separation, allowing them both a measure of freedom. There are varying accounts of what happened next, but the couple eventually left Paris for Italy together. In Italy, she gave birth to Joella, named for her biological father but recognised by Stephen, and two years later to her son with Stephen, John Giles.

At Villa Curonia, the elegantly dilapidated palazzo outside Florence owned by the American heiress Mabel Dodge, Mina encountered an eclectic gathering of international artists, writers, and hangers-on, including Gertrude Stein and the influential critic Carl Van Vechten. She became an expert at capturing in her writing the poses and postures, gestures and jests of these creative cliques who were always locked in anxious competition over who might emerge into greatness and who was doomed to irrelevance. Her story 'Gloria Gammage' is a keen satire on Dodge and her ilk – the 'millionheir class' as she dubbed them – and she frequently revisited these dilettantish milieus in her prose, poetry, and fragmentary plays in the 1910s and 1920s. Even when artists had claimed the stature of greatness, she still looked askance. Her 1925 essay 'Gate Crashers of Olympus' poked fun at Picasso and the Cubists, and the self-conscious modernity of their scene. 'Art is always "new" to the uninitiate,' she wryly declared.

The loudest proclaimers of the new, in pre-war Italy, were the Futurists, a chest-beating mini-movement of radicals obsessed with modernity's accelerated promise. Among its ringleaders was Filippo Marinetti, who yelled his message through the innovative American promotional device of the megaphone, spitting 'words like torpedoes', as Mina wrote. In Florence, his main competitor for attention was the more subdued Giovanni Papini – their rivalry was only sharpened when they both became Mina's lovers.

When the First World War began, Mina briefly volunteered as a nurse, while Marinetti eagerly joined up with the Italian army. Their affair became inextricable from the atmosphere of 'war fever', she later explained. She had appreciated his energy, vitality and his belief in rejuvenation, but was quickly disenchanted. Even as these artists and fascists (who so often overlapped) were trying to call a new future into being, they still consigned women to the past – or the unchanging present – obediently doing the dishes, raising the children and sleeping with their artist husbands when they came home from the bar. Loy's 1914 *Feminist Manifesto*, a riposte to the *Futurist Manifesto* that she dashed off in a letter to Mabel Dodge, is nevertheless one of her most enduring pieces of writing: at once a brilliant parody of the tone of those proclamations and an earnest engagement with the feminist questions of the time. Women's liberation was advancing but only by inches, and the progress was too slow for manifesto-Mina, who declared, 'There is no half-measure – NO scratching on the surface of the rubbish heap of tradition will bring about <u>Reform</u>, the only method is <u>Absolute Demolition</u>.'

As the war advanced, Mina tried to get out of Europe. In 1916, she made the dangerous crossing to New York, leaving her children in the care of their nanny in Florence. In New York she threw in with the avant-garde set, in downtown Greenwich Village, which was gathering to it an ever more eclectic mix of foreign exiles and refugees. In 1916, she performed in a one-act play, *Lima Beans*, alongside the poet William Carlos Williams, staged by the Provincetown Players, the theatre group founded by Mary Heaton Vorse and her friends the previous summer, who were now established in the Village. In February of the same year, Mina was identified by the New York *Evening Sun* newspaper as the quintessential 'modern woman'.

But it was not easy even for the most modern woman to escape the traps of men and marriage. Three years before Mina sailed for New York, Stephen had begun another affair and left Italy for Australia. Still, he refused to grant Loy a divorce – in part because he still needed her money. She soon found herself embroiled in another dramatic and destructive relationship.

Arthur Cravan was Oscar Wilde's nephew by marriage, and had been born Fabian Lloyd in Lausanne, Switzerland, five years after Mina, who liked the near-symmetry of their true last names. Nominally a poet, he was also a pugilist, both in person and in print, and had been on the move since getting kicked out of boarding school at the age of sixteen. Although he'd never met his uncle, who died in 1900, Cravan profited from the connection – occasionally impersonating Wilde and selling forged letters and memorabilia. In 1913, he even convinced the

New York Times that his uncle was not dead, and the body in Père Lachaise cemetery was a decoy. When war broke out, Cravan found refuge in neutral Spain then, like Mina, left Europe for the United States. He raised money for his passage with a showpiece boxing match in Barcelona against the reigning heavyweight champion, Jack Johnson, who knocked him out after six rounds. The two split the proceeds, and narrowly escaped a riot when the crowd figured out that the fight was rigged.

Mina met this unscrupulous showman in April 1917 when he gave a speech at an experimental art exhibition that opened just days after the United States entered the war. The Dada artists Francis Picabia and Marcel Duchamp got Cravan so drunk on absinthe he could barely stand, and when he started yelling obscenities and stripping off his clothes, four undercover detectives hauled him off to the police station. Despite this beginning, or perhaps because of it, the magnetic Cravan became the love of Mina's life.

But he could not stay still. That autumn, dodging the draft, he and a friend hitchhiked to Canada, from where Cravan took a boat alone to Mexico. He wrote to ask Mina to join him: 'send a lock of your hair,' he begged, 'or just come, bringing all of it.' She set off on a five-day train journey and met him in Mexico City. 'Our life together consisted entirely in wandering arm in arm through the streets,' she recalled in her autobiography *Colossus* – which was titled for the nickname she gave him. Passionately in love, desperately poor, and with Cravan pursued by the authorities, for them it was still an idyll: 'Somehow we had tapped the source of enchantment.' Seeking greater safety, they moved south to Salina Cruz, and were married in January 1918 – Mina had finally won her divorce from Haweis the previous summer. She left her new husband there, seemingly with a plan to reunite later in Buenos Aires, Cravan set off alone in a small fishing boat. He made it a few days' journey up the coast, then was caught in a storm and presumed drowned, although longing and legends kept his disappearance a mystery for years.

By this point Mina was pregnant again. In April 1919, back in England with her family, she gave birth to her daughter Jemima Fabienne, but by 1923 she had rejoined the expatriate crowd on the Left Bank of Paris, which was now lively with new blood and post-war energy. She, too, was different now: an old hand at the bohemian life, fluent in several languages, in her forties, and a mother. But there was more tragedy to come. In 1921, Stephen had taken their twelve-year-old son, Giles, to Bermuda despite her protests. Two years later, he died of cancer, without ever seeing his mother again. Mina's daughter Joella crawled into her bed as she grieved, to keep her from harming herself.

Mina Loy never had financial resources on the scale of other influential modernist women she would come to know: Gilded Age heiresses like Mabel Dodge, or Renée Vivien's lover Natalie Barney, with her salon in Paris, the art collector Peggy Guggenheim. So she wrote and painted, travelled and bartered, saved and laboured. Her need for money and her overflowing creativity fed each other. Over the course of her career she designed lampshades, dresses, theatrical sets and magazine covers, in addition to creating art and sculpture, and publishing stories, essays and poetry, much of which remained scattered around niche, often short-lived magazines and avant-garde journals. In 1923, her poetry collection *Lunar Baedecker* appeared, one of the only two books she published in her lifetime. The title alludes to, but misspells 'Baedeker', the ubiquitous brand of travel guidebook available at the time.

As a poet, Loy is sometimes compared to Emily Dickinson. Not only because she was a fan of the dash, the gap or the pause in poetry – the pause *as* poetry – but also for her singularity, the way she looked at the world and composed her words so differently from those around her. She liked to play with language and remake words and her poems are not easy to understand. The fragments glint brightly, there are lines that punch up through the strangeness, like the opening of 'Lunar Baedecker': 'A silver Lucifer/serves/cocaine in cornucopia.' But larger meanings often remain out of reach, unformed or unfinished.

In Paris with Joella and young Fabienne, Mina made a home on Rue Campagne Première in the heart of Montparnasse, and began or renewed friendships with several influential, creative women, including Gertrude Stein; Sylvia Beach, who ran the Shakespeare & Company bookstore; and Peggy Guggenheim, who underwrote Mina's latest venture – a shop selling her own lampshade designs, which opened in 1926. She and Joella worked together to renovate and furnish the space, in a fancy shopping district off the Champs-Élysées, and before long she was able to hire assistants and open a workshop to manufacture her designs. The lampshades featured water lilies, swans and images connected to the ocean. Mina loved the way that light and shadow could transform an interior, rendering it mysterious as the ocean floor. Her bestselling design was an illuminated globe. She advertised her creations widely, under the name *L'ombre féerique* (the fairyland shade), but success attracted cheap imitations. Her flower designs, in particular, attracted the interest of department stores and generated a flood of knock-offs. The artist did what she could to maintain control – filing patents and bringing lawsuits against her imitators – but, eventually in 1929, she decided to close and sell the shop, a decision no doubt made more urgent by the onset of the Great Depression.

By this point, Joella had married an artistically minded young American, Julien Levy, who was handsome and rich. The two moved to New York, where he opened a gallery that became a major showcase for Surrealist art. In Paris, Mina advised him on purchases and acted as agent, and she sent her own paintings to be shown there in 1933. She also completed a Surrealist novel, *Insel*, in the early 1930s. Its title character is a charismatic, down-on-his-luck artist based on her friend Richard Oelze – and, we might assume, her long experience with dissolute, possibly brilliant, and certainly careless men. Despite her reputation and connections, she was unable to publish the book – an indicator of how cultural tides were turning against artistic experimentation.

With the rise of fascism in Europe, the freewheeling spirit of inter-war Paris was rapidly darkening. Mina's Jewish heritage placed her and her family under an ever more present threat, so in 1935 she sent Fabienne, then sixteen, to live with her sister and brother-in-law in New York, and followed herself the next year. It was a struggle to adapt. She was fifty-four, and dependent on her children. She felt, at first, like a refugee rather than an artist. But as waves of émigrés and exiles found their way to New York, the artistic scene flourished anew. Mina's creativity was fired by her association with a new generation of artists, along with reconnections made with old friends like the writer Djuna Barnes, pictured with Mina at the start of this chapter, who had also moved back and forth between Left Bank and Greenwich Village bohemias since before the First World War.

In 1945, Mina became a U.S. citizen, and moved to the Bowery, an impoverished neighbourhood in lower Manhattan, where she lived among, and painted, the men and women who washed up on its desperate and unfashionable shores. She lived alone but in a shared household, and spent her time making collages and assemblages from discarded objects she collected in the streets. Her neighbours called her the 'Duchess'. They remembered her white face paint and wine-red robe, and her habit of poking in trash cans for material to make pieces like the collage *Communal Cot*, a collection of ten small figures moulded out of paper and fabric, seen from above as if sleeping on the ground. This tender attention to her unhoused neighbours was also reflected in her 1945 poem 'Hot Cross Bum', which despite its irreverent title, utilised her dazzling fragments of observation to create an epic of the broken lives on the Bowery – 'a lurid lane/ leading misfortune's monsters.'

In 1953, Mina Loy agreed to join her daughters and grandchildren in Aspen, Colorado, and lived out the rest of her life in the small mountain town that was slowly developing into a luxury resort – both Joella and Fabienne were, by this point, married to architects who were helping to develop the town. Against this backdrop, the eccentric Loy, draped in velvet, was a figure of some mystery to locals and a source of embarrassment to her daughters, as she continued to hunt through trash for art materials. She also seemed to have lost her grasp on two vital qualities for an artist: the ability to declare a work finished, and the power to convince an audience to look at it. After five years, she published her second volume of poetry, combining poems from *Lunar Baedeker* (its title spelling corrected) with newer work, *Time Tables*. She dialled in to the New York launch party from the mountains. But although a small coterie of new poets took up her cause, it did not find a wide readership.

That readership would come with the attention of feminist critics and biographers in the 1980s and 1990s, along with efforts to collect and assemble her scattered body of work. Yet the very eclecticism and impenetrability of her work make her continually elusive, an artist who tends to disappear into her biography.

That is understandable, perhaps, given that her life – with its constant movement, its undimmed artistic drive, and its flares of formative tragedy – was inseparable from the art she created.

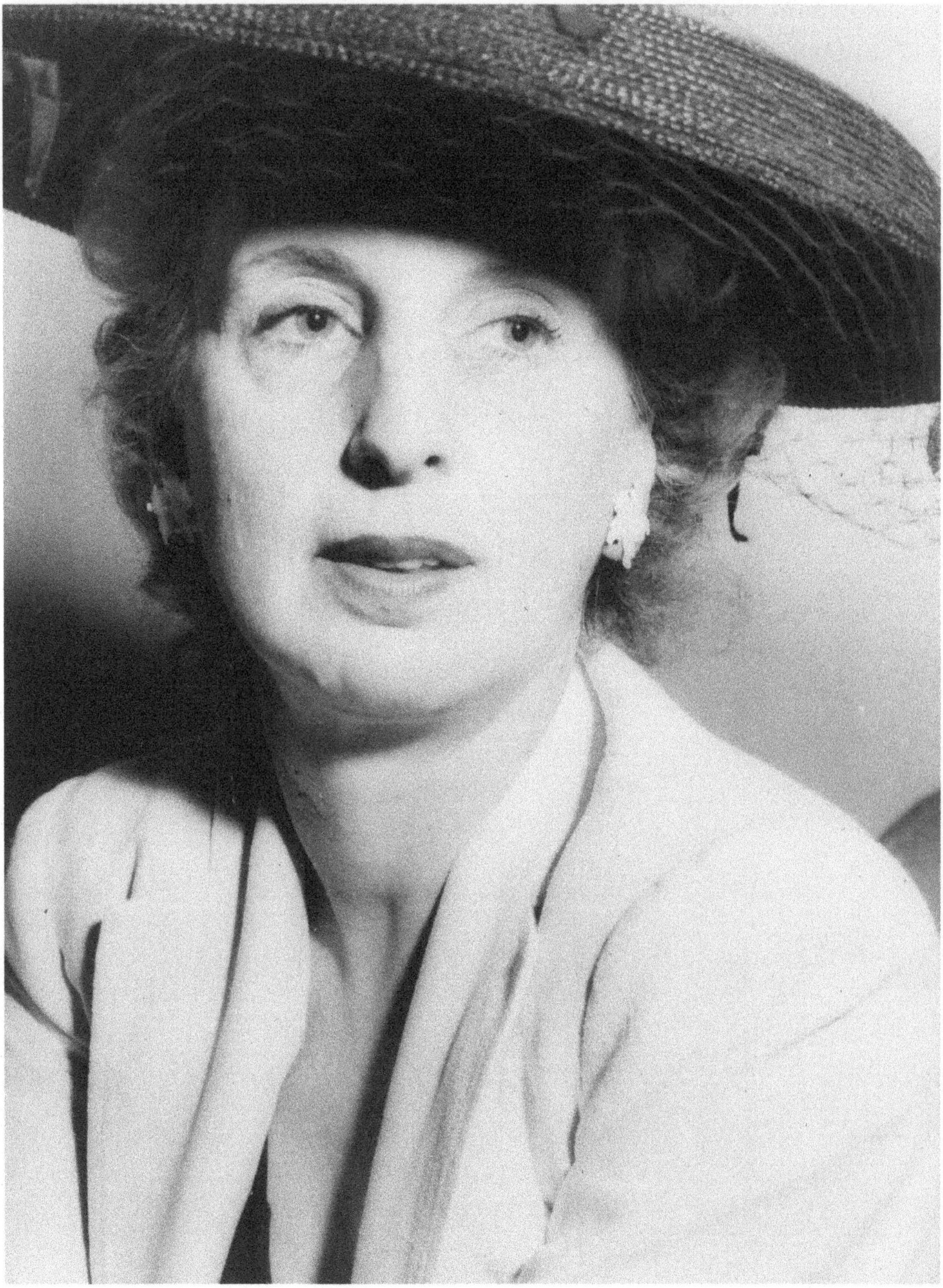

'Why do they call people rebels who are swinging into the wide, hot rhythms of life?'

KAY BOYLE
(1902–1992)

Kay Boyle's extraordinary creative life spanned almost the entirety of the twentieth century. A mother of six and the author of more than forty books, hers is a story of dazzling scope and energy, throughout which she insisted on the vital interconnectedness of art and social justice. She was there at the heart of 1920s Paris and co-wrote one of its most remarkable chronicles, *Being Geniuses Together*. She bore witness to the fascist takeover in 1930s Europe and became a victim of the McCarthy witch hunts in the United States in the 1950s. Finally settling in San Francisco, she protested the Vietnam War and fought injustice wherever she could. She won several important literary prizes and wrote bestselling books, but her popularity in her own time and the scale of her output were not enough to keep her a household name. Even as readers devour all they can of her male contemporaries in Paris she remains a writer in need of rediscovery.

Boyle's early life shaped her development as an artist and activist in decisive ways. She was born in 1902 in St Paul, Minnesota, the hometown of her fellow expatriate F. Scott Fitzgerald – another midwesterner who fled that wholesome, conservative milieu for the creative decadence of Europe in the 1920s. But unlike many who made that journey – and many of the women in this book, whose adventures were a form of rebellion against their parents – Kay had the rare good fortune of a mother who fully and eagerly supported her daughter's talent. The Boyle family depended financially on her paternal grandfather, a publishing executive, whose wealth meant that the family, Kay recalled, 'travelled expensively, and dined expansively' across the United States and Europe. But the money did not last. Kay was in her early teens when the family fortunes cratered, and they moved to Cincinnati, where her father took a job with his cousin repairing cars. Despite these reversals of fortune, her mother, Katherine Evans Boyle, remained the constant sun around whom Kay and her older sister Joan orbited.

Kay Boyle was born into a family of women who fought for other women. Her mother's sister, Nina Allender, was an artist who sued her cheating husband for divorce, then went on to become a prominent figure in the women's suffrage movement, spreading the message with her striking cartoons and illustrations. Kay's mother, Katherine, also jumped into the political fray, running for local office in Cincinnati even before women gained the right to vote, and bringing her daughters along to her campaign events. Katherine was as committed to Kay and Joan's artistic development as to their political engagement. In 1913, she took the girls to New York to see the enormous, electrifying Armory Show, an exhibition of modern art, where they contemplated paintings by Matisse, Picasso and Marcel Duchamp – whose Cubist masterpiece *Nude Descending a Staircase* was the show's most divisive piece. By the late 1920s, Kay would count Duchamp among her friends in Paris.

Although Kay's schooling, as she described it, was 'sketchy' at best, her mother's lessons were ambitious, and rooted in the belief that her children's developing talents ought to be nurtured. 'Mother accepted me and my word as she accepted James Joyce, Gertrude Stein, or Brancusi, or any serious artist,' Kay recalled. Her mother would read her daughter's writing aloud at political meetings and dinner parties. Kay's first published article was a letter to the magazine *Poetry* that lamented the unambitious state of modern music when compared to avant-garde poetry.

After brief stints studying architecture and music, Kay took a job as a switchboard operator in Cincinnati to save up the money to move to New York, where her sister was already working as an illustrator at *Vogue* magazine. Her plans were altered, although not seriously derailed, when she met a French exchange student at the local university, Richard Brault, and the two became engaged. While he finished his studies, Kay moved to New York, juggling art classes, odd jobs and experiments in writing. She began working with the modernist poet Lola Ridge on her literary magazine, *Broom*. Lola became a close friend and, through her, Kay started to forge connections in the city's artistic scene. She began to publish her criticism and poetry in the influential 'little magazines', like *Broom*, that offered a home to experimental writing.

Her time in New York was packed with creativity, but short-lived. After Richard graduated and moved to New York, the couple married in June 1922, and sailed the following spring to France, to stay with his family in Brittany for the summer. Kay had no way of knowing that the trip would mark the beginning of nearly two decades of exile. In France Kay quickly recognised her alienation from Richard's uncomprehending bourgeois family, who were kind enough to her, but could not understand why their son's wife neglected her domestic duties to spend her days writing. That experience of alienation and the slow suffocation of family life would form the basis of her 1931 novel *Plagued by the*

Nightingale, in which the American heroine finds herself trapped in her husband's claustrophobically close French family.

Kay and Richard escaped to Paris just as the legendary 1920s – christened 'the jazz age' by Fitzgerald, and *'les années folles'* by the French – were beginning to roar. Kay met the writer Robert McAlmon, whose reminiscences of this storied era she would later edit and supplement to create their hybrid chronicle, *Being Geniuses Together*.

But she couldn't afford to stay long in the centre of things. Richard found a job in the port town of Le Havre and the couple decamped to the cold and gloomy northern coast, where Kay spent her days trying to write and stay warm, fighting off a chest infection caused by the damp. While Richard was at work, she produced poetry, stories and a flood of letters to her family and her growing circle of literary friends. As her situation deteriorated over the winter of 1925, she was thrown a lifeline: Ernest Walsh, the editor of the literary magazine *This Quarter*, sent Kay money as an advance for her novel, and made her an appointment to see his doctor in Paris for the lung condition she had developed. When he extended a desperately welcomed invitation to stay with him and his co-editor Ethel Moorhead in the south of France, his friendship with Kay deepened into an intense romance. Walsh was, however, seriously ill with the tuberculosis he had contracted during the war. He died in October 1926, at the age of thirty-one, when Kay was five months pregnant with his child.

Although she and Richard had been estranged for over a year by now, Kay found herself with no other means of support, so she agreed to his offer to join him in Stoke-on-Trent, England, where he had found work. Not long after her daughter was born – Sharon, named for the biblical Rose of Sharon – she realised she could not stay, telling Lola Ridge, 'I cannot inflict a platonic wife upon Richard for the rest of his existence.'

By 1928, when Kay returned to Paris, she was – like Mina Loy – an older and sharper-eyed observer of a scene already intoxicated by its own mythology. Looking back years later, she sniffed that 'all this glorification of that wonderful Camelot period is absurd.' It was a scene, she judged, born out of a favourable exchange rate with the U.S. dollar as much as any Parnassian meeting of minds, and the people in it were far from gods. She disliked Gertrude Stein (who thought Kay was 'incurably middle class') and preferred to talk cookery with Stein's partner, Alice Toklas, than debate the intricacies of artistic experimentation. She had particular contempt for Ernest Hemingway, whom she thought a 'double-dealing bastard' for having a barely concealed affair with a friend of her sister's, Pauline Pfeiffer.

Kay's own literary experiments continued: inspired by William Blake, she rejected realism in favour of a belief in poetry's mystical power. Her connections in avant-garde Paris circles expanded but she lacked the comfortable financial security of many other 'bohemian' expats, and struggled to support herself and Sharon. She joined an artistic colony in Neuilly, on the Paris border (where Natalie Barney had established her avant-garde theatrical community twenty-five years earlier) and lived and worked in the commune's gift shop, while Sharon was cared for by the collective. But before long the arrangement soured – the head of the commune, Raymond Duncan, brother to the famous dancer Isadora, was a fraud who imported the supposedly handcrafted goods at the gift shop, and enriched himself at the expense of the group. Kay felt trapped and miserable, and began to drink heavily, fearing that she would somehow lose her daughter to the group. In August of 1929 she suffered what she called a general 'collapse' of her physical and mental state and, after some weeks in hospital, she successfully plotted with friends to reclaim her daughter from the colony.

The year 1929 was a transformative one for Kay. Dining with Robert McAlmon outside the storied Montparnasse brasserie La Coupole, she met the artist and writer Laurence Vail, who was nicknamed 'the King of Bohemia' and would soon become her second husband. Meanwhile, her first book, a short story collection, was published by the Black Sun Press, run by her friends Harry and Caresse Crosby, and she joined a group of other writers in signing her name to a literary manifesto in her friend Eugene Jolas's magazine *transition*. In stark block letters, and supported by quotations from William Blake, the manifesto joined many other such 1920s declarations that wanted to overthrow worn-out modes of literature – here defined as 'THE HEGEMONY OF THE BANAL WORD, MONOTONOUS SYNTAX, STATIC PSYCHOLOGY, DESCRIPTIVE NATURALISM – and declare a new style and a new dawn. Among the tenets of this new writing were 'THE WRITER EXPRESSES. HE DOES NOT COMMUNICATE' and 'THE PLAIN READER BE DAMNED.'

By the end of the year, during which the world economic collapse had driven many Americans home from their expatriate adventures, Kay had set up home in a village house outside Paris with Laurence Vail, Sharon, and Vail's son Sindbad, from his first marriage to Peggy Guggenheim. There, in December, their daughter Apple-Joan was born. In 1932, when both Kay's and Vail's divorces were finalised – still a slow, costly process at that time – they married and moved to the mountain town of Kitzbühel, Austria, where their second daughter Kathe was born. There, Kay witnessed the encroaching clouds of fascism gathering strength against a backdrop of joblessness and despair, and her writing turned more directly to engage with the growing threat of extremist politics. Her 1936 novel *Death of a Man* explored the threat of Nazi ideology. In this book and elsewhere she probed not only the threat but also the appeal of these movements. Why were people drawn to the politics of hate? What was the connection between gender dominance and the appeal of fascism? Those questions would take on an increasing urgency as the decade progressed.

The family moved back to France in 1937, to another Alpine home nicknamed *Les Cinq Enfants*, to include Sindbad's sister Pegeen, who frequently stayed with them. Five grew to six in 1939 with the arrival of another baby, Clover, as war drew ever closer. The months before the Nazi invasion were a frenetic, unreal moment in their mountain town of Megève. 'Here half the world is skiing while the other half dies, and the nightclubs are open until three in the morning,' Kay wrote to Caresse Crosby that winter. A year later, along with Vail, the six children, Peggy Guggenheim, and the latter's future husband, the German Surrealist artist Max Ernst, Kay managed to escape to America via Marseille and Lisbon. Kay also arranged passage to the United States via a different boat for the children's one-time tutor and ski instructor in Megève, an Austrian baron and anti-Nazi dissident named Joseph von Franckenstein. In 1943, after divorcing Vail, Kay would marry Franckenstein, who fathered her two youngest children, Faith and Ian.

In the United States, shocked by the shrugs with which many Americans regarded France's capitulation to the Nazis, Kay devoted herself to the urgent task of driving home the horrors of Nazism and the heroism of anti-fascists. She gave lectures and wrote stories based on her eyewitness accounts, while her novel about the French Resistance, *Avalanche*, published in 1944, became a bestseller. Franckenstein, meanwhile, became a naturalised U.S. citizen and joined the secret service. He returned undercover to his native Austria to help the Resistance, where the Gestapo arrested and tortured him. His survival and escape were a close call.

At the end of the war, Kay returned to Paris with Franckenstein, before moving to Germany, where her husband worked for the U.S. foreign service and she became a *New Yorker* correspondent – the magazine's editor, Harold Ross, was particularly interested in the literary scene as the country recovered. Yet their bravery and commitment during the worldwide conflict were not enough to protect them from the anti-Communist fanaticism sweeping the United States in the early days of the Cold War, under the influence of Senator Joseph McCarthy. They were hauled in front of a loyalty hearing in Marburg in 1952, at which Janet Flanner, the *New Yorker*'s longtime Paris correspondent, appeared as a witness, later describing to a friend her disgust at 'the humiliation, the degradation, the shocking injustice of all this'. Even though Kay and Franckenstein – whom Flanner described as 'haggard' and heartbroken by the hearing – were cleared of all charges, it was only a temporary reprieve. A few months later, both the State Department and the *New Yorker* revoked their respective employment, and the family had to return to America. They moved to Connecticut, where Franckenstein found a teaching job at a girls' school, while Kay was blacklisted and unpublishable by most major national magazines throughout the 1950s. It took years of dedicated fighting to fully clear their names finally in 1957, then a further five years before Franckenstein was allowed to rejoin the State Department. He achieved a longed-for overseas diplomatic posting, to the U.S. embassy in Tehran, but died shortly afterwards of an aggressive form of cancer.

In 1963, overcoming grief and anger at her husband's fate, Kay Boyle found a job teaching creative writing at San Francisco State College, where she remained until her retirement in 1979. During her time at San Francisco State, she lived in the Haight-Ashbury neighbourhood, at the city's counter-cultural heart, and embraced the radical activism of another much mythologised collision of time and place. She marched on picket lines and protested the Vietnam War, signed a writers' pledge to withhold taxes in protest, and was herself fired, arrested and imprisoned. She became an active supporter of Amnesty International and, when she moved into a retirement home at the age of eighty-seven, she continued to fight for progress and justice – she invited non-white friends to lunch, effectively forcing the community to integrate its dining room.

Although she had her doubts about the effectiveness of teaching writing in a classroom – she routinely told her students never to take another writing class after hers – Boyle advocated for her students to find their individual voices, whatever the cost. 'It takes courage to say things differently,' she wrote in an essay on creative writing. 'Caution and cowardice dictate the use of the cliché.' It was a lesson she might have learned from her mother, and one that she put into practice in her own writing throughout her career. Always seeking the truest, sharpest and freshest expression of her subject – whatever it was – she also communicated clearly with her readers, offering a sympathetic, resolutely human perspective on the tumult of the twentieth century.

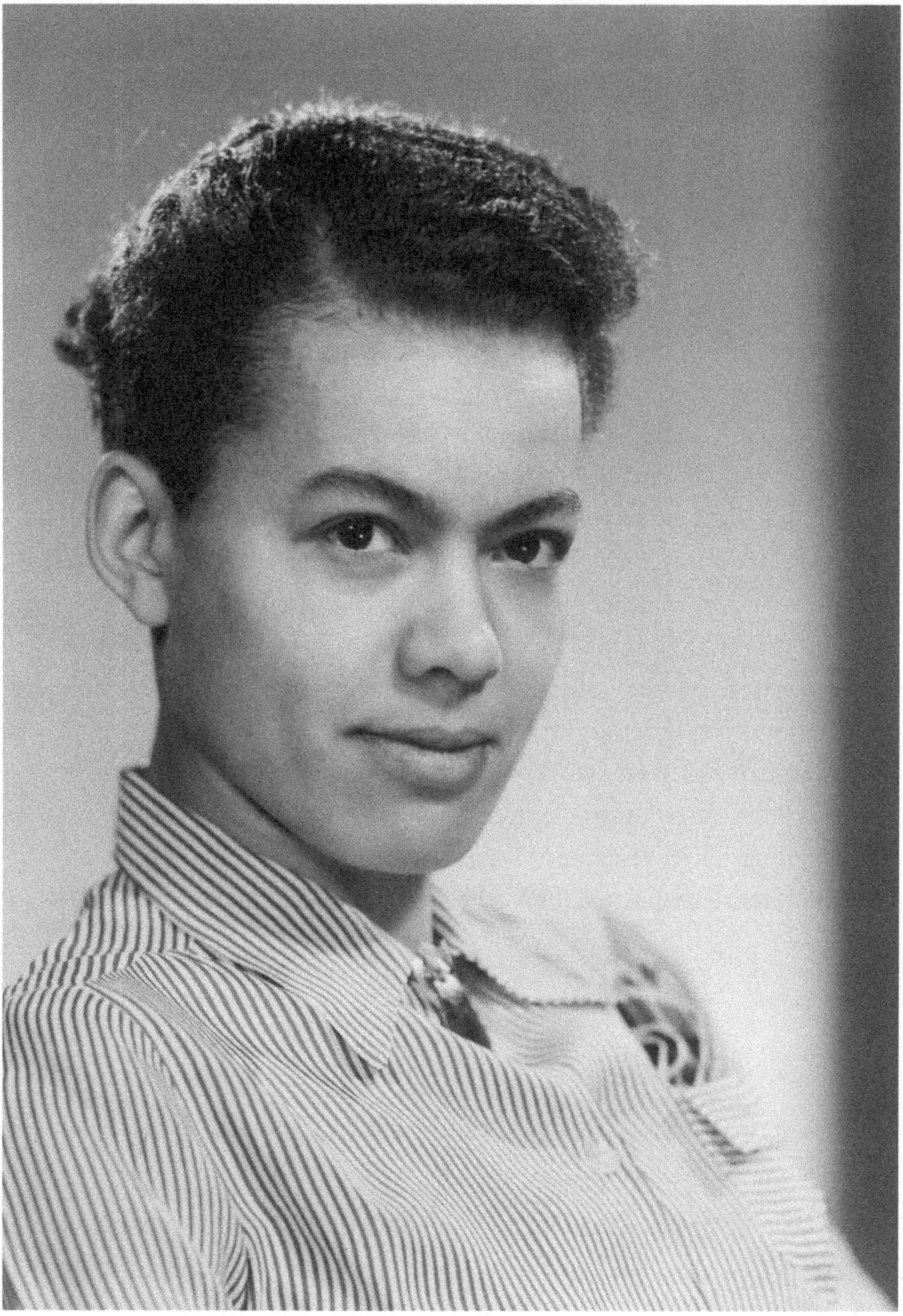

'Hope is a song in a weary throat.'

PAULI MURRAY
(1910–1985)

If it is rare for a poet to shape the rulings of the U.S. Supreme Court, it may be rarer still for a lawyer to be canonised as a saint. But Pauli Murray was a rare individual. A writer and lawyer born in the segregated South in 1910, she confronted discrimination on the basis of both race and gender, arguing that both, in parallel ways, violated the American Constitution. Despite a string of battles for women's rights, Murray struggled intensely from childhood with the conviction that her biological sex and gender identity did not align. Decades before modern understandings of the trans experience or gender fluidity, she frequently presented as male, and was sexually attracted only to women. Throughout her life, her religious faith sustained her with a vision of human equality and community, and in her late sixties, she left her role as a law professor to become an Episcopal priest. In 2012, her church recognised her as a saint: a testament to her remarkable, resilient, protean life.

Pauli Murray's development as a legal thinker is entangled with the history of race relations in the U.S. in the early twentieth century. After the Civil War opened the way to freedom and equality for African Americans, a violent backlash built among powerful whites, especially in the Southern states. At the end of the nineteenth century, a notorious Supreme Court decision reintroduced race-based discrimination under the banner of 'separate but equal' – the theory that segregation was permitted if facilities like schools and transportation were made available for both races. These separations, collectively known as Jim Crow laws, carved up daily life on racial lines across the former slave states. Lawyers were stuck with the exhausting task of challenging them one by one and arguing each time that the provisions were not 'equal' but substandard for Black people. As a law student, Pauli Murray proposed a new approach that attacked the separation itself, not the dubious equality, as unconstitutional. Inspiring a wave of ridicule from her peers, she made a bet with her professor that the law would eventually be overturned on these grounds. He took the bet, and a decade later brought Murray's audacious idea with him when he joined the team of lawyers arguing the pivotal case, *Brown v. Board of Education*, that ended racial segregation in American schools.

For Pauli Murray, the injustice of racial segregation did not exist in isolation. She coined the term 'Jane Crow' to point out the parallels between sex and race discrimination at a time when 'Help Wanted' advertisements could invite male or female only applications, and when Pauli could be refused entry to Harvard Law School on the basis of sex. Her argument was that the guarantee of equal treatment under the law, which was enshrined after the abolition of slavery as the Fourteenth Amendment to the U.S. Constitution, was a right that could also be applied to gender. It was an argument that helped propel another influential lawyer, the Supreme Court justice Ruth Bader Ginsburg, to pass legislation that ended legal sex discrimination. Decades later, another legal scholar, Kimberlé Crenshaw, citing Murray, would coin the term 'intersectional' to describe the way that different forms of oppression and discrimination could pile up. Long before the term was widely used, Pauli Murray's lived experience required her to find her own language for it. In 1970, she declared that

'If anyone should ask a Negro woman in America what has been her greatest achievement, her honest answer would be, "I survived!"' Not only for herself, but for her family, she knew the truth of that claim.

Anna Pauline Murray was born in Baltimore, Maryland, in 1910, and was one of six children who arrived in rapid succession. Their parents were a teacher and a nurse, whose marriage and precarious middle-class status could not survive the onslaught of children. After her mother died suddenly when she was just three, Pauline went to live with her namesake Aunt Pauline and her maternal grandparents in Durham, North Carolina. Her father, left with the three eldest of his children, was unable to cope and was committed to a mental institution – a place of brutality rather than care. Pauli saw him again only once, in his coffin, after he was beaten and killed by a white guard at the institution. She was twelve years old, and later wrote that being an orphan was her first way of identifying as an outsider. Race was another.

Proud Shoes, Murray's autobiography, tells the story of her complex mixed-race family, which blended enslaved Africans, Cherokee Indians and white Europeans – who themselves ranged from Quaker abolitionists to Protestant slaveholders – a mélange of a heritage she dubbed 'Euro-African-American' and for which the darker-skinned children at school bullied her. Her maternal grandfather, Robert Fitzgerald, was a free Black man and a teacher raised in anti-slavery circles in the north, while his wife, Cornelia, was born into slavery and was the product of her mother's rape – a fact of life for women held in bondage, as fellow North Carolina writer Harriet Jacobs had shown. That legacy of rape entwined Pauli Murray with one of the most prominent, politically influential white families in the state – a connection she tried unsuccessfully to leverage when she applied to the segregated University of North Carolina.

Aunt Pauline, a teacher, rose to the challenge of her unconventional niece with equanimity. Recognising early on that she was something unusual, a 'boy-girl', Pauline allowed her to choose and wear clothes from the boys' section on the condition she did not wear them at church. Self-described as 'thin, wiry, ravenous' – for both food and knowledge – Pauli bolted from school (where she was top of her class and in charge of the school newspaper) and the South at fifteen, having set her sights on New York. There, she lodged with a cousin in Queens and enrolled for another year of high school, in order to qualify as a state resident and secure a place at the then women-only Hunter College to study English. She moved to Harlem, where the storied cultural Renaissance was underway. She heard Duke Ellington play at the Apollo, befriended the poet Langston Hughes, and mapped out a glowing pathway to her dream life as a writer and social activist.

She had barely taken a step on that path when the Wall Street Crash brought the party of the 1920s to a crashing halt. Harlem was hit especially hard by the evaporation of wealth, with an unemployment rate hitting fifty per cent as the Depression began to bite. Pauli lost her waitressing job and left school to search in vain for other work. She shared a room with another student, surviving on the Southern staple of hominy grits for days at a time, to the point of malnutrition. Despite her struggles, she managed to finish her degree in 1933.

Upon graduation, she confronted the challenge of combining meaningful work with meaningful activism. It was not a dilemma she could resolve until she was, as she put it in her autobiography, 'Saved by the WPA'. The signature project of President Roosevelt's New Deal, the Works Progress Administration offered jobs in a wide variety of public projects – from infrastructure to literature – to unemployed Americans in the mid-1930s, saving Murray, and millions like her, from despair.

Throughout the 1930s, Murray was grappling with the question of who she was, and who she wanted to become, both professionally and personally. Her community's disproportionate suffering in the Depression had made clear the connection between class and race, and she joined a new wave of radicals making common cause against ruthless capitalism. She flirted briefly with communism, but didn't like the meetings. Along with this political confusion, she was in search of a resolution to questions about her gender and sexuality. She had started the decade, at twenty years old, by getting married to a man in a desperate effort to be a 'normal woman', as she put it, and force her life into a familiar shape. The union lasted a weekend. The stress and despair of her attraction to women caused a series of breakdowns during her life, and she spent hours reading up on theories of gender difference and the science of the day regarding sexual attraction. In vain she petitioned doctors for hormone therapy and, during surgery for appendicitis, asked a doctor to examine her for evidence of undetected male genitals – one theory that she thought might explain her condition. He found nothing.

Her literary and activist selves – and the 'poet and warrior/who grapple in my brain' – were also vying for supremacy. In 1934, not long after leaving college, Murray's first poem, 'Song of the Highway', was published in a doorstopper anthology of writing by and about the 'Negro', assembled by the British heiress and anti-racism activist Nancy Cunard. A celebration of the open road, in the vein of Walt Whitman, it was appended to a short story, 'Three Thousand Miles on a Dime', which fictionalised Murray's own cross-country adventure hopping the trains with hobos and outsmarting the policing 'dicks'. Next to the story appears a photograph of the author dressed in men's clothing and ostensibly depicting the hero of the piece, Pete. Along with Paul and Dude, this was one of the nicknames she adopted as a teenager, before settling on the androgynous Pauli in college.

Her family was worried about her and begged her to come home. In 1938, she agreed, despite her reluctance to return to the South. There, the confrontation with overt Jim Crow racism called her activism to the fore. She was turned down by the University of North Carolina when she applied to study sociology, and considered fighting the case in court. Not long afterwards, while travelling back north by bus, Murray and a friend were arrested and imprisoned for refusing to sit in the seats at the back – some fifteen years before Rosa Parks made civil rights history with a similar protest in Montgomery, Alabama. Murray might have had a legal case to fight the discrimination, but the authorities in Virginia fell back on the less divisive charge of disorderly conduct rather than violating segregation laws, and let the friends go.

Increasingly, Murray was coming to believe that politics and the law, rather than direct action, was the way to advance racial justice. In 1941, she enrolled at Howard University, a historically Black institution in Washington D.C., where the rest of her classmates were African-American men. Abruptly, her race faded from view and her gender – at least, the official one – came into prominence. She found herself facing the same old problem: being seen without being understood. But her influence was beginning to be felt more widely. After the First Lady, Eleanor Roosevelt, gave a speech at the University of North Carolina praising the school's commitment to social progress, Murray wrote a furious letter in response, detailing her own exclusion. Roosevelt wrote back, and the two began a correspondence that deepened into friendship after they made common cause in a failed campaign to prevent the execution of a poor Black farmer in 1942. Murray and the First Lady, despite their many differences, remained close throughout their lives.

While at Howard, Pauli Murray found her voice as a writer and poet, especially in her response to the outbursts of racist violence – so-called 'race riots' – in Detroit and Harlem in 1943, over which she excoriated President Roosevelt for his inaction. She published *Dark Testament*, a remarkable long poem that narrated the history of Black life in America, from the African villages where people were captured and then sold, to the horrors of the slave ship and the 'selling-block'. In her poem, the idealistic vision of an America that welcomed immigrants from all over the world is quickly 'twisted' into violence against Native Americans and the installation of capitalist logic, as 'planters bargained with traders/traders bargained with slavers' who, in turn, looked to Africa for human plunder. From this violent origin story, and its ongoing brutality – 'the hate, the old hate, keeps grinding on' – there emerges a desperate hope, a 'song in a weary throat' that would later become the title of her autobiography. Hope, for Murray, was rooted in her religious faith, which taught two inviolable truths: that all people are equal in the eyes of God, and that no human can truly be 'owned' by another.

Murray graduated first in her class at Howard, but when she applied to Harvard for further study, again it was sex-based discrimination that barred her way. Earnestly – more earnestly than the trustees could know – she begged, 'Gentlemen, I would gladly change my sex to meet your requirements.' They did not change their minds. So, instead, she went to Berkeley, California, for a master's degree, and returned to New York fully qualified as a lawyer, but found firms unwilling to hire a woman – let alone a Black one. She was now responsible not only for herself but also for her aunt Pauline, who had retired and moved north to live with her. So she took short-term jobs with progressive organisations. One task, a commission from the Methodist church, was to compile all the nation's racist segregation laws into one volume. Intended to help ministers comply with local statutes, it ballooned to a 700-page guide that laid bare the absurd, almost infinite variety of oppressions under Jim Crow. For the lawyers later working to overturn those laws, thanks to Pauli Murray's vision, *States' Laws on Race and Color* became a bible.

In the 1950s, Murray found a measure of stability. Although treatments for gender dysphoria were now being discussed and becoming more widely available – thanks in part to the widely publicised case of Christine Jorgensen, an 'all-American GI' who underwent sex reassignment surgery in Denmark in the early 1950s – Murray no longer sought out medical treatment for herself. It's possible that she had come to see her gender, and its rejection of binaries, as a strength which helped her resist and challenge all other boundaries that constrained people. She also found relief in the diagnosis and treatment of her hyperthyroidism – one physical cause of her thin frame and constantly racing heart – which calmed her without slackening the pace of her thinking.

In the middle of the decade Murray found a professional home at a New York law firm that set out to hire a diverse staff. It was there that she met Irene 'Renee' Barlow, a Yorkshire-born, British woman who was the office manager and who offered her love and acceptance for the first time. They never lived together as a couple, but shared a deep bond rooted in shared faith, commitment to family and a sense of being an outsider. Corporate law, however, did not hold Murray's interest for long, and in 1960 she took a job teaching law in the recently independent nation of Ghana, until increasing political unrest cut short her stay.

The women's movement in the U.S. took many cues from the fight for racial justice, and Pauli Murray, through her concept of Jane Crow, made the connection explicit. Shortly after her return from Ghana, in 1961, President John F. Kennedy included Murray on his committee assessing the status of women, and she began pushing for changes to American law that would guarantee women the same rights and privileges as men. Later in the decade, she joined a multiracial coalition in founding the National Organization for Women, the leading advocacy group of second-wave feminism, despite the dissonance of placing herself in that specifically gendered box. Her presence, at least at first, pointed to an inclusive vision, but she became disillusioned when the class and race biases of its predominantly white leaders began to exclude the poorest and most disadvantaged women. By that point, she had scored yet another first in her own career, when she became the first African American (of any gender) to earn a doctorate in law from Yale University. She was appointed a professor of law and politics at Brandeis University in Massachusetts – her most stable and high-earning job in a life of professional scrambling. In 1970, at the age of sixty, her collected poems were published – seemingly reconciling the warrior and the poet in such a way as to celebrate both.

It was not, however, the final turn in the course of her life. That came two years later, when Murray quit her job as a professor to enter the General Theological Seminary in New York. She was, yet again, the first Black woman to be ordained by the Episcopal church. Despite the very different nature of the work, she faced obstacles in her new career that mirrored the challenges of qualifying as a lawyer, including finding a permanent position that paid her enough to live comfortably. She gave sermons wherever she could, travelling widely in the stylish secondhand Mercedes she was able to buy after convincing a publisher to reissue *Proud Shoes*, first published in 1956 – she always prized car ownership for the freedom it offered from the hated public bus. But in 1982, church rules forced her into retirement. In her final years, she moved to Pittsburgh to be close to an old friend, and embarked with her on a cross-country train journey. She was finishing edits to her autobiography and increasingly being feted for her accomplishments by universities around the country, when a sudden and aggressive cancer took hold.

Song in a Weary Throat was published posthumously in 1987. In it, Pauli Murray articulated the belief that had guided her life: the vital necessity of 'a society in which individuals were free to express their multiple origins and to share their variety of cultural strains without being forced into a categorical mo[u]ld'. Across law, education, activism, the church and government, she made her case for radical inclusivity, and her fight was fired up anew by every door that was barred to her. Yet as a document of her personal life, the book withheld any mention of the private battles that shaped her. She could not have predicted the next four decades of growing visibility and backlash for queer and trans people, but she might have recognised the shape of that advance and retreat from her lifetime of fighting other battles. As she showed time and again, those battles were all versions of the same fundamental fight to see, acknowledge and welcome everyone, regardless of difference.

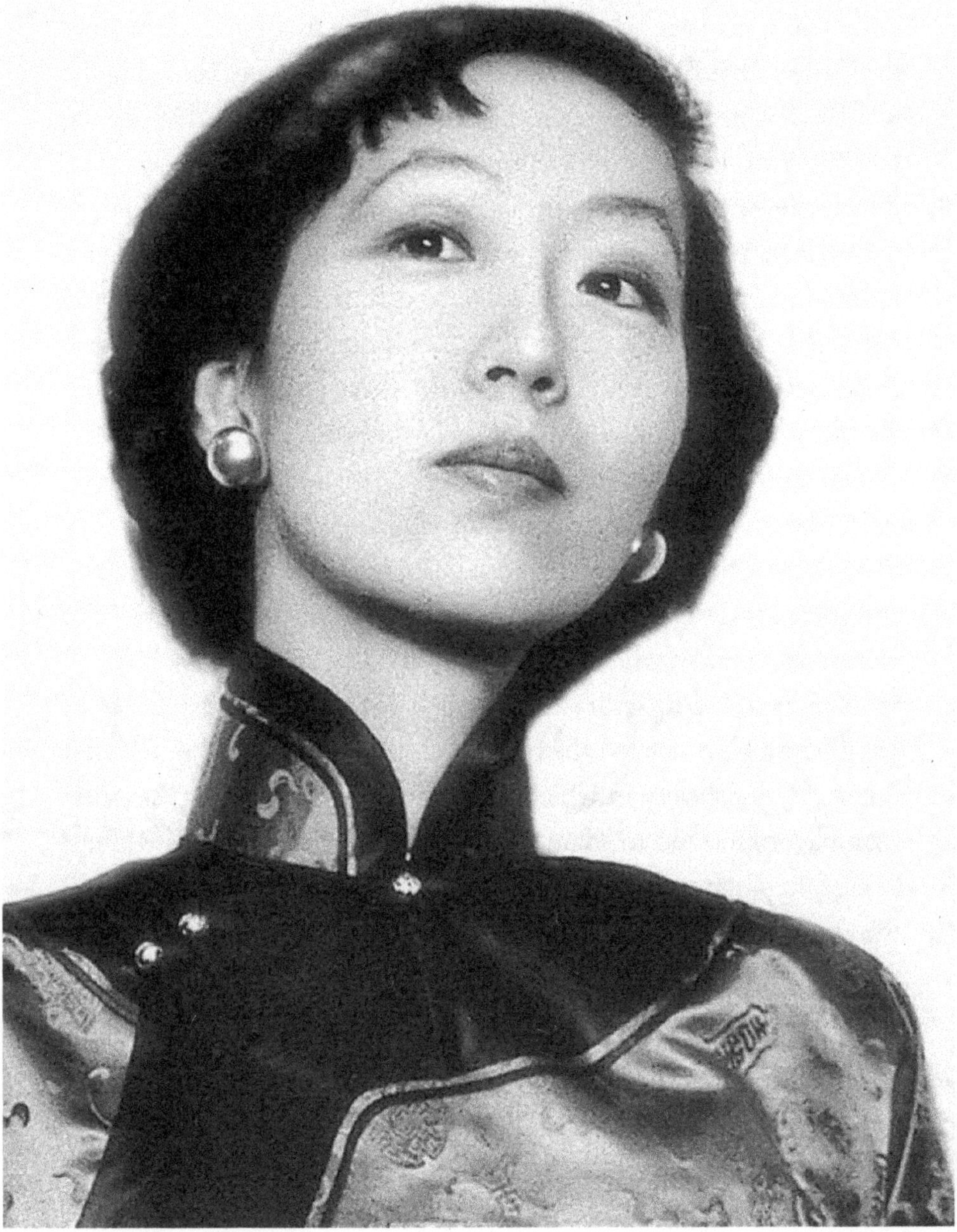

'All a writer can strive for is to live with integrity.'

EILEEN CHANG
(1920–1995)

By the time Eileen Chang died, alone in a sparsely furnished studio apartment in Los Angeles, she was a cult figure who had faded to a literary footnote. Her fan base was small and passionate, but to her detractors, she was a relic of imperial China and the decadent world that had otherwise sunk into myth. After early stardom as a prolific and self-consciously modern woman writer during the years of the Second World War, she left her homeland for good in the mid-1950s. Her early life was shaped by large forces far beyond her control so it is no wonder that, in her stories, she often channelled a kind of fatalism, creating characters resigned to the whims of power, resisting only as far as their sharp eyes and sharp tongues allowed.

Eileen was born into an uncertain world, and her upbringing tracked profound changes in China's fortunes, its identity as a nation and its place in the world. A few years prior to her birth in 1920, the last emperor of the Qing dynasty was overthrown. The Republic of China that was declared in place of the empire attempted to bridge the gap between the insular, hierarchical past and the rocketing adventure of modernity by embracing

Western values and concepts, such as democracy, loyalty to the nation-state and the protection of individual and women's rights. But before long, the First World War ripped the optimistic veil off the systems of capitalism and industrialisation. In its wake, the Chinese republic saw its own rights and territory trampled by Japanese interests, sparking fears inside the country of weakness and national decline. The centralised government faced constant threats from warlords determined to seize power in their provinces.

Chang's parents embodied the forward-and-backward tugging of her country between the world wars. Her father was descended from statesmen and aristocrats, but instead of wielding political power, he preferred to wallow in unearned privilege, losing his days to opium, keeping a concubine, and exerting his will over his women with his fists. By contrast with the decadent aristocrat she married, Chang's mother was a modern woman. The family, who spent time living in Tianjin, returned to Shanghai when Eileen was eight, living in a Western-style house. Despite his promises, her father's drug use and philandering continued, and he was committed to a hospital to treat his addiction after a morphine overdose. Freed from his shadow, for a time, Eileen studied music, art and English. 'That was probably the only time in my life when I luxuriated in the stylish ways of a pampered foreign girl,' she wrote in one of her earliest autobiographical essays, 'Whispers'.

The rift between her mother's modern ideas and her father's decadence was violently irreconcilable. 'They would fight with such fierce intensity that the servants were frightened into removing the children from the scene of battle,' she recalled. 'At such times, my little brother and I would sit quietly on the terrace on our little tricycles, without making a sound. It was late spring, and the terrace was shaded by a green bamboo trellis, striping the ground with sunlight.' Her laser-sharp attention to surface detail, especially at times of great stress, is a hallmark of her writing.

When she was ten years old, and to her great relief, Chang's parents divorced, and Eileen's world was cleaved in two: her mother's bright, modern apartment – the first place she saw a gas stove and a built-in bathtub – and the 'languorous, faded, dust-laden way of life' at her father's house. Yet she felt torn. Despite hating the backwardness at her father's house and the opium, 'I liked the sunlight filtering through clouds of opium smoke, hovering like a fog over an untidy room strewn with stacks of tabloids.' Paper stacks would continue, throughout her life, to give her 'the sensation of having come home'.

But when her father remarried, the tenuous bond between him and his bookish daughter snapped. After fighting with her stepmother, her father locked her in her room for several months, even refusing her treatment for severe gastroenteritis. 'I clasped my hands so tightly around the railings of the balcony that I might have squeezed water from wood,' she recalled of her imprisonment. It was 1937, and Shanghai was reeling under the Japanese aerial bombardment that destroyed much of the city. Eileen looked up into the bright blue sky, buzzing with airplanes, and willed a bomb to drop.

She managed to escape her father's house, but the machinations of global conflict did not let her go. The outbreak of the Second World War scuppered her plan to study English literature in London and she enrolled at the university of Hong Kong instead. Two years later, the Japanese invasion of Hong Kong shut it down. And so she returned to the 'bright little apartment' in the now Japanese-occupied Shanghai that her mother shared with her aunt. The Republic of China had been reduced to a puppet regime administered from Nanjing by the collaborationist Wang Jingwei, and Shanghai had become a place of scarcity and suspicion. The repressive atmosphere silenced many of the city's most prominent writers, or sent them into exile, and people were hungry for any kind of diversion. Chang, as her translator Karen Kingsbury put it, 'stepped into that silence like a diva entering the limelight'. She began contributing cultural commentary to an English-language journal, which praised 'young miss Chang' for her witty interpretations of Chinese culture for foreigners. Then, in search of a bigger readership, she translated her English writing into Chinese and published it again in some of the city's leading newspapers.

With a glamorous image enhanced by the stylish outfits she designed herself, Chang set out to be a sensation. She was tireless, turning her attention to subjects as diverse as Impressionist painting, the history of fashion and the constrained lives of the women she saw around her in the city, 'whose lives are consumed in talking about men, thinking about men, resenting men, now and forever'. In her fiction, she was influenced by the writers she'd read in English at university, such as D.H. Lawrence and Aldous Huxley, as well as by the insights of Freud and the glamour of Hollywood in its 1930s golden age. These cosmopolitan flourishes built on her thorough knowledge of Chinese culture and literature, and allowed her to create a vernacular literature that felt authentic and daringly modern. Within a single year, Chang published five novellas and innumerable stories and essays which were collected in two book-length collections late in the war, when their author was still just twenty-four.

With fame came attention from men – like Hu Lancheng, a prominent fellow writer some fifteen years her senior. They began an affair and she became his fourth wife (of five) in 1944, but the union barely slowed down his chronic infidelities. As a propaganda minister in the puppet government, Hu was a figure of suspicion, and his actions would taint Chang by association, even after the end of their short-lived marriage in 1946. The years of her marriage were her most prolific, during which she took seriously the implication of the title of her collection *Written on Water* – that life and history were flowing so fast it was impossible to leave a lasting mark.

Where she did speak directly about life under occupation, it was not to make political judgements – a dangerous task, even if she had wanted to – but rather to describe small, fleeting incidents that revealed the connection between individual human choices and the larger inhumanity of history. In a short essay called 'Beating People', she records a policeman beating a teenage boy with a knotted rope in broad daylight 'for no reason save his own momentary whim'. The watching narrator, who admits that she has a 'talent' for not seeing what she doesn't want to see, nevertheless finds herself unable to look away and fixes the policeman 'with a fierce and cutting stare'. But far from falling dead at her gaze, the man is puffed up, even aroused by her attention: 'With an exultant air, he adjusted the leather belt cinched around his waist.' The revenge she imagines for this brutality is not political – a popular uprising, perhaps – but intensely personal, a fantasy of becoming the man's superior, or 'the First Lady', who would be free to 'march over and slap' the policeman. At the same time, she recognises that, while this vengeance might feel justified, in reality it would be nothing more than another, equally unjustified exercise of power.

To her detractors, who grew louder after the war, Eileen Chang was a superficial writer, who ignored the horrors of war and occupation to focus on the emotional lives of the social elite. Her refusal to engage in political commentary may have been a survival tactic, but she also believed that writers ought not to stray far from the subjects they truly cared about, and that, like trees, they are strongest where they are rooted in native ground. 'A real writer can only really write about what he himself thinks,' she argued. 'He will write about what he can write; what a writer should or should not write is ultimately beside the point.'

After the defeat of Japan at the end of the Second World War, China remained embroiled in an increasingly broad and destructive civil war between the nationalist government and the Chinese

Communists, until Mao Zedong declared the creation of the People's Republic of China in the autumn of 1949. As a violently repressive new era dawned, Chang's visibility as a writer, her elite family background and her refusal to bend her writing to the will of power combined to make her vulnerable. Three years later, the pressure drove her from her beloved Shanghai for the last time, and the government banned her writing for the next three decades.

Chang went first to Hong Kong, where she worked as a translator for the anti-Communist United States Information Agency, producing Chinese-language versions of canonical works of American literature by writers like Ralph Waldo Emerson and Ernest Hemingway, and translating Chinese publications into English. During this period, she wrote and published two novels in English, which were a marked departure from her slick, wry, metropolitan stories. *The Rice Sprout Song* and *Naked Earth* explored the Communist government's land reform policies of the 1950s and their impact on ordinary families, highlighting the gulf between the high-minded purpose of the redistribution policy, which sought to wrest land from owners and return it to the people who worked on it, and the widespread suffering that resulted. The novels celebrated peasant culture and sympathised with those who had long been oppressed by their landlords and were now being encouraged to exact violent revenge. It's unclear how much time, if any, this resolutely urban writer spent immersed in the rural world she depicts, and there is some debate as to how far the U.S. government was involved in the creation of these novels. Some scholars argue that they were directly commissioned by the Information Agency to promote an anti-Communist message, albeit with Chang claiming a significant amount of authorial freedom. Whatever the genesis of the books, the author's work with the agency helped secure her permission to emigrate to the United States in 1955.

Although she continued to enjoy a passionate following in Hong Kong, Taiwan and among Chinese expatriates, Eileen Chang struggled to achieve literary success in America. If people there read Chinese stories at all, they were not looking for sharp psychological tales of urban alienation. Rather, they gravitated to the works of Pearl S. Buck, author of the sweeping family saga *The Good Earth*, which earned her both the Pulitzer and the Nobel Prize for Literature in 1938. The daughter of American missionaries, Buck grew up from babyhood in China and lived there until the early 1930s, so used her own observations and memories of Chinese rural life to craft her fiction. A powerful blend of sympathy and stereotype, *The Good Earth* helped sway readers' hearts toward her adoptive home as tensions built with the Japanese over the course of the decade. When the Communist regime rose to power, however, Buck found herself judged an 'American cultural imperialist' by the new leadership. Like Chang, she saw her work banned in China and was refused entry to the country for the rest of her life.

Despite the challenges of finding an audience, Eileen Chang kept writing, issuing her essays and translations through her Taiwanese publisher. But although she worked over and rewrote many of her earlier pieces of memoir and fiction, she did not produce much new fiction in America. After marrying an American writer, Ferdinand Reyher, she moved frequently around the country with him until his death in 1967.

In Los Angeles, where she spent her later years, Chang found work as a screenwriter, but increasingly withdrew from the world. The reports of her death in 1995 spurred a renewal of interest in her work, especially among a new generation less personally connected to, and scarred by, the events of the Communist Revolution and its cultural crackdowns. These readers connected with her cool, witty tales, in part because they refused to reduce the complexity of human lives to black-and-white political polarisation.

A little more than a decade after Chang's death, even greater attention followed the Taiwanese director Ang Lee's adaptation of her short story 'Lust, Caution' into an acclaimed film. The tale follows an innocent young student in Hong Kong on the eve of the Second World War who is swept up in a plot, with the members of her university drama group, to ensnare and assassinate a collaborationist official. They pursue the plan first in a kind of immersive dress rehearsal, which ends in bloody failure. Three years later in Shanghai, the group reunites to stage the deadly serious, emotionally wrenching performance.

The film is a gorgeous modern noir, that fills in the gaps in Chang's restrained, deflective writing with bursts of graphic violence and sex. But although the adaptation focuses intently on clothing and visuals, it cannot interpret them the way Chang does through words in her story, which spends a great deal more time 'reading' clothing than it does explaining characters' relationships or histories. The messages embedded in fashion – the price of fabrics, clothes and soft furnishings – communicate richly to the women who can speak that language, while passing utterly unnoticed by the men who cannot. While the heroine Chia-chih plays Mahjong with the wives of functionaries in the puppet government, she describes their black capes secured with heavy gold chains. These signify wealth and power – especially as the occupation has spiked the price of gold – while also, because the chains have a functional purpose, avoiding 'the taint of vulgar ostentation'. These clothing choices and how Chia-chih interprets them tell the reader everything we need to know about these women, but on film, some of the layers are inevitably lost.

During the climactic scene of the story, the heroine lures Mr Yee – the target of the assassination, who has become her lover – to a jeweller's shop. She contemplates him as he's picking out a rare, expensive pink diamond for her, and considers whether she has fallen in love, despite her 'fierce scepticism' toward the idea. Since her mid-teens, she tells us, she has been 'fully occupied in repelling romantic offensives', and has thus 'built up a powerful resistance to forming emotional attachments'. This military-infused language of offensives and resistance is doubly ironic given the setting – the jeweller's shop is where she has tipped off the Resistance to assassinate him, while he is undefended. Watching his 'sorrowful smile', an expression of unexpected happiness, Chia-chih reads in it his love for her. Shocked into feeling and action, she tells him to run, knowing that doing so is to sign her own and her fellow resistors' death warrants – literally, with her lover's pen. The film gives us no final word from Mr Yee as to his feelings or regrets, but Chang's narrative in the book seamlessly shifts to his perspective as he reassures himself that the swift executions of the would-be assassins were necessary to maintain secrecy. His own doubts about the progress of the war and his own fate are soothed by the sense that having loved Chia-chih, he can die without regret. And, further, that by executing her he has turned her into a ghost, who is his own possession more thoroughly in death than her body was in life. 'She must have hated him at the end,' he concedes to himself. 'But real men have to be ruthless. She wouldn't have loved him if he'd been the sentimental type.' Which, of course, he is – it is only through sentiment that he became vulnerable to the Resistance scheme at all.

As Chang demonstrates throughout her work, sentiment and ruthlessness belong together, and one can flip into the other without warning – much like the opposing forces that shaped her life: peace and war, loyalty and treason, good and evil. For this reason, she does not offer up heroes and villains who reliably belong on one side or other of a moral fence. This nuance makes her a prickly and unpredictable writer, especially on subjects like war and nationalism, where the urge for black-and-white thinking is especially strong. But, for that reason alone, she remains a vital voice.

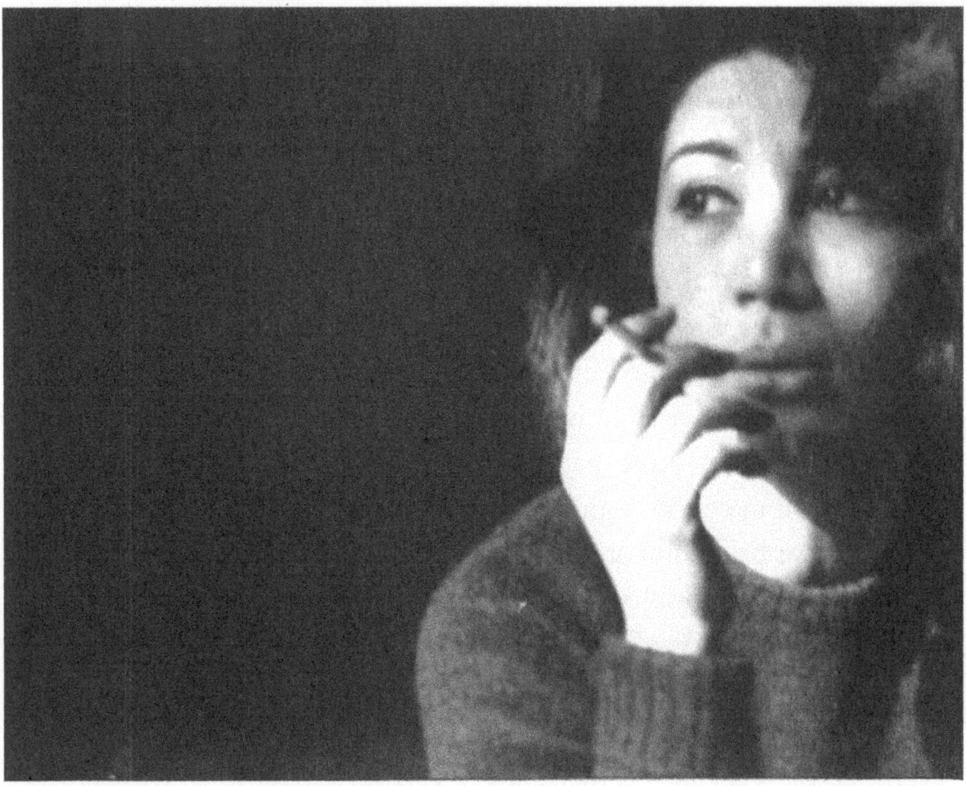

'Perhaps because no woman before me took steps toward breaking the shackles binding women's hands and feet, and because I am the first to do so, they have made such a controversy out of me.'

FOROUGH FARROKHZAD
(1934–1967)

In 1954, a nineteen-year-old woman walked unannounced into the literary editor's office at *Roshanfekr* (The Intellectual), one of Iran's most prestigious magazines. Her fingers were stained with green ink, and she trembled with nerves as she handed over three poems. One of them, the twelve-line 'Sin', described in explicit detail her affair with the magazine's editor-in-chief. Different translations give different nuances to the opening of the poem: 'I have sinned a rapturous sin/in a warm enflamed embrace' (Sholeh Wolpé); or 'I have sinned, a delectable sin,/In an embrace which was ardent, like fire' (Hasan Javadi and Susan Sallée); or 'I sinned/it was a most lustful sin/I sinned in arms sturdy as iron,/hot like fire and vengeful' (Farzaneh Milani). Across these variations, there are a few scandalous constants: the heat, the embrace, the pleasure and the boldly unashamed 'I'. The speaker declares herself as a sinner, but there is no repentance in the poem, no punishment. She is not her lover's victim, but a joyous co-conspirator, exhilarated by her power to arouse him: 'Lust enflamed his eyes,/red wine trembled in the cup,/my body, naked and drunk,/quivered softly on his breast' (Wolpé).

The magazine printed the poem. At a time when many Iranian poets wrote under pseudonyms, the author of 'Sin' not only used her real name, but her poem appeared alongside her photograph and a short biography, which revealed her to be a married mother of a two-year-old son. It also described her physical appearance in sexualised terms, drawing attention to her 'dishevelled hair' and 'penetrating eyes'. Here was a young woman confessing to a sexual awakening in the arms of a man who was not her husband, a provocative invocation and inversion of Persian literary tradition, which for hundreds of years had been rich in sensual poetry written by men – and only men – about their lovers. The accompanying biography collapsed any distance between the loving wife and the libidinous poet, implying that this was not a work of imagination, but a report on experience that would make male readers wonder what their own wives might be getting up to.

Few poetic debuts can have exacted as high a price as Forough Farrokhzad's. Men in Iran were free to take other wives and have lovers, but an adulterous woman was taking her life into her hands – she could be killed for her transgression and her killers would go barely punished. Even if she escaped violence, she could be punished in other ways, as Farrokhzad would discover. When she divorced her husband not long after 'Sin' was published, the decision cost her custody of her son, Kamyar. The stress of that loss pushed her to a breakdown and a suicide attempt, after which she spent a month in a psychiatric institution and underwent electroshock therapy. She was forced to choose, in effect, between her child and her art. The anguished 1957 'Poem For You', dedicated to her son, ends with the hope that their connection can somehow live on through her poetry: 'You will search for me in my words/and tell yourself: My mother, that is who she was.'

Farrokhzad is sometimes called the Persian Sylvia Plath because the two overlapped in era, style and untimely death – in Farrokhzad's case, a car accident at the age of thirty-two. Although the two writers did not read each other's language, they both grew up cramped within their cultures' reductive and repressive visions of women, from which they managed to break free and write. In their poetry, Plath and Farrokhzad register the struggle to hold onto the artistic self under the pressures of marriage, motherhood and mental illness. Both deploy the ambivalent image of the mirror, a gendered symbol of vanity as well as a deceptive tool for self-examination.

In Farrokhzad's poems 'The Forgotten' and 'The Broken Mirror', a female speaker waits for her lover, gazing at her reflection and questioning the point of beauty in the absence of a man to admire it. In the first poem, the speaker calls on her mother to 'break this mirror' as she realises she has been abandoned, demanding 'what do I gain by adorning myself?' In the latter, it is the mirror itself that listens to the tale, and the mirror that ends up destroying itself, crying out that the woman's 'woes' have broken its heart. In her poem 'The Mirror', written around five years later, Sylvia Plath turns the perspective around. The mirror is the speaker, and an implacable witness to a woman's quest for the truth about who she is below the surface: 'I am not cruel, only truthful/The eye of a little god, four-cornered.' The conflict between appearances and value, between the eyes of the world and the truth of the soul, would mark both Plath's and Farrokhzad's lives and work indelibly.

A pretty, rebellious child, Forough Farrokhzad was born into an upper-middle-class family in Tehran in January 1935, one of seven surviving children of a strict, military-minded father and his much younger wife. She went to a co-educational elementary school, which was unusual for the time, and then a technical high school, where she studied painting and dressmaking. Her mother was obsessed with dolls, surrounding herself with them in the home and petitioning (unsuccessfully) to be buried with her favourites. One of Farrokhzad's most powerful poems, 'The Wind-Up Doll', equates femininity to the glass-eyed doll, immobilised 'inside a felt box/body stuffed with straw,/wrapped in layers of dainty lace.' With its enforced blindness and silence, the claustrophobia of its lace-trimmed confinement, the doll evokes the superficial beauty and docility demanded of women in a patriarchal society. The doll, or the doll-like woman, has no choice over how she is handled or used, but is under the constant obligation to be pleasant and grateful: 'With every salacious squeeze of one's hand,/for no reason one can cry:/Ah, how blessed, how happy I am!'

The Iran of Farrokhzad's childhood was a nation whiplashing between the medieval and the modern. As one of her translators, Farzaneh Milani, puts it, Tehran was 'a city of mosques and cabarets, designer clothes and chadors'. For women, this era of rapid change was especially disorienting. Just after Farrokhzad was born, the Shah's pro-Western regime passed a law banning the hijab, and schools and universities began to open their doors to women. But, even as the possibilities for women expanded, patriarchal ideas and systems lingered. Marriage was still meant to be the main goal of a woman's life, although it spelled dependence and domestic seclusion. As a teenager, Forough fell in love with her older neighbour, a distant relative of her mother's, and a satirist and cartoonist who worked for the ministry of finance. The couple married over the objections of both families, and Farrokhzad later said, 'that ridiculous marriage at the age of sixteen destroyed my future life.'

Her first collection, *Captive*, published in 1955, did not include the incendiary 'Sin', but still had poems that spoke openly, and shockingly, of the conflict between artistic freedom and domestic confinement, which was sharpened by the intensity of maternal love: 'O sky, if I want one day/To fly from this silent prison,/what shall I say to the weeping child's eyes:/forget about me, for I am a captive bird?' The poems are addressed to unnamed men, the captive speaker's loving jailers, who are both her oppressors and the objects of her desire.

In the book's afterword, Farrokhzad wrote that she expected her poems to be controversial, '[p]erhaps because no woman before me took steps toward breaking the shackles binding women's hands and feet'. But isolated controversies only build into sensations – moments into movements – through the raising of many voices together. In the late 1950s and early 1960s, women all over the world were beginning to identify that same sense of confinement, and experience that same longing for freedom. The American feminist Betty Friedan would memorably call this 'the problem that has no name'. To name the problem and to voice the struggle would strike a blow for women's liberation, but men still held the power.

Forough Farrokhzad dedicated *The Wall*, her second collection, to her ex-husband, calling the book a 'worthless gift' that she hoped he would receive as a token of her gratitude – and in return, grant her access to her son. If the self-abasing gesture was intended to soften him, it didn't work – he and his family continued to enforce their separation and cut off her visitation rights. Farrokhzad left Iran soon afterward, scraping together the money to take a cargo plane to Italy and then to Germany, where she studied languages and poetry. The relative cultural freedom she felt over her several months in Europe was liberating, and her next poetry collection, *Rebellion*, shows her laying claim to a bolder poetic identity that fused her experience as a woman with her Persian literary heritage. But it was hard to shake the weight of her scandalous beginnings. On her return, she published *Dar Diyari Digar* (Elsewhere), an eight-part account of her journey to Italy, in an Iranian literary magazine. In this thoughtful, self-reflective narrative, which constantly questioned its own value, she made it clear that her journey had been undertaken as part of her recovery from the trauma of her separation from her son and suicide attempt. Nevertheless, she found herself once again attacked as a licentious hedonist.

In 1958, missing her own language and people, and in need of money, Farrokhzad returned to Iran. Through mutual friends, she met the filmmaker and intellectual Ebrahim Golestan, who offered her a job filing and answering phones at his large studio in northern Tehran. Golestan was married, but a few months after she began working for him, they embarked on an intense affair that would continue for the rest of her life. Golestan left Iran in 1975 and has lived in England ever since. In 2017, he broke a fifty-year silence to speak about his relationship with Forough. 'We were very close, but I can't measure how much I had feelings for her,' he told the *Guardian*. 'How can I? In kilos? In metres?' Although he has often been credited with influencing Farrokhzad's best poetry and inspiring her interest in film, Golestan denied this, saying 'she had the biggest influence on herself'. Farrokhzad herself once claimed to respect poetry 'in the very same way that religious people respect religion', and Golestan likewise compared her to a 'seminary student', dedicated monastically to her art. 'I never saw her in a state of not being productive,' he said.

While she was working at Golestan's studio, Farrokhzad developed the project that would result in her short 1962 documentary, *The House Is Black*, made in collaboration with a leprosy charity. The film would prove transformative both creatively and personally. After an initial visit to a leprosarium in Tabriz County, she returned three months later with a five-man crew and lived among the residents for twelve days, observing and capturing their lives on film. Her immersion in the colony was such that she went on to adopt a young boy, Hossein Mansouri – he now lives in Germany and has translated her poetry into German.

The twenty-two-minute film, which is available online, is intimate and unflinching, reflecting Farrokhzad's interest in states of imprisonment and the lives of social pariahs. In long takes training the camera on faces of all ages, she invites the viewer to see the people instead of their condition. The film opens with the image of a veiled, disfigured face reflected in a mirror edged with flowers – a continuation of the mirror imagery that appears throughout Farrokhzad's poetry. The voiceover narration poses philosophical and religious questions about the nature of ugliness, before giving a more straightforward account of the symptoms and treatment of leprosy. Emphasising that the disease is made worse by poverty and can be managed by hands-on care, the voiceover plays over uncomfortable images of patients undergoing treatment. But then the visuals change in tenor, showing us patients receiving physical therapy; children and babies playing; music and celebrations; and women preparing food, brushing one another's hair, and applying heavy kohl. Through the tight focus on a small group of people in an unfamiliar, isolated world, Farrokhzad manages to gesture at the much larger story of how societies function, how people thrive in communities, and how beauty can grow out of deprivation.

The poetry collection she published two years later, titled *Another Birth* (*Reborn* in some translations), is dedicated to Ebrahim Golestan and is considered, by critics and by Farrokhzad herself, to be her most accomplished. In this collection, her intensely personal gaze widens to encompass Iranian politics and society at large. The long poem 'O Bejeweled Land!' takes its title from a patriotic song, and satirises government bureaucracy and the reduction of human life to a name and number on an ID card: 'long live number 678, precinct 5, Tehran.' Everything is reduced to this number 678: poets, nightingales, plastic roses, 'faddish electric kebab grills', Rolex watches, and '678 lungs-full of air smelling/of shit, garbage, and piss'. In an interview after the collection was published, Farrokzhad explained her impulse to present an unvarnished picture of the world around her. 'When I want to talk about a street which is full of the smell of urine, I can't put a list of perfumes in front of me and choose the most fragrant one to describe this smell. This is deceit, which man first practices on himself and then on others.'

The year before her death, Farrokhzad wrote to Golestan to tell him, with a kind of ironic prescience, 'I love you to an extent that I am terrified what to do [sic] if you disappeared suddenly. I'll become like an empty well.' In the end, it was Farrokhzad who disappeared – killed in a car accident on the way home from her mother's house on February 14, 1967. Her work survived, passed around in secret after the 1979 revolution, when it was banned and then heavily censored. In recent years, Forough's status as a rebel icon has only risen in Iran, where she's usually identified just by her first name. Her words continue to resonate powerfully, especially her work linking women's personal experiences with political protest, which became more overt in the early 1960s, amid an atmosphere of increased protest against the Shah's unpopular and oppressive regime. Her poem 'Red Rose', for example, compares a baby growing in the womb to a 'red rose/red/like a flag in/an uprising'.

Since 2022, Farrokhzad's words and her image have frequently been invoked by protestors in the 'Woman, Life, Freedom' movement, which surged up in protest at the death in custody of a young Kurdish woman, Mahsa (Jina) Amini, in September of that year, following her arrest by Iran's so-called 'modesty police', allegedly for incorrectly wearing her hijab. Responding specifically to Amini's death, but also to the government's recent crackdowns on abortion and birth control, and its harsh new penalties for appearing unveiled in public, these protests, in Iran and around the world, have featured women publicly cutting off their hair or burning the hijab – taking aim at these loaded symbols of femininity. The influential Iranian artist and filmmaker Shirin Neshat created a new digital artwork, projected in London and Los Angeles in late 2022, to express solidarity with the protestors. The piece reworked her 1993 photograph 'Unveiling', in which a woman in a chador appears with text from Forough's poetry superimposed across her face. It remains unclear whether the 'Woman, Life, Freedom' protests will lead to greater freedom for women in Iran, but there is no doubt that the authorities are well aware of the risks to their power of women speaking openly, and following Farrokhzad's call, to 'Seek your rights, Sister/From those who keep you weak,/From those whose myriad tricks and schemes/Keep you seated in a corner of the house.'

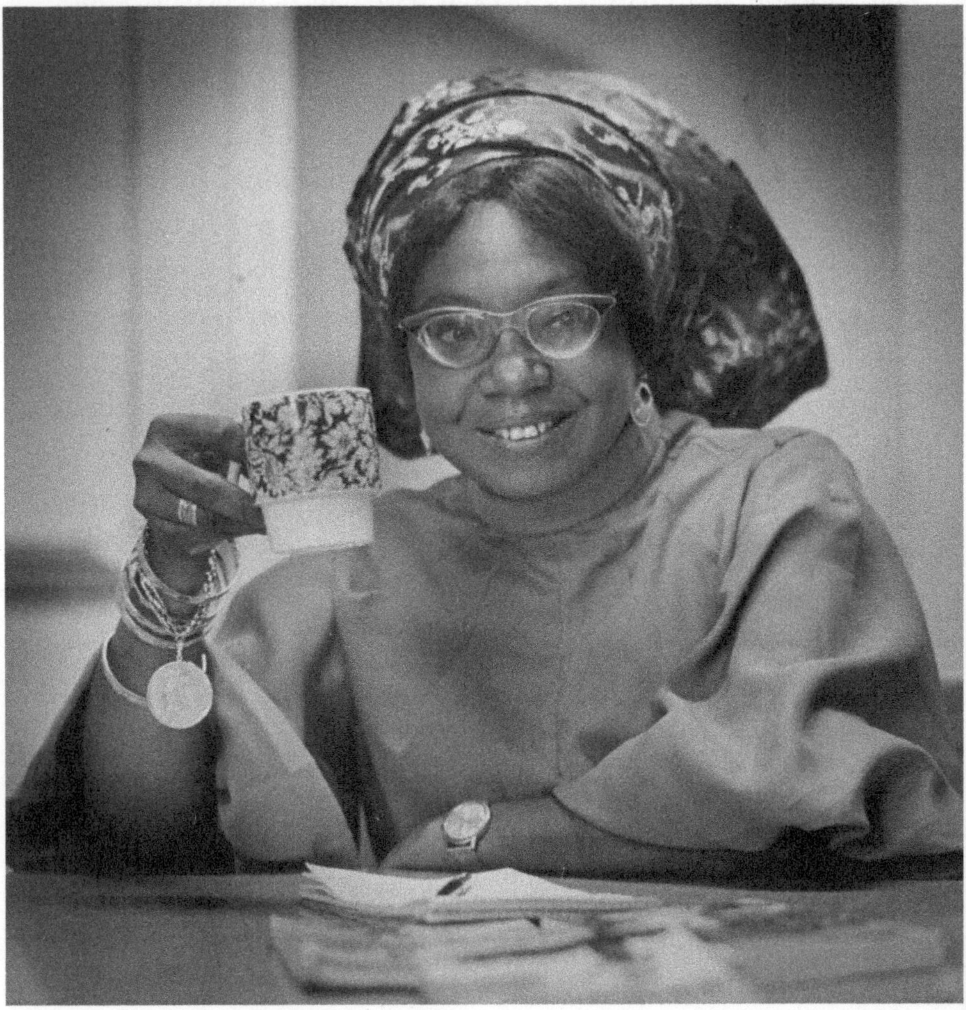

'You know women's conversation never ends.'

FLORA NWAPA
(1931–1993)

In her still-radical pacifist essay of 1938, *Three Guineas*, Virginia Woolf argued that nationalism and gender were fundamentally at odds. 'As a woman, I have no country,' she declared. 'As a woman, I want no country.' It was up to women, she believed, to recognise and resist the entwined forces of patriarchy and militarism, and to reject the false promise of patriotism. Barely two decades later, as former British colonies seized their independence after the cataclysm of the Second World War, nationalism had transformed into a source of identity and power for newly independent states. Modern post-colonial nations drew on an array of symbols and mythologies as they worked to unite the people within these new borders, bridging the gulfs of religion, region and tradition.

In this new world order, could women, too, claim their country? Or would they be claimed, against their will, as a symbol? Among post-colonial nations in Africa, the 'mother continent' who had the strength and desire to unite her children scattered in a global diaspora was a powerful idea. Yet the idealisation of the African mother as a symbol tended to obscure the absence of real women at the upper echelons of politics and power. The link Woolf had laid bare between patriotism and patriarchy held strong, and many new nations enforced rigid gender hierarchies under the banner of tradition. A mythic Mother Africa, no matter how venerated, was little comfort to individual women who were systematically excluded from the arenas of politics and literature – from power itself and the ability to pass judgement on it. A lack of educational opportunity and the sexist attitudes of both colonial and nationalist authorities combined to make female African writers a rarity, before and after their countries gained independence. Men's voices overwhelmed women's – an influential English-language anthology of 'African voices' published in 1958 included just two female authors among thirty-seven men. Even thirty years later, novelist Buchi Emecheta contrasted the attitudes to men and women writers in her native Nigeria, pointing out that the men were encouraged by friends and 'doting families' while aspiring women writers 'are invariably viewed with suspicion'. As a literature professor in Nigeria, her classes were exclusively male: further evidence that 'the world, especially the African world, still regards serious writing as a masculine preserve.'

Enter Flora Nwapa. Working at the University of Lagos in the years following Nigeria's independence in 1960, she found enough spare time to write short stories – one of which she boldly sent to the writer Chinua Achebe. His enormously influential novel *Things Fall Apart* had been published a few years earlier, in 1958, making him the internationally lauded voice of Nigerian history, culture and post-colonial promise. To Nwapa's surprise, Achebe's response was to give her moral and material support, and he encouraged her to send her work to his British publisher, Heinemann, for consideration in its African Writers series. Enclosed in his letter was one guinea, the cost of postage to London. Her first novel, *Efuru*, was published by

Heinemann in 1966. The author was thirty-five years old, and the first African woman to have a novel written in English and published internationally.

Like *Things Fall Apart*, Nwapa's novel depicts village life among the Igbo people of southeastern Nigeria during the era of colonisation. But unlike Achebe, Nwapa places the lives of rural women at the centre of the story. She crosses to the female side of the village to bring back stories that matter – about marriage, childbirth, and all the joy and pain that, buried within the supposedly trivial domestic experience, cut to the heart of human experience. In paying attention to women's voices, their relationships and their power, by representing them as full, complex and infinitely variable people, she subverts the stereotypes found in the writing of her male contemporaries, including Achebe, of victimhood and silence: women whose roles are confined to the kitchen, the nursery and the bedroom. 'The male writers have disappointed us a great deal by not painting the female character as they should paint them,' said Nwapa, who strove to place women in a 'positive' light. Her characters, however, are not simple.

Efuru tells the story of an unconventional Igbo woman, the beautiful and strong-willed daughter of a prominent tribal leader. 'One moonlit night' she meets and falls in love with a poor farmer, and runs away with him in defiance of convention – she does not wait for her family to investigate his and approve the match, nor for him to pay her bride price. When she moves into his house, the local community of women begins to buzz with speculation about why, how and with what consequence she has acted. The novel transmits tradition and superstition in a stream of chatter as the story unfolds through the discussions of women – especially between Efuru's mother-in-law and the latter's sister, Ajanupu, who delivers Efuru's baby daughter and becomes a mother figure to her.

'When the baby was five days old, Ajanupu told her sister that it was time to put alligator pepper in her mouth so that her tongue will be free. If this was not done, Ajanupu said, the baby might be deaf and dumb. So early the next morning, some alligator pepper was brought and Ajanupu chewed it very well and then put it under the tongue of the baby. The baby yelled and yelled. She was quickly breast-fed, and she stopped crying.

"Ajanupu, my daughter will talk like you. I am afraid she will be very talkative." Efuru's mother-in-law teased her sister.

"That is all right. Aren't you lucky that I am near to put alligator pepper in her mouth? Who wants to be quiet these days?"'

Nwapa's stories are built from women's talk, while the plot plays out, in a sense, offstage. The women's voices are constantly turning over what has happened, offering commentary and warning, like a Greek chorus in which individual voices emerge and retreat into the collective. Arguments repeat and events are retold – the telling and retelling both making and sustaining the community and its values. The women are never silent, but constantly gossiping and arguing, building and undoing the world through their speech, unheard by anyone but themselves.

Even though their lives are tightly bound by the limits of patriarchy, their conversations enliven experience within those confines, and reveal that information can be powerful. Everything is a subject: families, children, straying husbands, but also the price of goods and the vicissitudes of the market. The novel emphasises the vital economic role women play as market traders and supporters of the family, and the resulting potential for independence through savvy trading. While the distinction between men's and women's worlds may be wide, there is no simple division of public and private. Women's worlds encompass the domestic and the worldly, the home and the market, and Nwapa displays the fullness of their lives from the inside. As readers, we are invited in – as listeners, participants and fellow insiders.

Efuru is a character operating firmly within her culture, resisting some traditions and demands, and submitting to others, but her rebellions come at a cost. After her baby dies, her husband abandons her to marry another woman – news that she learns indirectly, through women's marketplace gossip. Efuru refuses to stay in her home and wait for him to come back to her, and instead returns to her father's house. She marries again, this time a comparatively elite, educated man, but the two cannot have children – a failing that was considered to be entirely a woman's responsibility. As her 'barrenness' becomes evident, Efuru's husband takes a second and then third wife. Efuru is comforted by becoming a chosen worshipper of the lake goddess Uhamiri, whose gifts include wealth and beauty but not children, although there is a note of uncertainty about the value of these gifts as compensations. Efuru dreams 'of the woman of the lake, her beauty, her long hair and her riches', but thinks, 'she had never experienced the joy of motherhood. Why then did the women worship her?' Her questions are indicative of the way that Efuru challenges Igbo values without fully rejecting them: she remains an obedient daughter and wife and accepts without question the practices of polygamy and cliterodectomy (removal of the clitoris, a form of female genital mutilation). Her story allows Nwapa to consider how women can pursue self-determination, happiness and power in the context of their traditional society.

Nwapa's specifically African vision of female solidarity also resonates beyond the novel. Although Efuru is not blessed with 'the joys of motherhood' by the goddess, this phrase from the end of the novel gave Buchi Emecheta the title of her 1979 novel, suggesting the existence of a powerful alternative lineage through women's literature. The contemporary Nigerian novelist Chimamanda Adichie has also credited Flora Nwapa, along with Chinua Achebe, as literary inspirations: 'If they had not written the books they did, when they did, and how they did, I would perhaps not have had the emotional courage to write my own books.'

Efuru does not place its events clearly in a historical setting, but nor does it depict a world untouched by European colonialism. Instead, Nwapa hints at the ways in which the community's traditions have already been irrevocably altered by the hierarchies of wealth and power that structure the village and, by extension, the elite English education reserved for wealthy sons. She also makes clear exactly how Efuru's family has earned its high status. When her father dies, his funeral is marked by the firing of cannons. 'No poor man could afford to fire seven rounds of a cannon in a day,' the narrator observes, adding that 'the shooting of the cannon did not only announce the death of a great man, but also announced that the great man's ancestors had dealings with the white men, who dealt in slaves.' The slave trade, the most brutal incursion of colonialism, often enlisted the support and collaboration of local people, and this detail pushes against any fantasy of rural African life as an Eden untouched by the white men's violence.

There is a fascinating historical backdrop to the novel's exploration of female power and justice in an event known as the Igbo Women's War. In late 1929, just over a year before Flora Nwapa was born, a huge contingent of Igbo women rose up to protest the corrupt, male-dominated Native Courts, a system set up by the British to dispense judgements and punishments across the southeastern provinces. Beginning as a revolt against taxes levied on women traders, the protest took a traditional form, known as 'sitting on' a man, which involved targeting a particular transgressor in a loud and public way. Women would band together to surround a man's home, damage his possessions, and loudly sing and shout his wrongs to the world. Traditionally, other men did not intervene, but let the women dispense their justice until the man in question had apologised and atoned for his crimes. However, when women launched their 'sitting' protest against the Warrant Chiefs, leaders of the Native Courts, the protestors were met with force. Soldiers and police, baffled and intimidated by the vehemence of the women, opened fire into the crowds, causing injuries and around fifty deaths. The scale of the protest and the speed of its organisation showed the power of women's collective action. In the aftermath, the British established a commission to report on the events, interviewing hundreds of witnesses, and recommending an overhaul of the court system. Colonial officers saw the protests as a sign of an 'organised sisterhood' of Igbo women and compared them to the actions of the militant British suffragettes. Mother Africa, these warring women had warned, could be not just a nurturer but an avenger.

Florence Nwanzuruahu Nkiru Nwapa, known as Flora, was born in January 1931, in the town of Oguta in southeastern Nigeria. She was the first daughter of six children born to a prominent Igbo family. Her father managed an exporting company and her mother was a teacher, who encouraged all her children to read widely. Flora absorbed a wealth of Victorian novels but was also influenced by a local feminine oral tradition: 'moonlight stories told by women in Oguta'. She attended a prestigious girls' high school, and at a time when women's university education was still unusual, went on to study English, history, and geography at University College, Ibadan. After graduating in 1957, she travelled to Edinburgh to study for a diploma in education, returning to Nigeria on the eve of its independence to teach and work in university administration. She had three children, the younger two from her marriage, in 1967, to Chief Gogo

Nwakuche, a wealthy businessman. He was a staunch nationalist, who encouraged her to write to raise the profile of Nigerian women, but also a traditionalist, who took two other wives after Nwapa.

Flora's life and her writing career both reflect the deep and widening tensions in the new nation between tradition and modernity. During the late 1960s, those tensions exploded in violence, swallowing up the immediate impact of *Efuru*'s publication in 1966. Civil war erupted between the Nigerian government and the breakaway Biafra republic, formed of Igbo territory in the east of the country. Massacres of Igbo people in northern Nigeria in 1967 forced Flora Nwapa to flee her job in Lagos, and through the ensuing war, the Igbo people suffered horrifically through famine and disease. In the wake of the war, in 1970, Flora joined the government to help with the work of tracking down children evacuated and displaced during the war, and reuniting them with their families. She followed up this role with one focused on infrastructure and urban development, overseeing the rebuilding of towns and cities destroyed by the fighting.

Despite the intensity of her political work in the early 1970s, Nwapa continued to write and publish novels that elevated and humanised the Igbo people in the wake of the war's ethnic violence. Her novel *Idu* (1970) showed her continued interest in women's lives, but focused more extensively on marriage, and the challenge of finding love and happiness within its fundamentally unequal contours. She published a collection of short stories, *This Is Lagos*, in 1971, and followed it up with her first children's book. However, she found it hard to sustain the interest and support of foreign publishers, who wanted African writing to fit into certain narrow parameters that would be easily understood by international readers, whose expectations and prejudices had been shaped by colonialism.

In response, Nwapa set out to publish and promote Nigerian authors through her own publishing company, Tana Press, which she established with state funding in 1974. A pioneering venture, it was among the first publishing houses in Africa to be headed by an indigenous woman, and had a mission to provide affordable fiction and poetry for a primarily female audience. In addition to the goal of publishing local authors, Nwapa declared her aim to 'inform and educate women all over the world, especially Feminists (both with capital F and small f) about the role of women in Nigeria, their economic independence, their relationship with their husbands and children, their traditional beliefs and their status in the community as a whole'. But, despite early support, the venture did not last, although its impact earned Nwapa the honour of being called 'the mother of African literature' – an accolade that drew on the maternal myth to gloss over the material difficulties of bringing African women's writing, especially, to a global audience.

Undeterred, Nwapa consolidated her reputation as a writer in the 1980s with novels, story collections, poetry and more children's books, and was awarded the prestigious Order of the Niger in 1982. Her reputation grew among the international literary audience, and she was frequently invited to give talks and lectures in the United States, Europe and elsewhere in Africa. She was preparing to spend a year at a university in North Carolina when she died of pneumonia in 1993, at the age of sixty-two. Towards the end of her life, she reflected on the dominant theme of her thirty-year literary career: 'My interest has been on both the rural and the urban woman in her quest for survival in a fast-changing world dominated by men.' Her career tracks the rise of second-wave feminism in the West, from the 1960s on, and shares with that movement the concern to centre and lift women's voices. Although she found a keen readership outside Nigeria, she remained unapologetic in living and writing as an Igbo woman, and drawing on her own customs and history to present her unique vision of women's 'quest for survival'.

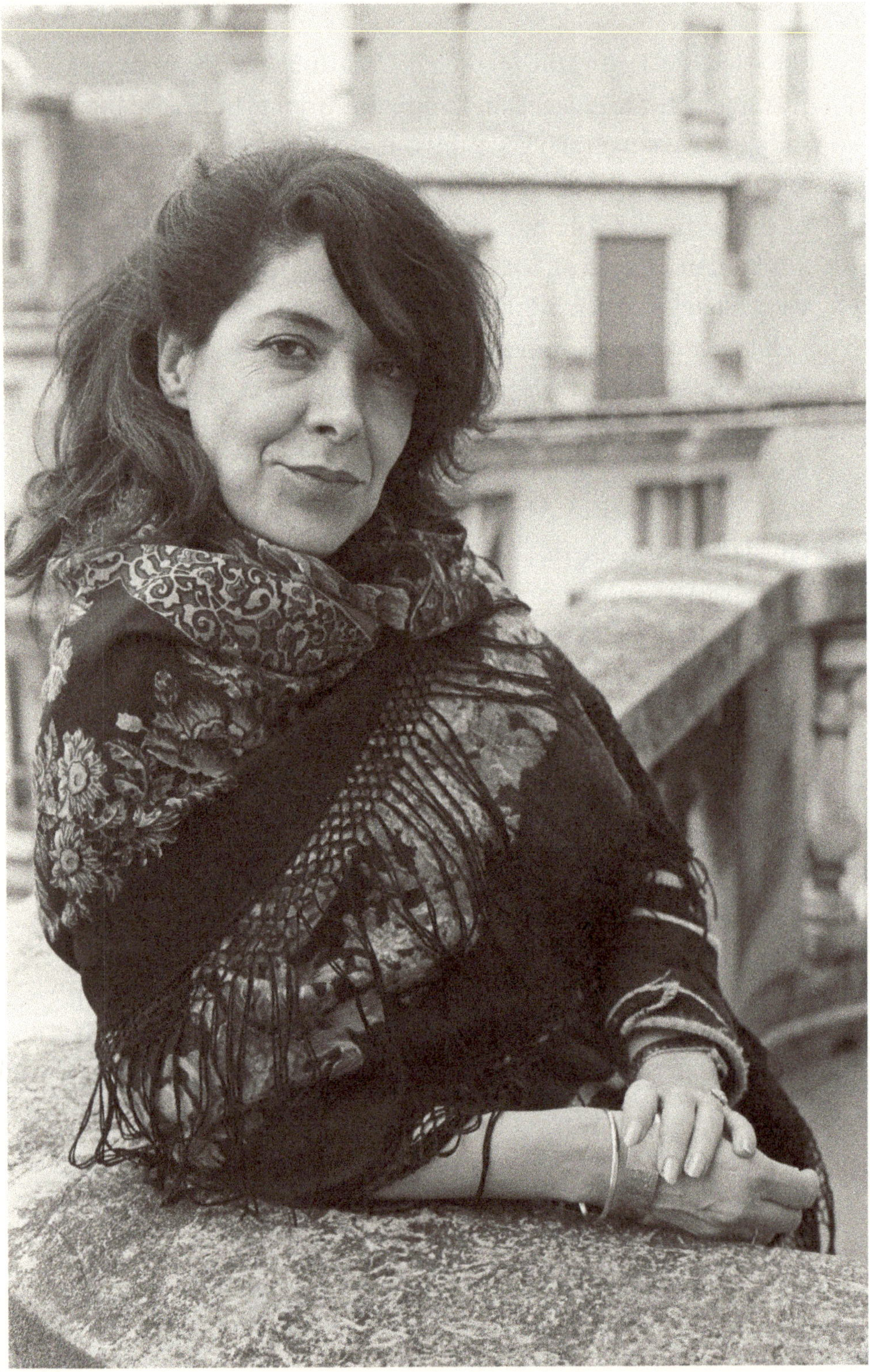

'I am not a symbol.'

ASSIA DJEBAR
(1936–2015)

Fatima Zohra Imalayene was born in the Algerian town of Cherchell in 1936. Located on the Mediterranean coast west of Algiers, the town was once a Roman colony, passing through Byzantine, Berber and Arabic hands before the French invasion in the early nineteenth century. From these intermingled cultural roots, the girl who would become the writer Assia Djebar grew up between languages. With the women in her family she spoke Arabic and Berber dialects, but French was the language of the written word, education and status. It was also the language of the enemy – or, as Djebar often, more gently, put it – of a stepmother, held within the family, but at a potentially antagonistic remove from the mother tongue. In a further complication, it was her father, a teacher, who educated her in French – at the time, it was against the law to teach in Arabic. He insisted she stay in school, even after her female cousins had left to take the veil, so she became a skinny cropped-haired girl alone among the boys. Literacy opened the door to liberty, but a woman who could read and write was harder to control. 'The written word will take flight from the patio, will be tossed from a terrace,' Djebar wrote years later. 'The blue of heaven is suddenly limitless.'

After attending her father's school, Djebar went to a colonial boarding school for girls in Blida, where only a handful of students were Algerian. It was an environment that she later compared to the stifled women's world of the harem. She continued her unusual scholastic career in Paris, where she became the first Muslim student to attend the prestigious École normale supèrieure de jeunes filles in Sèvres, a school set up in the nineteenth century to train women for careers as teachers. It was another cloistered enclave, but its walls could no longer hold back the world. Decades of French oppression in Algeria had recently exploded into war and, before graduating, Djebar joined a general strike of Algerian students in protest at the violence at home. When the school expelled her for this action, she began to write, publishing her first novel in 1957 at the age of twenty-one. She adopted the pseudonym Assia Djebar – which combined words meaning 'consolation' and 'intransigence' – in order to shield her family from the scandal of their daughter's publication. In becoming the first Algerian woman to publish a book outside Algeria, she embarked on a career that would bear out her community's deepest fears about educating girls: that they might then have something to say, and the means to say it.

Djebar's novel *La Soif*, published in English the following year as *The Mischief*, was issued by the same Paris publishing house that had scored a hit, three years earlier, with eighteen-year-old Françoise Sagan's *Bonjour Tristesse*, the tale of a bored rich girl's summer misadventures. *La Soif* echoed Sagan's tale, playing out in an Algerian beach resort popular with Europeans, where Nadia, the motherless daughter of an indulgent, distracted father, passes her time in a whirl of casinos, parties, jazz, cigarettes and 'mad drives in sports cars as skittish as thoroughbred horses'. The constant motion of her existence fails to dispel her abiding sense of emptiness, which she compares to 'the brackish fatigue of a morning-after' – that hungover hopelessness that washes over in the 'grey, grey dawn'. When her old school friend arrives to stay at the villa next door with her husband, Nadia's vanity and boredom launch the mischief of the English title – as she sets out to seduce her married neighbour. But the story's tensions are more explosive than just sexual competition and fraught family dynamics. With a French mother and an Arab father, Nadia is 'on the borderline between two civilisations' like her creator. Although the shadow of politics is barely perceptible in *La Soif*, it would deepen and entrench for Djebar throughout her life and her literary career.

Djebar returned to North Africa after the publication of *La Soif*, despite the intervention of General de Gaulle, who demanded that she be readmitted to school in 1959, in recognition of her literary talent, and the enthusiasm of her publishers at having an exotic ingénue on their hands. She moved first to Rabat, Morocco, where she studied and taught modern history at the university, and continued to write. Her third novel, *Les Enfants du Nouveau Monde* (Children of the New World) appeared the day after Algeria declared its independence in 1962. A departure from the haute bourgeois settings of her earlier books, this was a novel of war and resistance. Set in a small mountain town, it gave voice, in chorus, to a group of women who are beginning to question whether the promised liberation of their nation will also set them free. The book was remarkably prescient in bringing together questions of gender and freedom in post-colonial or post-liberation countries. In the wake of the war, Djebar returned to Algeria to teach history, French literature and cinema at the University of Algiers.

Now in her late twenties, Djebar had been married since 1958 to Ahmed Ould-Rouïs, a scholar and playwright who wrote under the pseudonym Walid Garn, and with whom she collaborated on a play, *Rouge l'Aube* (Red is the Dawn) in 1969. After the war, the couple adopted a young Algerian boy, Mohammed, who had been born as a result of the rape of his teenage mother by French soldiers in a prison camp. The story her son has told since Djebar's death is a disturbing one. He claims that her husband was physically abusive toward them both and that, when the couple split up and divorced, they sent him back – then aged fifteen – to the orphanage where he was born. As an adult, he worked to locate his birth mother and has fought to have her officially recognised as a victim of war.

At the core of Algeria's transition to a post-colonial nation was the installation of Arabic as a national language. This was despite enormous linguistic diversity among the mostly illiterate population, and indicated the wholesale rejection of French, the language spoken by almost all of the country's small, educated elite. Unable to continue teaching in French, Assia Djebar moved back to Paris in 1965, and would spend the next decade crossing back and forth between the two continents. In this period of semi-exile and uncertainty, she turned her creative attention to film where she found a new visual language and narrative approach to the question that now haunted her: how, and whether, Algerian women could reconcile the pull of their home nation's culture and the culture of the West. Her 1978 film *La Nouba des femmes du Mont Chenoua* (The Party of the women of Mount Chenoua) which won the International Critics' Prize at the Venice Film Festival, hovers between fiction and documentary, centring on a woman who returns to Algeria a decade and a half after independence. Through a narrator who describes her task as listening to 'the sound of broken memory', the film foregrounds ordinary women as witnesses to war, and emphasises their unsung role, as survivors, in rebuilding the nation's identity through their own stories. The short film that followed it, *La Zerda ou les chants de l'oubli* (The Zerda or the songs of the forgotten), in 1979, combines archival footage of life in the Maghreb region whilst under colonial rule in the early twentieth century, over a soundtrack of words and music that resist and subvert the story that the images tell. *Zerda* is a religious ceremony while *Nouba* is a form of military music, which became another word for 'party' – both titles therefore embed Arabic-derived 'foreignness' within French, in a way that reflects the inextricable history of coloniser and colonised.

In 1980, Djebar married the poet and literary critic Malek Alloula, with whom she collaborated on *La Zerda*. She also returned to Paris because, as she explained to the newspaper *Le Monde*, 'there were only men in the streets of Algiers'. After the war, Algeria's leaders struggled to establish a strong government that could fulfil the promises of independence, and increasingly faced challenges from Islamist groups who wanted to install a repressive religious regime in their place. As the fundamentalists tightened their grip, the capital city had become a place where, Djebar believed, the only way to respond to the situation of women was through journalism and overt militant protest. She wanted to write differently, drawing on the techniques she had used in her films of subverting official history with personal testimony.

Her story collection *Femmes d'Alger dans leur appartement* (Women of Algiers in their apartment) takes its title from a famous painting by Eugène Delacroix, which was painted just after France's invasion of Algeria. It shows a group of women in elaborately decorated, but somewhat dishevelled robes, blankly staring at the viewer, and offered European viewers a titillating glimpse into the sensuous, torpid world of the women that they imagined inside the walls of a harem. In her book, Djebar offers her own reading of this Orientalist image, although her own writing sometimes shows the difficulty of escaping this generalising and reductive Western view of downtrodden Arab women.

Assia Djebar's writing from the late 1950s to the 1990s is entangled with the history of modern feminism. That history is often assumed to be irreparably divided between a Western individualistic approach and the community-centred incarnation articulated in the non-Western world, but Djebar's vision disrupts this binary. She suggests that women need to work together to combat political oppression, but never loses sight of the way that personal experience shapes us, and of how hard it can be to tell our own unique story in any language, let alone that of the coloniser. At the age of forty, Djebar realised that she 'was incapable of saying words of love in French'. Out of that mismatch of language and feeling, of expression and self, would be born her next project, an ambitious series of four books that blended autobiography with fiction, history and national myth, and that placed women at the centre of the story.

The first novel *L'amour, la fantasia* (published in English as Fantasia: An Algerian Cavalcade), opens with a prelude that draws on her childhood and education through the image of 'A little Arab girl going to school for the first time, one autumn morning, walking hand in hand with her father'. A tall man in a 'fez and a European suit', her father offers his daughter the gift of learning, despite the judgement of their community, and his own fear that it will lead to 'that fatal letter' and the beginning of a love affair and the end of her innocence. Communication becomes more tempting the more strenuously it is forbidden. At seventeen when she is at boarding school, a boy writes to her. Her father tears up the letter, which he claims is 'completely indecent'. When she pieces the fragments together, the boy's offer of correspondence is perfectly innocent, but to her father seems to be 'tantamount to setting the stage for rape'. This imagined threat holds women captive, for their own supposed protection. The story ends with the narrator imagining herself as a mother holding a spectral daughter's hand and leaving the town without turning back.

Intertwined with this personal narrative of a woman clutching for freedom through education is the broader history of modern Algeria. The story picks up in the silent, sparkling dawn of a June day in 1830, as an 'immense flotilla of frigates, brigs and schooners, bedecked with multicoloured pennons' streams into the bay of Algiers, the 'Impregnable City', setting in motion the French conquest. Drawing on the stories buried in the colonial archives, this historical tale is threaded with the author's memories of coming of age and written in her stepmother tongue of French. In that language the word for 'history' and 'story' is the same, suggesting that there is no clear division between fact and fiction, events and the way they are interpreted.

Djebar's ten-year literary project that began with *L'Amour, la fantasia* continued to interlace national, colonial and personal histories, culminating in *Vaste est la prison* (So Vast the Prison). In this novel, the breakdown of a modern marriage becomes part of a long matrilineal story which incorporates the search for the Berber language her grandmother spoke. It extends to become a quest for a women's language, through which stories can be shared in safety and secrecy.

By the early 1990s, the Algeria of Djebar's childhood and the early years of liberation had disappeared as the tension between nationalists and Islamist fundamentalists, building throughout the 1980s, finally slid into a decade-long and brutal civil war. Her writing in this period became more overtly political in response to the atmosphere of religious oppression and anti-intellectual hatred, which led to the assassination of several of her friends, including her second husband's brother, who was a playwright. *Le blanc de l'Algérie* (Algerian White) is, like some of her earlier works, a kind of chorus and a collective requiem for the loss of both her friends and a number of other Algerian writers and intellectuals, from the writer Albert Camus, killed in a car accident in 1960, up to and including a female teacher murdered in 1994. A subsequent novel, *La disparition de la langue Française* (The disappearance of the French language), returns again to the tension around language in Algeria, and the larger cultural violence that linguistic erasures unleash. Here, and across her body of work, Assia Djebar – rather like Juana Manuela Gorriti more than a century earlier in Latin America – conjures ghosts that embody traces of the past which are never fully buried or forgotten. Colonialism and the French language do not disappear when they are outlawed, but nor do they remain a stable source of identity and authority for the Francophone writer. Instead, they are a persistent haunting.

In 1995, Assia Djebar moved to the United States, to direct the Center for French and Francophone Studies at Louisiana State University – a part of the country with an especially strong French and Creole heritage – before moving to New York. In 2005, she made history in becoming the first person from the Arab world to be elected to the Académie Française, the highest literary honour in France. She won several international literary prizes, was awarded honorary doctorates by universities in Canada and Europe, and was frequently touted as a candidate for the Nobel Prize for literature. In this period of honours and visibility, however, she took pains to emphasise that her work was not done. 'I am not a symbol,' she declared, insisting that she was a working writer who was still exploring the many 'imaginary worlds' buried in the multiple layers of her culture. In 2007 there was another, less heralded but just as important, first when her novel *Nulle part dans la maison de mon père* (Nowhere in my father's house) became her first to be translated into and published in Arabic, the mother tongue in which she did not learn until adulthood to write in.

In 2015, Djebar died in Paris, and the city commemorated her three years later with a majestic new public library. She was, however, buried in her birthplace of Cherchell, the town that was the site of her earliest encounters with the crosscurrents of history. Her immersion in the multiple histories and cultural legacies of Europe and the Maghreb meant that in her work, she could call upon a kaleidoscopic – that is, dazzling and fragmentary – array of references and literary traditions. 'Ever since I was a child, the foreign language was a casement opening on the spectacle of the world and all its riches,' she wrote in *L'Amour, la fantasia*. But the richness her education offered was not without danger in a world that deeply fears an educated, outspoken woman: 'In certain circumstances it became a dagger threatening me.' Djebar's story is unavoidably bound up with the colonial and post-colonial; with French and Muslim history; with ancient and modern stories of Algeria; and with the country where she felt both alienated and rooted as a cosmopolitan, educated woman, but also a native daughter, holding her father's hand on the way to school.

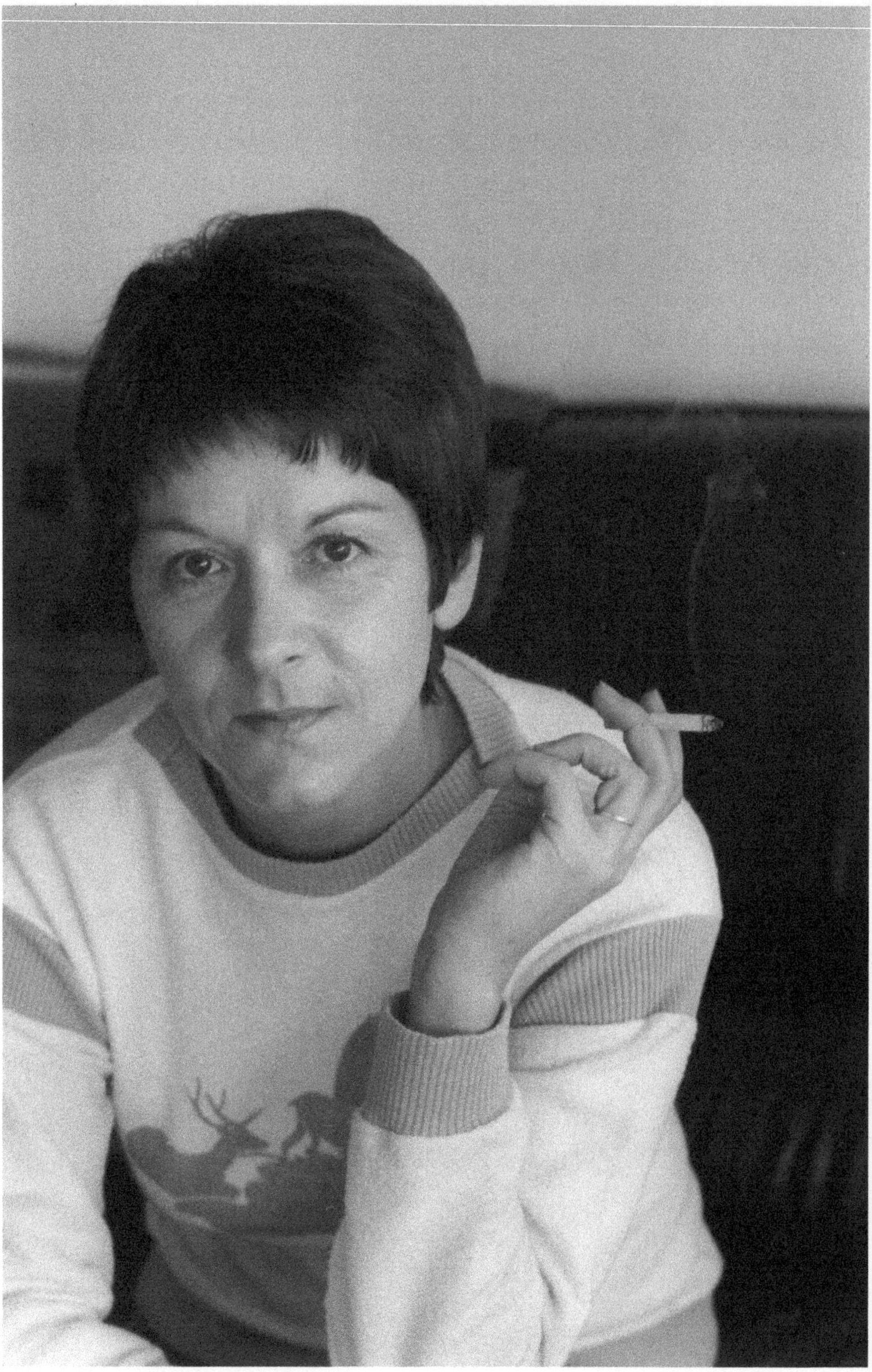

'A child is life's memory of itself.'

INÈS CAGNATI
(1937–2007)

How is a literary career to be mapped and measured? What's the relationship between fame, acclaim and endurance? These questions come up over and over again in the assessment of women writers, but in her refusal to play the game of literary celebrity, the French-Italian author Inès Cagnati presents a particular challenge. Far from unknown during her lifetime, Cagnati was profoundly unwilling to inhabit the public role that helps a writer secure a place in the canon or spread her fame beyond national borders. Her writing illuminates a forgotten era in French history, and offers an astute assessment of the hardships of a rural, working-class girlhood in the years after the Second World War. She published three novels over the course of the 1970s, and each won or was nominated for France's most prestigious literary prizes, but it wasn't until 2019 that her work first appeared in English, with the translation of her debut novel *Le jour de congé* (Free Day).

There is an irony in Cagnati's embrace by the French literary establishment which lies in her deep sense of alienation from the country in which she was born and raised. The daughter of Italian immigrant farmers, Inès grew up with five sisters, poor and isolated, in the tiny town of Monclar-d'Agénais, in south-western France – not far from Montauban, where Olympe de Gouges was born almost two centuries earlier, who also felt like an outcast from mainstream French society for her working-class status and regional dialect. Cagnati's parents were both Italian and Inès spoke no French until she went to school. Although she eventually became a teacher and a novelist in the language, she described her naturalisation as a French citizen as a 'tragedy' for the way it overwrote her origins. The weight of multiple forms of estrangement – of language, culture, class and gender – settled heavily on her when she was a child and shaped her as a writer.

The popular vision of rural France as a place of sun-dappled ease and beauty is not the version that appears in Cagnati's books. The countryside of her upbringing is, rather, a place where tough, taciturn people scratch out a thankless existence. Her parents arrived from Italy as part of a wave of immigration to the Aquitaine region that took place between the wars, where the twin depopulating forces of the First World War and mass migration to cities had left a gap that urgently needed to be filled. Lured with the promise of lush and abundant farmland, the Italian agricultural workers found themselves faced instead with a 'marshy, rocky' and unforgiving reality, but they nonetheless dug in and helped revive the rural economy.

By the time Cagnati was born in 1937, more than 80,000 Italians were living in the region around Monclar and were running more than half of the farms. Their presence complicates the widely held French faith that the country's rural areas are the home of a single, unsullied national identity. Although most immigrants were impelled more by economic than political forces, the rise of fascism in Italy in this period undeniably played a role in encouraging some people to leave. Others might have brought fascist sympathies with them, and established or joined right-wing groups in France, but the incentive to integrate into the new society limited their influence – if anything, the anti-fascist impulse seems to have been stronger. However, because the stories of poor rural people, often unable to read and write, are easily lost, it's a period and place that has largely been forgotten – its nuances of identity and affiliation obscured. Cagnati's novels, therefore, are of vital importance in shaping the memory of this era, and bearing witness to an otherwise buried history.

Le jour de congé is a story stuck in a young girl's head. Like her creator, fourteen-year-old Galla is one of five daughters of an insular immigrant farming family, who has managed to persuade her parents to let her attend high school, twenty miles away. She rides back home for a visit every two weeks on her decrepit but beloved bicycle. The narration follows the structure of this regular journey home, but it is an unscheduled visit and for reasons that are only slowly revealed and thus shadowed by a sense of doom. The narrative is constantly interrupted by forays into Galla's past and memories that lurch between extremes of affection for her mother and younger sisters and sudden eruptions of brutality at the hands of her father. Her emotional vocabulary is likewise dominated by extremes: like and dislike, love and hate, wonderful and terrible. When she can, she sings to express what she can't articulate, though this is often misunderstood. At her little sister's funeral, she sits on the wall and sings to comfort her sister in the cemetery, then finds herself scolded for her perceived heartlessness.

From the beginning, we are plunged into Galla's perspective – she is defiant, solitary, tough, argumentative, but also tragically limited in her power to change things. This is how the book opens:

> 'I leaned my bicycle against the wall of the barn and left it there. I could have kept on dragging it until it was in front of the house, as usual. It's not more than fifty yards. But

> 'I'd had enough of my bicycle. Of pedalling. Of pushing it. Of pedalling. Of pushing it. And, in the end, carrying it. Completely enough. I'd had it. Because all of that had been going on for three or four hours, maybe more, even, and there comes a point when things have gone on long enough, and you say: No.'

Within a paragraph, we are mired in the stubbornness of the narrator, pushing against the equally stubborn force of her circumstances. She traps herself in obsessive circles around repeated phrases and recurrent images, and has to work to dig herself out. Her arrival home is delayed by this same kind of impasse, the forward motion of her journey grappling with her reluctance to arrive, to face her family and the reality of her circumstances.

Galla's voice fluctuates between the boldness of an instinctive rebel and the fearfulness of an abused and haunted child – often in the same breath. Cagnati's translator, Liesl Schillinger, explains the challenge of accurately conveying the idioms of Galla's speech, written in French by an author whose first language, like her character's, was Italian. That duality 'guided and narrowed the breadth of her expression, which, I think, focused and concentrated the authenticity of her voice,' Schillinger writes in her introduction to the 2019 English edition of the novel. 'Her narration, the inner thoughts she revealed, seemed to me more devoid of pretense than any I'd encountered before.'

A chain of violent incidents runs through the book, looping through Galla's memories as she slogs onwards on her bicycle. There are the everyday eruptions of her father's beatings, too common to warrant description, and more intensely rendered scenes of physical suffering endured by animals or younger children, which underline how little power Galla has over her circumstances or her memories. The crying of a salamander, left to die slowly impaled on a hook, unconsciously becomes the sound of her ancient bicycle, which starts to squeak like a salamander. This transference of suffering happens repeatedly. When she hits a patch of black ice and tumbles off her bike, her concern is all for her rusted ride: 'As for me, I banged my knee again, which started to hurt a lot. Poor bicycle.' Her memory can be a safe place to store stories, songs and poems, but it's treacherous, too: 'I don't have many good memories, and if I go on recalling the same ones, they get used up, and they're no good anymore. After that, there's nothing left.'

The high school is Galla's sole escape and a place she has fought her parents for the right to attend on a scholarship. Yet it is far from a haven. Instead, it is where she is made to feel her strangeness and her poverty most acutely. Her bright-green smock, which she's sewn from remnants of a hand-me-down dress, contrasts loudly with the regulation pink blouses the other girls wear. 'Most people just assume that, if you have something, you simply bought it,' Galla notes, in a brilliantly concise encapsulation of poverty. If she has something, it's been handed down, begged from her family or stolen from Prisunic, the unglamorous chain store in town. Founded in 1931, Prisunic was a fixture in French towns until the early 2000s, and for many years the 'Prisunic cashier' was political shorthand for an ordinary working-class woman – yet to Galla, it's a place of such abundance that nothing she takes will be missed.

The fourteen-year-old Galla's awareness of herself as female is only nascent, throbbing at the edge of her consciousness. She takes note of her mother's back-to-back pregnancies, of the vague bogeymen of 'the old Spaniard' in the marshes and the caretaker at her school who 'looks at bottoms', and of her teachers' insistent belief that any girl playing truant from school must be doing so to see a boy. But for the moment, these are lessons learned but not felt. Galla notices beauty and ugliness in her classmates but doesn't connect it to sexual value: her friend Fanny is beautiful the way sunshine is, unreachable and somehow part of a different order of existence. Being beautiful is a sign, for Galla, that Fanny must have been wanted by her parents, not a sign that she's going to be wanted by a man. When Fanny tells Galla that she's beautiful, too, or when Galla glimpses herself in a mirror propped in a shop window in town, she doesn't recognise herself.

Though Cagnati was hyperaware of her own immigrant identity, Galla does not understand herself explicitly as an ethnic outsider. In a school lesson dealing with racism, she freely sorts her few Vietnamese and Black classmates by intelligence, and mocks her teacher's display of emotion while telling the class about the anti-slavery leader Toussaint Louverture. Distracted and bored, she interrupts to ask whether black and red ants can mate, earning herself a detention. Her foreignness is a difference among differences and another load to bear.

There is a recording of a rare interview on Swiss television made in 1989, on the occasion of the publication of Cagnati's short story collection *Les Pipistrelles*. The transcript of the interview is included as an appendix in the English edition of *Free Day* but onscreen, it's blunter. The author comes across as soft-spoken, serious, and utterly uninterested in alleviating anyone's discomfort – certainly not that of the male interviewer making sentimental generalisations about childhood, nature, French identity and writing. Cagnati, chain-smoking in a red sweater and twisting her necklace in her fingers, rebuffs the interviewer. Is it a comfort to write? 'It's terrible to write,' she replies. She lives in the countryside, she says, as she's unhappy in town – unhappy with people. 'With everyone?' the interviewer asks, and gets another firm '*Oui*.' It's why her main theme is isolation, why she cares about telling the stories of the poor and the silenced, of children, the elderly, and those deemed mad.

Like Galla, Cagnati escaped her impoverished childhood through education, although she, too, felt acutely like an outsider at her high school, unable properly to understand the language or what was being asked of her. Her studies, nevertheless, allowed her to qualify as a teacher, and for most of her career she taught literature at a prestigious *lycée* in northwest Paris. In 1977, after she won the Prix des Deux Magots for her second novel, *Le Monde* noted that she was living in Brasília with her engineer husband and her son. Two years later, when her third book was published, Cagnati was back in France, where she was photographed for *Paris Match* in her country home, playing, reading and roasting chestnuts with her young son. Her husband is present in one picture, leaning out of their tight circle. In the 1989 interview, Cagnati does not mention him, describing her son as her only true family. 'Is that not excessive?' the interviewer asks, to which she responds with a shrug. 'Not if I don't make him feel it that way, no.' Yet as she makes clear in her fiction, familial love is not so easily directed or controlled as that.

The helpless love of a child for its mother, the desire to be noticed and welcomed, runs through *Le Jour de congé* and continues through *Génie la folle* (Génie the Crazy) as well. The second novel is narrated by Marie, the young daughter of the 'crazy' Génie, who has been cast out by her middle-class family for becoming pregnant while unmarried. Génie, whose name also means 'genius', clings to an erratic, precarious existence as a farmworker and refuses to speak to anyone. Marie trails behind her, desperate for any sign of affection. It's a love that is always partly hedged with the terror of loss.

Le Jour de congé predates by a few years the vogue for autofiction, the term coined by the French novelist Serge Doubrovsky in 1977 for the creative blurring of imagined and lived experience. Yet in its evocation of the looping, obsessive, unpredictable movement of memory, it could easily be seen as a forerunner of the genre. In Doubrovsky's words, '*L'autofiction, c'est comme le rêve; un rêve n'est pas la vie, un livre n'est pas la vie.*' ('Autofiction is like a dream; a dream is not life, a book is not life.') In the hands of writers like Karl Øve Knausgaard, Sheila Heti or Rachel Cusk, autofiction has tended to examine the interplay of life and art in relatively privileged settings. Cagnati is a bracing antidote to that. In this sense, her work deserves to be read alongside that of Annie Ernaux, a close contemporary of Cagnati's, who was born three years after her in Normandy, and also raised in a working-class family. When Ernaux won the Nobel Prize for Literature in 2022, she was the first Frenchwoman to receive that honour, and President Emmanuel Macron called her the voice 'of the freedom of women and of the forgotten'. Similar to Cagnati, Ernaux's education took her down a different path to the one her parents followed. She earned a teaching degree and taught at high schools in eastern France and then in a suburb in northwest Paris, where she still lives. In her debut autobiographical novel *Les Armoires Vides* (published in English as Cleaned Out), which appeared a year after *Le Jour de congé*, the protagonist, a young woman, reflects on her childhood and education as she waits for an abortion, a procedure Ernaux herself underwent as a student in the early 1960s, before it was legal in France, and revisited years later in her 2000 novel *L'Evenement* (Happening).

Le Jour de congé is also a story constructed from memory and darkened by a sense of not-quite-definable tension. The narrative often moves like a dream – or a nightmare, down unwanted pathways. Just as fog and darkness turn the familiar marshy landscape of Galla's family's farm into a place of hidden horrors, so unwanted memories yank her out of complacency into grief. Throughout the novel, Cagnati denies the reader the comforts of distance, the knowledge of Galla's survival into adulthood and the absorption of her memories into a longer timeframe of mature reflection. She refuses to mitigate the pain and isolation of childhood, which she seems to pull, unvarnished, out of the past.

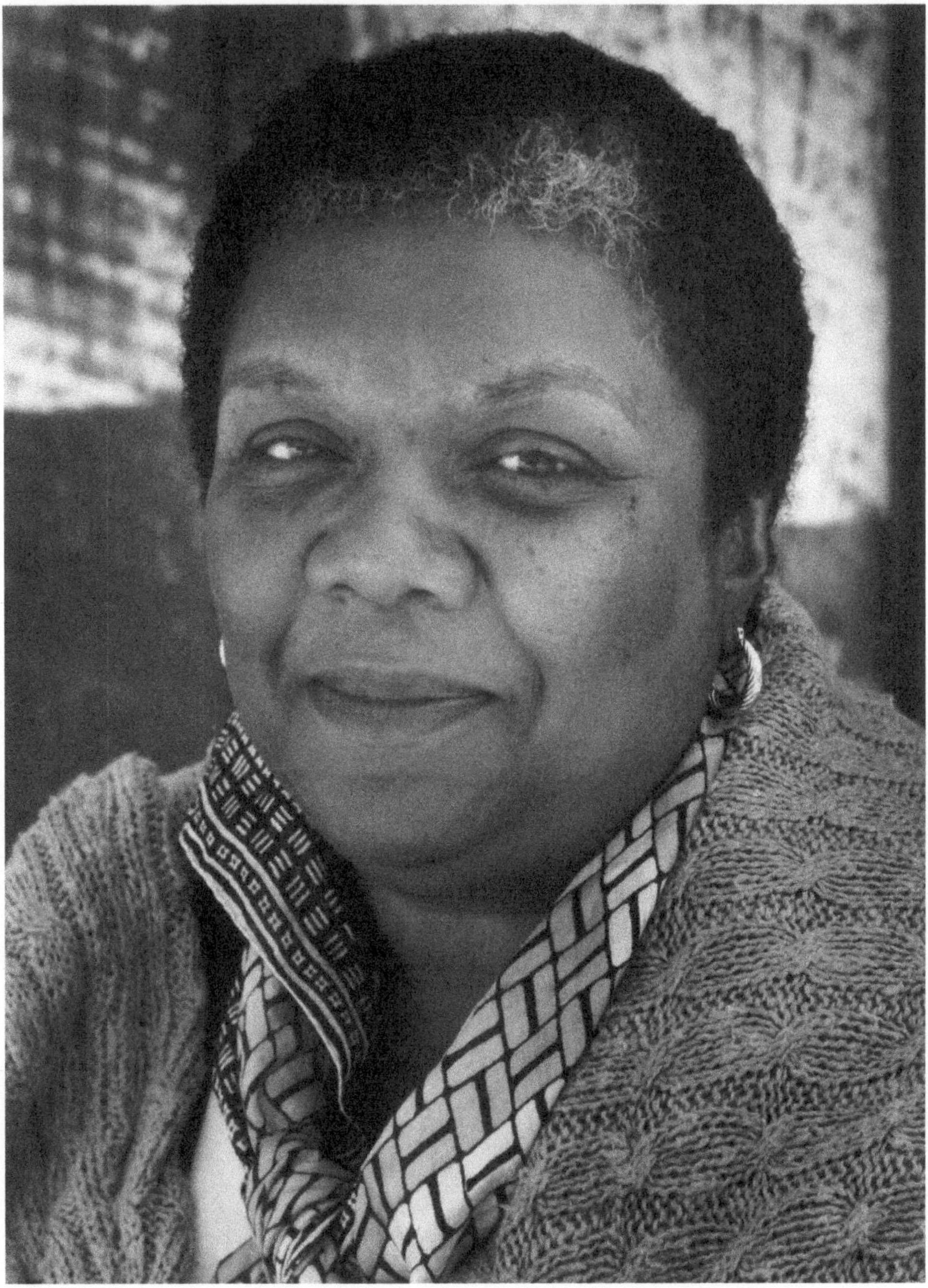

'what did i see to be except myself?'

LUCILLE CLIFTON
(1936–2010)

Lucille Clifton is a poet who inspires devotion. Her poetry is distinctive on the page: no capital letters, often no punctuation, short yet flowing lines and lots of white space. Her words are written to be spoken aloud, sung and shared – the rhythms of jazz and sex meeting the interruptions of children, of necessity. They exude gentleness and care and humour, even when the subject of her poems is the tough truths of African-American history, or the indignities of mothering and living as a Black woman. The 'I' of her poems isn't a towering column, and that is on purpose. It's lower case, a body with a head, an individual, no more or less important than the other letters. An open *i*.

> 'won't you celebrate with me
> what i have shaped into
> a kind of life? i had no model.'

Lucille Clifton was born Thelma Lucille Sayles in 1936 – the deep middle of the Depression and what she calls 'Roosevelt time' – in Depew, in upstate New York, twelve miles from

Buffalo: 'a small town, mostly Polish, all its life turned like a machine around the steel mill.' Her father had moved there from Virginia during the Great Migration, the mass early-twentieth-century movement of African Americans from the rural South to the industrial cities of the northern United States in pursuit of better jobs and safer lives. In many cases, however, workers realised they had been brought in to disrupt union activism, break strikes and drive down wages. Black workers often found themselves in direct conflict with a previous wave of newcomers who were fighting for better conditions in the factories. In her family's small town, Lucille's was one of very few Black families, and she learned to speak Polish as a child. The sprawling city of Buffalo was a landscape of abandoned buildings, 'potted as if by war'. It was the fading echo of a boomtown, but still a place where thousands of people lived. In this survival, the communities holding together and families seeking joy and love, Clifton found the essence of her poetry.

Like many bright children growing up in tough circumstances, young Lucille was often told that she should get away from her hometown. Uncertain but dutiful, she did so, winning a scholarship to the prestigious historically Black college Howard University in Washington D.C., where Pauli Murray had studied law two decades earlier. Despite finding herself among a dynamic peer group, she felt out of place – older, somehow, than her fellow students – and lonely. She had no model for how to study or how to be that far from her family. After two years, she transferred to a college closer to home. At a local community drama workshop, she met Fred Clifton, a philosophy professor at the University of Buffalo, who would help establish what was then called the 'Afro-American studies' department at Harvard University. Starring together in their theatre group's production of *The Glass Menagerie*, Lucille and

Fred fell in love. They married when Lucille was twenty-two and went on to have six children in quick succession. But for motherhood, too, Lucille had no model – her own mother, Thelma, had died suddenly in 1959, a month before her eldest child was born. Her poem 'Dear Mama' is a lament for that life cut short – the plants Thelma never grew, the poems she never wrote. Lucille remembered her as a 'dreamwalker' who loved to read, an imaginative, fragile woman who was terrorised by her violent husband, who burned the poetry she wrote.

When her first collection of poetry, *Good Times*, appeared in 1969, Clifton was thirty-two, and her six children were still under the age of ten. When she was later asked about her involvement in the civil rights movement of the 1960s, she excused her relatively low political profile by pointing out that 'I was pretty much constantly pregnant'. In the same vein, 'Why do you think my poems are so short?' she'd bounce back when she was asked about her poetic style. Hers was literature snatched from the endlessly demanding mouths of babes, the work of someone who, as she put it, 'finds a pen between the cushions/on the couch' and scribbles a few words at a time. This mother-poet may strike us (she certainly strikes me) as heroic, even miraculous; but can we celebrate her life without diminishing her craft? Do her circumstances suggest that she was brilliant by accident? Her friend Toni Morrison, who edited and wrote the introduction to her memoir *Generations*, declares that in loving Clifton, as so many readers do, they miss her 'cold hard intellect'. But that doesn't seem quite right either. Intellect is certainly evident in her rigour and deep historical research, but there is nothing cold in Clifton's work, even when she's writing about hard truths, hard lives, 'the terrible stories' as the title of her 1996 collection has it. She tells stories of enslavement, bereavement, abuse – but also of survival, family and, that determined word, celebration.

Although her family obligations made it hard for her to march in the streets, Clifton's literary career was nevertheless part of the fight for racial justice, which was not just about gaining political rights – or undoing political wrongs – but asserting the human dignity of Black Americans, which encompassed cultural and artistic recognition. The Black Arts Movement, at the same time, was putting forward a vision of poetry that emphasised its power to communicate with everyday readers, by using the rhythms and vocabulary of vernacular speech to create a 'public poetry' that could connect with a wide audience, and build pride in the artistic heritage of African Americans. Although Lucille Clifton was a poet not clearly aligned with any single movement, her writing shared this same commitment to speaking in an ordinary voice and finding poetry in the sharp observation of overlooked lives. *Good Times* belonged to a moment that was bringing the history of Black Americans into the light and imagining a brighter future – one that would have to be imagined over and over again.

From the beginning, her poetry belonged to a distinctly African-American lineage, though there is some confusion about its origins. According to her friend, the writer Ishmael Reed, her career was launched when he shared her poems with Langston Hughes, the elder statesman of the Harlem Renaissance, who considered them for a major anthology he co-edited. *The Poetry of the Negro 1746–1970* included poems by Alice Dunbar-Nelson, Jessie Redmon Fauset, and Pauli Murray, but Clifton's poems didn't actually appear in the volume. However she got her start, those 1960s poems, forged in the love and desperation of family life, won her a prestigious award from a New York cultural centre, and the rare honour of her first collection being named one of the best books of the year by the *New York Times*, eclipsing the moonshot dreams of most debut poets.

That early recognition didn't transform the Cliftons' material circumstances, though. Perhaps there's no level of success for a poet, and certainly for a mother of six, that can lift her out of the realm of worrying over money and survival. Lucille and Fred had moved to Baltimore in 1967, and she had teaching and poet-in-residence positions at prestigious universities around the U.S. She published thirteen poetry collections in her lifetime, along with a series of children's books featuring a protagonist named Everett Anderson, a Black boy from a poor background whose creative spirit transforms his ordinary surroundings into adventures. In 1988, two of her books were nominated for the Pulitzer Prize in the same year, an unprecedented feat. Yet the Cliftons had also lost their family home to foreclosure some years before. Her daughter Sidney bought it back in 2019 with plans to establish it as an arts centre.

Poetry, to Clifton, was the gift of her foremothers, a legacy that stretched back to the Kingdom of Dahomey in West Africa (part of modern-day Benin), from where hundreds of thousands of Africans were kidnapped and then transported to work as slaves on Caribbean and American plantations. Clifton's great-great-grandmother, Caroline, was captured there as a young child, sold into slavery and, at just eight years old, was chained up and marched from New Orleans to Virginia. Lucille's ancestry was a source of defiant strength, echoing down the generations, from 'Mammy Ca'line', through Clifton's father who would tell his daughter, 'Get what you want, you from Dahomey women.'

Her memoir *Generations* narrates the journey that she made as an adult along with her husband and brother to her father's funeral. She describes their laughter in the car, driving from her home in Baltimore back to upstate New York, their celebration as a part of their grief – two impossible-to-separate moods that live together in her poetry. Around that story, in expanding circles, is traced ancestry, lineage and the way her foremothers shaped her voice. The challenge is always finding someone to listen. The memoir begins with a telephone call from a 'thin voiced white lady' carrying out genealogical research on her family, who share the last name, Sayles, that Clifton's father had adopted. The woman was confused by the connection and curious about these ancestors she didn't know. 'Who remembers the names of the slaves?' Clifton asks her. 'Only the children of slaves.' An uncomfortable silence follows, stretching across the gulf of realisation. When the woman sends Clifton her family history, the poet sees the names of her own family members 'thick in her family like an omen'. Her own given name was Thelma, after her mother, but she became known as Lucille after her great-great-grandmother Caroline's daughter, 'an afrikan name', she wrote, that invokes both light and the devil. Lucifer becomes a figure of fascination, almost a kindred spirit. In one poetic sequence, she speaks in Lucifer's voice, as one who has the power to speak an involuntary truth: 'illuminate i could/and so/illuminate i did.'

Who remembers the names of slaves?

For Clifton, history came alive in the intimacy of the family. When she writes about her ancestors, she's writing about inheritance and the endurance of women whose bodies were subjected to so much, and who seized whatever they could. She's writing about her namesake, her great-grandmother Lucille, who shot dead the white man who raped her and fathered her son. Because that Lucille's mother, Caroline, was a respected midwife, the community did not condemn her immediately, but she was eventually found guilty at trial, giving her the dubious distinction of being the first Black woman legally put to death in Virginia. Clifton imagines the grim silence of mother and daughter at the execution, and lets their grief take over her own body and voice: 'I turn in my chair and arch my back and make this sound for my two mothers and for all Dahomey women.'

That ancestral fortitude lives in her own body, 'plain as bread/ round as cake', and yet imbued with enormous and, at times, almost supernatural power. Fighting is not the only show of strength, in other words: there is strength in care, in love, in the nurture of babies and the hurting and healing of the body. The home, as Clifton knew from life and from history, was not a sanctuary for Black women, not the domestic idyll that theoretically sheltered wives and mothers from the world. The angel in the house was white: a Black woman had to build her own home and defend it from terrors within and without.

'My father burned us all,' she wrote. He sexually abused Lucille, and her memoir is in part an effort to recover and understand the ways in which her family's story connects with a longer, wider history of abuse, at the centre of which are the bodies of Black men and women, treated as commodities and broken without remorse. Her father, a miner, suffered from lung problems and survived a brain tumour, and eventually needed his leg amputated after an accident. Looking into his coffin, she noted the carefully hidden injury. 'oh stars/and stripes forever,' she asks, 'what did you do to my father?'

And yet it was her father, Sam, grandson of the avenging great-grandmother Lucille, who insisted that she take pride in her Dahomey heritage, the strength of her ancestors. That pride depends on seizing joy, which lives most intensely in the body. Clifton writes with a broad grin about sex and her body, her mighty hips that have 'never been enslaved', with the power to 'put a spell on a man and/spin him like a top!' As she gets older, she writes about the surging of desire in her ageing body – she is 'randy as a wolf' – and composes an elegy for her last period, that bringer of trouble and mess and relief. In a poem for her sons, she again conjures menstruation as a blessing and a curse, wishing on them cramps, white skirts, no more tampons, and the terror of being late – those routine indignities of womanhood that her boys cannot share.

Sexy in its ordinariness, her body was also marked, as we all are, by individual quirks and particular pains. Lucille inherited from her mother a condition called polydactyly, being born with an extra finger on each hand, which were surgically removed when she was a baby. This peculiarity, along with her limited vision in one eye implanted, early on in Lucille, a sense that she had a connection to witchcraft and to forms of sight and knowledge that other people lacked. In later life she had to have other parts of her body removed, cut away, closed off: her uterus, fibroids, her parathyroid gland, her kidneys – her daughter donated her own kidney for a transplant operation.

Those physical ordeals were amplified by more resounding losses. Her husband Fred died of cancer in 1984, at just forty-nine, and two of their six children also died before their mother, in 2000 and 2004. The losses shaped her late work, which was increasingly drawn to the mysticism of African religions and the spiritual seeking of poets like William Blake, who had inspired Kay Boyle. Her 2004 collection *Mercy* included writing that she described as transcripts of messages from the spirit world, attempts to comprehend loss and find comfort in the continuity of memory. Prophecy, in her personal mythology, was one of the gifts of Lucifer, the devil whose name meant light, like her own.

Lucille Clifton died in 2010, leaving a legacy that gives the lie to ordinariness, to the idea that there are people who don't matter, who can be silenced. Her early poems still resonate powerfully for their insistence that joy comes through paying attention to the present moment, however fleeting: to the relief that comes when the rent is paid; the release of celebrating in the kitchen, drunk; dancing and singing together – *good times*. She explores what it is to have children, to be part of a lineage, to recognise how your life is enmeshed with those who came before and after and to marvel at how enduring those connections are. They are threads that go on and on and don't snap. 'Things don't fall apart,' she writes at the end of *Generations*, defying Yeats and Achebe, defying the men who say so, who give in to the constant temptation and the false promise of despair. No, she says – insistent on the endurance of lineage and inheritance, of memory and family, of mothers and their children – it is not like that. 'Things hold.'

CREDITS AND FURTHER READING

This book is built on a foundation of labour and insight from an enormous number of researchers, past and present. As a former academic myself, I know firsthand how deeply knowledgeable, thoughtful and passionate scholars are about their subjects, and I am endlessly grateful for the work that they share with the world. This book is dedicated to those scholars whose curiosity and persistence in the archives and libraries has brought to light forgotten voices and helped re-evaluate those who were fading into history. Especially for those translators bringing foreign voices to an Anglophone readership, I am grateful for your efforts of literary and cultural translation.

What follows is not a traditional bibliography but an effort to acknowledge both the specific sources that were most useful to me in writing these profiles as well as the scholars who have been most important in maintaining or promoting individual writers' legacies. I have also included information on where to find the authors' work, in the most accessible, in-print editions, which I encourage readers to seek out and order from independent bookstores, in person or online. I hope this will serve as inspiration to readers and to publishers alike. Finally, I apologise for any omissions or oversights in this broad project, and welcome reports of any new publications.

ENHEDUANNA

'*I, Enheduanna...*': From the poem 'The Exultation of Inanna'.

I first encountered Enheduanna (sometimes spelled 'Enheduana') in 2022 at the exhibition *She Who Wrote: Enheduanna and Women of Mesopotamia, ca. 3400–2000 BC* at The Morgan Library and Museum in New York. Here I gleaned information from a presentation by co-curator Sidney Babcock and the museum texts. Scholar and translator Sophus Helle maintains the website Enheduana.org, which features texts of several poems, as well as links to further reading and interviews. Helle is also the editor and translator of *Enheduana: The Complete Poems of the World's First Author*, published by Yale University Press in 2023. His essays on ancient literary forms, especially 'What Is an Author? Old Answers to a New Question' (*Modern Language Quarterly* 80:2, June 2019), offer a provocative way to think more broadly about the history of authorship and Enheduanna's place in that long tradition. Elizabeth Winkler's essay in the *New Yorker*, 'The Struggle to Unearth the World's First Author' (November 19, 2022) is an excellent overview of the controversy among scholars around Enheduanna's status, including the arguments of sceptics W.G. Lambert, Paul Delnero and Eleanor Robson, who called Enheduanna a 'wish-fulfilment figure' for feminists; and Assyriologists Benjamin Foster and Zainab Bahrani, an expert in ancient Near Eastern art and archaeology, who has written extensively about gender in Mesopotamia, who support her claim to authorship.

MURASAKI SHIKIBU

'*Among her assemblage of tales she found accounts, whether fact or fiction, of many extraordinary fates, but none, alas, of any like her own*': from *The Tale of Genji*, chapter 25.

The Tale of Genji was first translated into English in six volumes (1925–1933) by Arthur Waley. The first volume is the translation Woolf read and reviewed in 1925 for *Vogue*, and the review is featured in Volume IV of her collected essays, edited by Andrew McNeillie (Harcourt, 1994). Subsequent English translations appeared in 1976 by Edward G. Seidensticker, in 2001 by Royall Tyler, and in 2015 by Dennis Washburn (W.W. Norton). I drew on two extended review essays, first of Tyler's translation by Janice Nimura ('Courtly Lust', the *New York Times*, December 2, 2001) and then Ian Buruma's review of Washburn's translation in the *New Yorker* (July 13, 2015). Tyler assembled an abridged version of *The Tale of Genji* for Penguin Classics in 2006, which has a valuable introduction. Penguin Classics also publishes *The Diary of Lady Murasaki*, translated with an introduction and notes by Richard Bowring (2005). For an understanding of *Genji* in its time, and of its later influence, I am indebted to Brian Phillips for his essay '*The Tale of Genji* as a Modern Novel' (*The Hudson Review*, Autumn 2010) and to leading Murasaki scholar Michael Emmerich, author of *The Tale of Genji: Translation, Canonization, and World Literature* (Columbia University Press, 2015). For anyone interested in the changing reception of the novel over time, Columbia also publishes *Reading The Tale of Genji: Sources from the First Millennium*, edited by Thomas Harper and Haruo Shirane (2015).

CHRISTINE DE PIZAN

'There is not the slightest doubt that women belong to the people of God and the human race as much as men': from *The Book of the City of Ladies*, II.54.1.

A wealth of information is available about Christine de Pizan (sometimes spelled de Pisan), and she is often cited as an early feminist foremother. Judy Chicago's iconic 1979 artwork *The Dinner Party* features a place setting for her. Her writing is readily available in English translation and the digitised illuminated manuscript of the *Book of the City of Ladies* can be viewed online at the websites of the British Library (bl.uk) and Bibliothèque Nationale de France (bnf.fr). *The Book of the City of Ladies* has been translated and is available in a revised 2013 edition from Persea Books, translated by Earl Jeffrey Richards and with a foreword by Natalie Zemon Davis, as well as in a Penguin edition (1999), translated and introduced by Rosalind Brown-Grant. Penguin Classics publishes *The Treasure of the City of Ladies: Or the Book of the Three Virtues*, translated and edited by Sarah Lawson (2003), while the 1997 Norton critical edition of *The Selected Writings of Christine de Pizan*, translated by Renate Blumenfeld-Kosinski and Kevin Brownlee, contains several useful critical and historical essays on the author, with a full bibliography. The article 'Five Poems from the French of Christine de Pisan' by Charles Martin and Johanna Keller (*The Hudson Review*, summer 1999) gives a taste of her early work. Further critical analyses of Pizan's life and thought can be found in Charity C. Willard's *Christine de Pizan: Her Life and Works* (Persea Books, 1984) and Margaret Brabant's *Politics, Gender, and Genre: The Political Thought of Christine de Pizan* (Westview Press, 1992).

APHRA BEHN

'A Female Sweetness and a Manly Grace': from the dedication to *Poems on Several Occasions*.

Like Christine de Pizan, Aphra Behn is well known as a representative figure in early women's writing, the exception that proves the rule of female silence. As Virginia Woolf wrote in *A*

Room of One's Own, 'all women together ought to let flowers fall upon the tomb of Aphra Behn [...] for it was she who earned them the right to speak their minds.' Those interested in early twentieth-century views of Behn should seek out the biography *Aphra Behn, the Incomparable Astrea* by Woolf's friend and lover, the novelist Vita Sackville-West, published in 1927. Today, Behn's plays and her short novel *Oroonoko* are widely available in Norton Critical and Oxford World's Classics editions. The 2003 Penguin Classics edition of *Oroonoko* has an excellent introduction by leading Behn scholar Janet Todd, also the author of the biography *Aphra Behn: A Secret Life* (Fentum Press, 2017) and several related essays and articles. The biographical essay (unattributed) at the Poetry Foundation website offers a thorough and detailed analysis of Behn's poems, as well as the outline of her life story, while Mary Ann O'Donnell's essay 'Aphra Behn: The Documentary Record' in *The Cambridge Companion to Aphra Behn* edited by Derek Hughes and Janet Todd (Cambridge University Press, 2004) is an essential guide to what is known, and what is not, in Behn's mysterious life.

CHARLOTTE LENNOX

'The ladies must allow me once more to repeat to them that the only means of charming, and of charming long, is to improve their minds; good sense gives beauties which are not subject to fade like the lillies and roses of their cheeks, but will prolong the power of an agreeable woman to the autumn of her life': from 'Of the Studies Proper for Women', *The Lady's Museum*, Volume I, Issue 1, 1760 (via ladysmuseum.com).

Charlotte Lennox's *The Female Quixote* is easily available in editions from Oxford and Penguin Classics, although her other works are somewhat harder to find. Her novel *Henrietta* is available from the University Press of Kentucky (2010) with an introduction and notes by Susan Carlile and Ruth Perry. An excellent website, The Lady's Museum Project (ladysmuseum.com), offers an open-access critical edition of Lennox's magazine of that name, produced by Karenza Sutton-Bennett and Kelly Plante, with contributions from Lennox scholar Susan Carlile, whose biography *Charlotte Lennox: An Independent Mind* (University of Toronto Press, 2018) is a lively guide to her life and writing. I also drew upon insightful scholarly essays by Jessica Kane ('Rewriting the Quixotic Novel in Charlotte Lennox's *The Female Quixote*', *Style*, Volume 57, Number 1, 2023); Laurie Langbauer ('Romance Revised: Charlotte Lennox's *The Female Quixote*', *NOVEL: A Forum on Fiction*, Autumn 1984) and Margaret Anne Doody ('Shakespeare's Novels: Charlotte Lennox Illustrated', *Studies in the Novel*, Autumn 1987).

OLYMPE DE GOUGES

'Women have the right to mount the scaffold, they must also have the right to mount the speaker's rostrum': from 'Declaration of the Rights of Woman and the Female Citizen', Article X.

Much of Olympe de Gouges' writing is not published in book form in English, although various scholarly and biographical works are available. Sandrine Bergès' *Liberty in Their Name: The Women Philosophers of the French Revolution* (Bloomsbury Academic, 2022) tells Olympe's story intertwined with that of her fellow revolutionaries Sophie de Grouchy and Manon Roland, while Sophie Mousset's short book *Women's Rights and the French Revolution: A Biography of Olympe de Gouges* (Transaction Publishers, 2014) gives an overview of her life. 'The Declaration of the Rights of Women and the Female Citizen' is available in English online, or in a short illustrated book with brief commentary from other famous women

(Octopus Publishing, 2018). For those who read some French, I highly recommend the graphic biography *Olympe de Gouges* by illustrator Catel Muller and writer José-Louis Bocquet (Casterman, revised edition 2021) which combines a lively visual telling of her life with extensive supporting material. Online, the best resource for the English reader who wants to read more of her work is the website of translations maintained by Clarissa Palmer, at olympedegouges.eu.

FANNY FERN

'What a pity when editors review a woman's book, that they so often fall into the error of reviewing the woman instead': from 'Some Hints to Editors' in *Ginger-Snaps*, 1870.

Fern's *Ruth Hall* is available in several editions, none recently published. The Penguin Classics edition, *Ruth Hall: A Domestic Tale of the Present Time*, edited and introduced by Susan Belasco, appeared in 1997, while a scholarly edition, *Ruth Hall and Other Writings by Fanny Fern*, edited by Joyce W. Warren and containing a selection of Fern's newspaper columns, was published by Rutgers University Press in its American Women Writers series in 1986. Joyce Warren's biography *Fanny Fern: An Independent Woman* was also published by Rutgers in 1992, followed a year later by a shorter biography by Nancy A. Walker, which is now out of print. The best current resource for reading about Fern's journalism is the website fannyfern.org, edited by scholar Kevin McMullen, which offers full-text transcriptions of her columns for the *New York Ledger* from 1856–1858 (so far).

HARRIET JACOBS

'Slavery is terrible for men; but it is far more terrible for women': from *Incidents in the Life of a Slave Girl*.

Unlike some profiles in this book that involve the consolidation of a wealth of scattered writings, the story of Harriet Jacobs is contained in her own book, and amplified by the commentary and work of scholars surrounding it, and anyone interested in her life story should begin with that arresting and unforgettable story. *Incidents in the Life of a Slave Girl* is a widely available text in a number of editions of varying quality. I relied on the comprehensive 2023 Broadview Press edition *Incidents in the Life of a Slave Girl, Written by Herself*, edited and with an excellent introduction and notes by Koritha Mitchell. Other accessible editions include those edited by Nell Irving Painter (Penguin Classics, 2005), R.J. Ellis (Oxford, 2015), and Frances Smith Foster and Richard Yarborough (Norton Critical, Second Edition, 2019). These all owe a debt to Jean Fagan Yellin, whose scholarship and biography of Jacobs in the 1980s, building on the work of Dorothy Sterling and George Stevenson, laid to rest the longstanding myth that her story was an invention, or the work of Lydia Maria Childs, her white editor.

GEORGE SAND

'It seems to me that we change from day to day and that after some years we are a new being': George Sand, quoted in the introduction to Belinda Jack's *George Sand: A Woman's Life Writ Large*.

The Oxford World's Classics 2008 edition of *Indiana*, translated by Sylvia Raphael and edited by Naomi Schor, is George Sand's most readily available novel in English. Biographies of the author written in English include Belinda Jack's *George Sand: A Woman's Life Writ Large* (Knopf, 2001), Elizabeth Harlan's *George Sand* (Yale University Press, 2004), and Benita Eisler's provocative *Naked in the Marketplace: The Lives of George Sand* (Counterpoint, 2006). A new graphic biography *George Sand: True Genius, True*

Woman is forthcoming in English in 2024, by author Séverine Vidal and illustrator Kim Consigny. Online, the website for George Sand's house at Nohant, maison-george-sand.fr, contains a wealth of information about the author, as does the Musée de la Vie Romantique (Museum of the Romantic Life) in Montmartre Paris, which has a permanent display of objects and artworks relating to Sand, who was a regular visitor to the house when it was owned by the artist Ary Scheffer. It is a beautiful evocation of Sand's life in Paris and the vibrancy of her salon, her friendships and her writing.

JUANA MANUELA GORRITI
'Do you know anything which is so sought after and yet so sad as travelling?': from *Panoramas de la Vida*, 1878.

Juana Manuela Gorriti's work and remarkable life remain fairly unknown to English readers. To write this profile, I drew on the collection of her fiction published as *Dreams and Realities* (Oxford University Press, 2003), translated by Sergio Gabriel Waisman, and with a valuable introduction by Francine Masiello. This collection includes her story 'La Quena', among several others. To interpret the fiction, I was indebted to English-language studies by Luz Hincapié ('Exile, Displacement and Hybridity in Juana Manuela Gorriti', in *Aesthethika* Vol. 2, May 2006) and Beatriz Urraca ('Juana Manuela Gorriti and the Persistence of Memory', *Latin American Research Review* Vol. 34, No. 1, 1999). In the UK, the small independent Clapton Press, which specialises in Spanish and Latin American literature, publishes three titles by Gorriti, translated by Kathryn Phillips-Miles and introduced by Simon Deefholts: her memoir *Our Native Land*, and the short novels *An Oasis in Life* and *The Yocci Well*.

CREDITS AND FURTHER READING

SUI SIN FAR/EDITH MAUDE EATON

'Individuality is more than nationality': from 'Leaves from the Mental Portfolio of a Eurasian', *The Independent* (New York), 21 January 1909.

Sui Sin Far/Edith Maude Eaton remains best known today for her 1912 collection *Mrs Spring Fragrance*, which has appeared in several editions, most recently published by Broadview Press (2011) and edited by Hsuan L. Hsu. In the 1980s and 1990s, scholars Annette White-Parks and Amy Ling worked to bring Eaton's work, and that of her sister Winnifred, to a new scholarly audience. They co-edited an edition of *Mrs Spring Fragrance*, and in 1995, White-Parks published *Sui Sin Far/Edith Maude Eaton: A Literary Biography* with University of Illinois Press. More recently, Mary Chapman has worked diligently to unearth and attribute Eaton's scattered journalism and stories, detailing her efforts in the 2012 essay 'Finding Edith Eaton' (*Legacy* Vol. 29, No. 2) and the edited collection *Becoming Sui Sin Far: Early Fiction, Journalism, and Travel Writing by Edith Maude Eaton* (McGill-Queen's University Press, 2016). I'm also indebted to the wonderful *Lost Ladies of Lit* podcast, which featured Sui Sin Far and *Mrs Spring Fragrance* in their December 29, 2020 episode, with journalist Victoria Namkung.

ALICE DUNBAR-NELSON

'To an independent spirit there is a certain sense of humiliation and wounded pride in asking for money, be it five cents or five hundred dollars. The working woman knows no such pang; she has but to question her account and all is over ... There is an independent, happy, free-and-easy swing about the motion of her life': from 'The Woman', *Violets and Other Tales*, 1895.

After spending many decades in the shadow of her more famous first husband, Alice Dunbar-Nelson is now receiving an overdue posthumous reassessment. This began in the early 1980s with the new publication and critical appraisal of Dunbar-Nelson's writing by scholars R. Ora Williams and Akasha (Gloria) Hull. Hull, in particular, went on to become Dunbar-Nelson's literary champion, editing three volumes of her writing for the Schomburg Library of Nineteenth-Century Black Women Writers, as well as her diary, published in 1984 as *Give Us Each Day*. In 2016, scholars Katherine Adams, Sandra A. Zagarell and Caroline Gebhard took note of the growing interest in Dunbar-Nelson and co-edited a special issue of women's literature journal *Legacy* titled 'Recovering Alice Dunbar-Nelson for the Twenty-First Century' (University of Nebraska Press, Volume 33, Number 2), which provides many new avenues for research and reappraisal. Eleanor Alexander's account of the Dunbars' relationship, *Lyrics of Sunshine and Shadow: The Tragic Courtship and Marriage of Paul Laurence Dunbar and Alice Ruth Moore* (NYU Press, 2001), was followed up more recently by Tara T. Green's biography *Love, Activism, and the Respectable Life of Alice Dunbar-Nelson* (Bloomsbury Academic, 2022), which attempts to expand the author's story beyond her relationship with Dunbar. Also in 2022, Gene Andrew Jarrett's biography *Paul Laurence Dunbar: The Life and Times of a Caged Bird* marks the 150th anniversary of the poet's death and re-evaluates his literary legacy. Alice's poetry is included in a number of anthologies but her prolific publications still require some digging for. A recent new collection, *The Goodness of St. Rocque and Other Stories* (Random House, 2022), introduced by Danielle Evans, offers a good overview of her short fiction.

RENÉE VIVIEN

'The Amazon smiles above the ruins': from 'Amazone', *A Crown of Violets*, 1901, translated by Samantha Pious.

CREDITS AND FURTHER READING

Renée Vivien's story remains elusive in English, and her works more so, although visitors to Paris can pay homage at her tomb in Passy Cemetery and the square named for her in the Marais. In the 1970s, publisher Barbara Grier's Naiad Press, a small U.S. press specialising in lesbian literature, brought out Vivien's novella *A Woman Appeared to Me* (translated by Jeannette H. Foster), the poetry collection *The Muse of the Violets*, translated by Margaret Porter and Catharine Kroger, and *At the Sweet Hour of Hand in Hand*, translated by Sandia Belgrade. The press no longer exists, but newer versions of her work are appearing from dedicated independent publishers, including *A Crown of Violets*, translated by Samantha Pious, from Headmistress Press (2015), and a new 2020 edition of her shapeshifting short stories *The Woman of the Wolf and Other Stories*, translated by Yvonne M. Klein and introduced by Karla Jay, from Gallic Books. To write her profile, I relied on biographies available online in English and French, especially the essay by Julie R. Enszer at Lambda Literary (lambdaliterary.org) as well as Suzanne Rodriguez's vital biography of Natalie Barney, *Wild Heart* (HarperCollins, 2003). Colette's *The Pure and the Impure*, with its portrait of Vivien, is available from New York Review Books, translated by Herma Briffault and introduced by Judith Thurman. Among the many biographical and cultural histories of early twentieth century Paris, Diana Souhami's recent *No Modernism Without Lesbians*, stands out as a lively, woman-centred overview of the scene (Bloomsbury, 2020).

MARY HEATON VORSE

'I am part of the avant-garde. I have overstepped the bounds!': Mary Heaton Vorse, from an unpublished story, 1897.

The late Dee Garrison's 1989 biography *Mary Heaton Vorse: The Life of an American Insurgent* (Temple University Press, 1990) remains the only comprehensive guide to Vorse's life and work. Garrison also collected and edited her journalism in *Rebel Pen: The Writings of Mary Heaton Vorse* (Monthly Review Press, 1985), but most information about Vorse today now comes from books about her friends, such as Amy Aronson's biography *Crystal Eastman: A Revolutionary Life* (Oxford University Press, 2019) or about the activist circles in which she moved in the early twentieth century, such as Christine Stansell's *American Moderns* (Princeton University Press, 2000). In New York, Vorse was a member of the secret feminist club Heterodoxy and is therefore one of the subjects of my 2022 book *Hotbed: Bohemian New York and the Secret Club that Sparked Modern Feminism*. Her own autobiography *A Footnote to Folly* (1935) is available online in an archival edition as well as some of her novels including *I've Come to Stay*, which is an entertaining chronicle of bohemian Greenwich Village. In Provincetown, Massachusetts, where she owned a home that became the launchpad for the innovative theatre group the Provincetown Players, she is now something of local celebrity, partly thanks to her book *Time and the Town: A Provincetown Chronicle* (edited by Adele Heller, Rutgers University Press, 1991). Since 2020, her home in Provincetown has been redeveloped as the home of the Provincetown Arts Society, which hosts events and exhibitions in the town.

MARY BORDEN

'There are no men here, so why should I be a woman?': from *The Forbidden Zone*, 1929.

Mary Borden is another enormously prolific author whose oeuvre has essentially vanished from modern bookshelves. Jane Conway, author of the 2010 biography *A Woman of Two Wars: The Life of Mary Borden*, maintains a website (maryborden.com) with links to works by and about the author. As a celebrity graduate of Vassar College, Borden has an extensive biography on the Vassar Encyclopedia, available online at vcencyclopedia.vassar.edu. Scholars of the First World War have long been interested in Borden's work. To write about *The Forbidden Zone*, I drew especially on work by Margaret Higgonet, Ariela Freedman ('Mary Borden's Forbidden Zone: Women's Writing from No-Man's-Land', in *Modernism/modernity*, Volume 9, Number 1, January 2002), Sandra M. Gilbert, author of *Behind the Lines: Gender and the Two World Wars* (Yale University Press, 1987), and Christine E. Hallett's book *Nurse Writers of the Great War* (Manchester University Press, 2016). The most recent edition of *The Forbidden Zone* was published by Hesperus Press, with a foreword by Malcolm Brown, in 2008, while the 2015 Dare-Gale Press collection *Poems of Love & War*, edited by Paul O'Prey, is the most comprehensive source for her poetry.

JESSIE REDMON FAUSET

'The world's ours as much as it is theirs': from *There Is Confusion*, 1924.

Jessie Redmon Fauset's poetry, including her translation of Massillon Coicou's poem, 'Oblivion', appeared in the 1922 anthology *The Book of American Negro Poetry*, compiled by James Weldon Johnson, which also featured Alice Dunbar-Nelson. Over the years, her work continued to feature in anthologies of African-American and Harlem Renaissance writing, like Cheryl A. Wall's 1995 collection *Women of the Harlem Renaissance* (Indiana University Press) and the *Gale Critical Companion to the Harlem Renaissance* (Cengage Gale, 2003), which includes her 1922 essay 'Some Notes on Color'. After decades of being neglected or disparaged as overly class-conscious and conservative, her novels are enjoying a new appreciation. *Plum Bun* appears in the Library of America Collection five-book anthology of Harlem Renaissance novels, edited by Rafia Zafar (2011) and a new edition of *There Is Confusion*, introduced by Morgan Jerkins, was published in 2020 by Random House. A richly illustrated anthology of stories and art for Black children, *The New Brownies' Book* (Chronicle Books, 2023), reimagines Fauset and W.E.B. Du Bois's short-lived anthology. Despite this new attention, however, the only existing biography of Fauset remains Carolyn Wedin Sylvander's 1981 study *Jessie Redmon Fauset: Black American Writer* (Whitson Publishing).

MINA LOY

'*The woman*
As usual
Is smiling as bravely
As it is given to her to be brave': from 'Cafe du Néant', *Lunar Baedecker*, 1923.

Appropriately perhaps, given the fragmentary nature of her work and its interplay of word and image, one of the best ways to explore Mina Loy's work is via the website maintained by Suzanne W. Churchill, Linda Kinnahan and Susan Rosenbaum, Mina Loy: Navigating the Avant Garde (mina-loy.com), which includes biographical information, timelines, and links to her work. Her longtime editor and literary executor Roger L. Conover, who referred to her as a 'binarist's nightmare', is the editor of the *Lost Lunar Baedeker*, which is still the most comprehensive collection of her poetry (1997). Other works of hers appear in small press editions: *The Stories and Essays of Mina Loy* edited by Sara Crangle (Dalkey Archive Press, 2011), and her unpublished novel *Insel* which was published by Melville House's Neversink series in 2014, while Yale University Press is publishing two unseen novels in the 2024 edition *Lost Writings*, edited by Karla Kelsey. A recent exhibition of Loy's art at Bowdoin College in Maine (*Strangeness is Inevitable*, 2023) is accompanied by an extensive catalogue. Carolyn Burke's 1996 biography *Becoming Modern* remains the most comprehensive biographical study, recently joined by Mary Ann Caws's *Mina Loy: Apology of Genius* (Reaktion, 2022). Tara Prescott's *Poetic Salvage: Reading Mina Loy* (Bucknell University Press, 2017) sets out to make her poems more readable and accessible. Finally, in the absence of a full biography of the remarkable Arthur Cravan, I'm grateful for Jaap Harskamp's enlightening article 'Poet-Boxer Arthur Cravan: The Man Who Shocked Greenwich Village' (*New York Almanack*, 2023).

KAY BOYLE

'Why do they call people rebels who are swinging into the wide, hot rhythms of life?': Kay Boyle to Lola Ridge, 1923.

Much of Kay Boyle's writing today is out of print, a fate that seems especially to befall more prolific writers. The Virago Modern Classics series features three of her novels: *Year Before Last*, *My Next Bride* and *Plagued by the Nightingale*, which are only available from resellers. Sandra Whipple Spanier is the author of *Kay Boyle: Artist and Activist* (Southern Illinois University Press, 1996) as well as the editor of *Kay Boyle: A Twentieth-Century Life in Letters* (University of Illinois Press, 2015). I'm grateful to online resources including Barbara Bair's essay 'Six Degrees of Kay Boyle' for the Library of Congress website (March 30, 2020) and Shannon Levitzke's essay 'Holding the Artist Accountable: Kay Boyle in the Modernist Press', published in the digital journal *e-Rea* 10.2 (June 2013). Boyle's curious revision of Robert McAlmon's Paris chronicle

Being Geniuses Together first appeared, with her own reflections interspersed, in 1968. The UK's Pushkin Press recently released Boyle's short 1938 novel *The Crazy Hunter* in a new paperback edition, perhaps signalling her overdue revival.

PAULI MURRAY
'Hope is a song in a weary throat': from *Dark Testament*, 1942.

Pauli Murray's influence on many figures and decisions of the Civil Rights movement is much better appreciated today than a few years ago, largely thanks to Rosalind Rosenberg's landmark biography *Jane Crow: The Life of Pauli Murray* (Oxford University Press, 2017). Kathryn Schulz's review essay in the *New Yorker*, 'The Many Lives of Pauli Murray' (April 10, 2017) summarised many of the twists and turns of the story, while the non-profit Pauli Murray Center, headquartered at her childhood home in Durham, North Carolina, maintains an informative website. In my essay on Murray, I follow Rosenberg in using 'she' pronouns, but the Center acknowledges the fluidity of Murray's gender identity by alternating between she, he and they/them. New appreciations of Murray tend to focus on her political legacy, but I am also grateful for the essays on her poetry by Christina G. Bucher ('Pauli Murray: A Case for the Poetry' in *North Carolina Literary Review*, no. 13, June 2004) and Ed Pavlić ('Ours is No Bedtime Story', Poetry Foundation). Murray's memoirs are not currently in print, but her poetry is available in the collection *Dark Testament And Other Poems* (Liveright/W.W. Norton, 2018).

EILEEN CHANG
'All a writer can strive for is to live with integrity': from 'What Are We to Write?' in *Written on Water*, 1944.

CREDITS AND FURTHER READING

Several of Eileen Chang's novels and short stories are available in recent translations, especially from Penguin Classics and New York Review Books. *Little Reunions* is translated for NYRB by Jane Weizhen Pan and Martin Merz, while Karen Kingsbury, the translator of *Love in a Fallen City* (Penguin Classics, 2007) and *Half a Lifelong Romance* (Penguin Classics, 2014) also provides a useful biographical overview in her introduction to the latter book. Biographical writing on Chang, of which there is not much in English, tends to draw on Chang's own account of her life, 'Whispers', which is collected in *Written on Water* (New York Review Books, 2023, translated by Andrew F. Jones, with an afterword by Nicole Huang). Ang Lee's film *Lust, Caution* was the impetus for the republication of Chang's novella of the same name, as well as useful critical commentary. In a 2007 edition, Pantheon Books published the story alongside the film's screenplay, by James Schamus, and an account of the film's production.

FOROUGH FARROKHZAD

'Perhaps because no woman before me took steps toward breaking the shackles binding women's hands and feet, and because I am the first to do so, they have made such a controversy out of me': from the afterword to *Captive*, 1955.

Forough Farrokhzad's impact is now decisively felt outside her native Iran, as a poet and a rebel against an oppressive culture. Saeed Kamali Dehghan's interview with Ebrahim Golestan appeared in *The Guardian* on February 12, 2017, and a new obituary was written by Amir-Hussein Radjy for the *New York Times* series 'Overlooked No More' in 2019. Several other translators and critics have been vital in explicating her poetry and impact for a Western audience, including Leila Rahimi

Bahmany, author of *Mirrors of Entrapment and Emancipation* (Leiden University Press, 2015) which compares Farrokhzad and Sylvia Plath, and Farzaneh Milani of the University of Virginia, author of *The Literary Biography of Forough Farrokhzad with Unpublished Letters* (Persian Circle, 2017), *Words, Not Swords: Iranian Women Writers and the Freedom of Movement* (Syracuse University Press, 2011), and *Veils & Words: The Emerging Voices of Iranian Women Writers* (Syracuse University Press, 1992). Her poetry is available at forughfarrokhzad.org and farrokhzadpoems.com, the latter site maintained by Sholeh Wolpé, who also published a collection of her poems, *Sin* (University of Arkansas Press, 2010). Susan Sallée and Hasan Javadi are co-translators of *Another Birth & Other Poems*, revised edition published 2010 (Mage), while the collection *Forugh Farrokhzad, Poet of Modern Iran*, edited by Dominic Parviz Brookshaw and Nasrin Rahimieh (I.B. Tauris, 2010), explores the poet's influence on her contemporaries and her lasting impact on Iranian culture. Most recently, a new translation and selection of her poems by Elizabeth T. Gray Jr. was published by New Directions in April 2022.

FLORA NWAPA

'You know women's conversation never ends': from *Idu*, 1970.

Some of Nwapa's novels are out of print, and hard to find online, though *Efuru* and *Idu* are most easily sourced. There is, however, considerable scholarship on her, and biographical accounts that give a picture of her life, although not without some internal conflicts and contradictions. I used Kathryn Gibson's entry on Nwapa in *Women in World History: A Biographical Encyclopedia* (via Encyclopedia.com) as a starting point. I am indebted to prominent post-colonial scholars for a deeper reading, including Elleke

Boehmer and Susan Z. Andrade. Boehmer's 'Stories of Women and Mothers: Gender and Nationalism in the Early Fiction of Flora Nwapa' in *Stories of Women: Gender and Narrative in the Postcolonial Nation* (Manchester University Press, 2005) was especially enlightening, as was Susan Z. Andrade's 'Rewriting History, Motherhood, and Rebellion: Naming an African Women's Literary Tradition' (*Research in African Literatures*, Spring, 1990, Vol. 21, No. 1). On Nwapa's death in 1994, an obituary and more personal reminiscence by Gay Wilentz and Susan Gardner, respectively, appeared in the *Women's Review of Books* (Volume 11, Number 6, March 1994). Buchi Emechata's 1986 biography *Head Above Water* was a frank account of the challenges Nigerian women of her generation faced in getting their work published, while Chimamanda Ngozi Adichie acknowledged her debt to Nwapa in a lecture in 2014 in honour of the Governor of Anambra State, Chief Willie Obiano. Detailed information about the Igbo Women's War can be found online at the blog of the UK National Archives by Sarah Castagnetti and Elizabeth Haines, published March 30, 2023.

ASSIA DJEBAR

'*I am not a symbol*': Assia Djebar in an interview with *Le Figaro*, 2005.

The most detailed account of Assia Djebar's life and writing in English is Jane Hiddleston's *Assia Djebar: Out of Algeria* (University of Liverpool Press, 2006), while biographical information also appears in obituaries by Maïa de la Baume (the *New York Times*, February 13, 2015) and Lindsey Moore, in *The Journal of Commonwealth Literature* 2015, Vol. 50 (2). Moore's piece is also a critical analysis of Djebar's work, which is also considered in detail by Soheila Ghaussy in her essay 'A Stepmother Tongue:

"Feminine Writing" in Assia Djebar's *Fantasia: An Algerian Cavalcade*' (*World Literature Today*, Summer, 1994, Vol. 68, No. 3) and in Dorothy S. Blair's introduction to *Fantasia: An Algerian Cavalcade* (also translated by Blair, Heinemann, 1993). Lucy Scholes's article on *La Soif* in *The Paris Review* online (December 2, 2019), in her excellent 'Re-Covered' series, is a great overview of the book, its reception, and its connections to *Bonjour Tristesse*. In English, Djebar's writing is scattered. Her story 'There Is No Exile', translated by Marjolign de Jager, is included in the *Oxford Book of French Short Stories* edited by Elizabeth Fallaize (Oxford University Press, 2002), while her novel *Children of the New World: A Novel of the Algerian War*, also translated by de Jager, is published by the Feminist Press (2005).

INÈS CAGNATI
'A child is life's memory of itself': from *Free Day*.

In contrast to many of the writers in this book, information about Cagnati is extremely limited, in French or English. Liesl Schillinger's translation of *Free Day*, published by New York Review Books in 2019, includes her vital introduction and the transcribed television interview between Cagnati and Pierre-Pascal Rossi from 1989, footage of which I was able to watch on YouTube. As Schillinger notes, Cagnati's importance as a witness to the forgotten history of Italian immigrants in France between the wars was explored in a symposium in Bordeaux in 1997, the proceedings of which were published as *Sur les Pas des Italiens en Aquitaine* by Monique Rouch and Carmela Maltone and reviewed briefly in English in *The International Migration Review* Vol. 33, No. 2 (Summer, 1999). This is in contrast with the wealth of biographical and critical information about Annie Ernaux, Cagnati's contemporary, but so far no critical study has linked the two.

CREDITS AND FURTHER READING

LUCILLE CLIFTON

'what did i see to be except myself?': from 'won't you celebrate with me?' in *The Book of Light*, Copper Canyon Press, 1993.

A 'poet's poet', Lucille Clifton's work circulates widely online, especially in the United States, and a detailed biographical essay and selected poems are available at the Poetry Foundation website. A comprehensive collection of her work is available from BOA editions (2014), edited by Kevin Young and Michael S. Glaser, with a foreword by Toni Morrison and afterword by Young. When Clifton died in 2010, the prominent poet Elizabeth Alexander's remembrance in the *New Yorker* (February 17, 2010) was a testament to her influence and her enormous personal warmth. Her 1976 memoir *Generations* was published in a new edition, introduced by Tracy K. Smith, by New York Review Books in 2021 and her selected poems, edited by Aracelis Girmay and published as *How to Carry Water*, appeared from BOA editions in 2020, which inspired an extended review essay by Andrea Brady, 'Lost Names', in the *London Review of Books*, April 22, 2021. Since the property was saved in 2020, the Clifton House in Baltimore is working to preserve and promote the artistic and political legacy of Fred and Lucille both on site and online.

ACKNOWEDGEMENTS

My interest in literary canons, and their curious habit of 'losing' women writers, is longstanding. I owe the critic Sam Sacks a debt of gratitude for first giving me the space to write about the topic at the online journal *Open Letters Monthly*. In 2019, I was honored to be asked by editor Nadja Spiegelman to take over the *Paris Review*'s online column 'Feminize Your Canon' from its founding writer Emma Garman. I'm grateful for the opportunity to include my contributions here, in substantially revised form.

While I'd always secretly thought the project would make a good book, it was Rowan Cope, then my editor at Duckworth Books, who made the idea a reality. I'm indebted to her for her vision, and to the whole Duckworth team – especially Daniela Ferrante and Clare Bullock – for their patience and dedication in shepherding the book into the world. I am deeply honored that The Royal Society of Literature recognised the book with its work-in-progress Antonia Fraser Award.

This book is dedicated to the writers and readers who work so hard to uncover and champion women's writing, including those who have inspired me personally, especially Lauren Elkin, Anne Boyd Rioux, Lucy Scholes, and Allison Devers of The Second Shelf. As ever, I count myself lucky to have the support of my wonderful agent, Kate Johnson. To my family, especially my husband Tony and our son Felix, thank you for everything, every day.

IMAGE CREDITS

Disc of Enheduanna, 150424, courtesy of Penn Museum; Murasaki Shikibu, H.O. Havemeyer Collection, Bequest of Mrs. H. O. Havemeyer, 1929; Harl 4431 f.4 Christine de Pisan writing at her desk, from 'The Works of Christine de Pisan', Parisian copy, *c.* 1410-15 (vellum) © British Library, London, UK, From the British Library archive/Bridgeman Images; Aphra Behn © Dean and Chapter of Westminster; Charlotte Lennox (née Ramsay) by Francesco Bartolozzi, after Sir Joshua Reynolds, stipple engraving, published 1793 © National Portrait Gallery, London; portrait of Olympe de Gouges by Alexandre Kucharsky © Fine Art Images / Bridgeman Images; portrait of George Sand by Luigi Calamatta, after Eugène Delacroix, 1837; Sara Payson Parton, known as Fanny Fern, held in the Library of Congress; Harriet Jacobs, 1894; Juana Manuela Gorriti, Photo © JBP/AIC / Bridgeman Images; portrait of Sui Sin Far by George H. Braas (Seattle) 1900, Gift of Mr. Charles F. Lummis © Braun Research Library Collection, Autry Museum of the American West; Alice Dunbar-Nelson. The New York Public Library Digital Collections, 1923; portrait of Renée Vivien by Otto Wegener, held in the archive of the Smithsonian Institution (number SIA2015-006918); Mary Heaton Vorse, Schlesinger Library, Harvard Radcliffe Institute; Mary Borden, 1931 © National Portrait Gallery, London; Jessie Redmon Fauset. Photographer unknown, held in the Library of Congress; Djuna Barnes (*left*) and Mina Loy (*right*), Carolyn Burke Collection on Mina Loy and Lee Miller. Yale Collection of American Literature, Beinecke Rare Book and Manuscript Library; Kay Boyle by Al Ravenna, held in Library of Congress; Pauli Murray © Everett Collection / Bridgeman Images; Eileen Chang © Pictures from History / Bridgeman Images; Flora Nwapa © John Preito/Getty; Assia Djebar © Sophie Bassouls. All rights reserved 2024/Bridgeman Images; Ines Cagnati © Sophie Bassouls. All rights reserved 2024/Bridgeman Images; Lucille Clifton © Chris Felver. All rights reserved 2024/Bridgeman Images.